Scripture in the Church

Scripture in the Church

The Synod on the Word of God
and the Post-Synodal Exhortation *Verbum Domini*

James Chukwuma Okoye, CSSp

A Michael Glazier Book

LITURGICAL PRESS
Collegeville, Minnesota

www.litpress.org

A Michael Glazier Book published by Liturgical Press

Cover design by David Manahan, OSB. Photo courtesy of ThinkstockPhotos.com.

Excerpts from documents of the Second Vatican Council are from *Vatican Council II: The Basic Sixteen Documents*, by Austin Flannery, OP © 1996 (Costello Publishing Company, Inc.). Used with permission.

Scripture texts in this work are taken from the *New Revised Standard Version Bible: Catholic Edition* © 1989, 1993, Division of Christian Education of the National Council of the Churches of Christ in the United States of America. Used by permission. All rights reserved.

1   2   3   4   5   6   7   8   9

Library of Congress Cataloging-in-Publication Data

Okoye, James Chukwuma.
    Scripture in the church : the synod on the Word of God and the
post-synodal exhortation Verbum Domini / James Chukwuma Okoye.
        p. cm.
    "A Michael Glazier Book."
    Includes bibliographical references (p.   ) and index.
    ISBN 978-0-8146-5761-4 — ISBN 978-0-8146-8026-1 (e-book)
    1. Bible—Criticism, interpretation, etc.   2. Bible—Use.   3. African
Synod (2008 : Rome, Italy)   I. Title.

BS511.3.O36   2011
220.6088'282—dc22   2011010932

To the students of
the Catholic Theological Union, Chicago

Contents

Foreword

In the Gospel of Luke, there is a famous passage in which a scholar of the law asks Jesus what he must do to "inherit eternal life." In response, Jesus asks him, "What is written in the law? What do you read there?" (Luke 10:25-26). Jesus' answer conveys two important things: first, to engage the most serious questions in life, a believer turns to the Scriptures; second, not everyone will read the Scriptures the same way.

In this book, James Chukwuma Okoye, CSSp, explores questions concerning who should read the Scriptures, what is the nature of the biblical word, how to interpret it, how to pray with it, and how to live it. The occasion of the synod of bishops that took place throughout the month of October 2008 in Rome to reflect on the significance of the Word in the life and ministry of the church provides the impetus to take up these questions in the wider church. With his clear style and balanced approach, Okoye helps the novice reader of the Bible easily understand the complicated world of biblical exegesis and hermeneutics. Scholars and seasoned readers of the Bible will also find his expositions engaging and helpful.

Okoye's wisdom comes from his many years of teaching and guiding graduate students of theology and ministry at Catholic Theological Union as the Carroll Stuhlmueller Professor of the Old Testament. In addition, he has led his Nigerian Congregation of Spiritan priests and brothers, has served on the International Theological Commission, was *peritus* in the Synod of Bishops for Africa, and is a missionary who has ministered with people from many different cultures. Okoye's passion for the Word is sure to draw the reader of this book not only into greater understanding but also into an increased love and commitment to the Word of life.

Sr. Barbara E. Reid, OP, PhD
Vice President and Academic Dean
Catholic Theological Union, Chicago

Introduction

I participated in the preparation of the first Synod of Bishops for Africa (the one held in Rome in April 1994) in the capacity of a *peritus* (expert) who worked closely with the secretariat of the synod of bishops to prepare the documents and other administrative matters pertinent to the synod. It was then that I realized how much work went into a synod, how much documentation accumulated, and how much a vital exercise of the collegiality of bishops a synod really was. The media were then all taken up with why the synod was not being held somewhere in Africa. They called its being held in Rome a slight on Africa, a continent exploding with new adherents to Catholicism. They did not realize that a synod in the Roman Catholic Church was an exercise of the universal church (involving the pope and the college of bishops), even if with particular reference to the pastoral or other issues of a continent, country, or particular church. Theologically, the correct terminology is not the African synod, or the Asian synod, but the Synod of Bishops *for* Africa (*for* Asia, *for* Holland, etc.). Holding a synod in Rome opens up the entire resources of the universal church and its solidarity to the delegates. During the synod itself bishops and other participants have the opportunity of meeting with the pertinent officials of the Roman Curia and receiving advice and/or help with whatever they may need.

My participation in that first Synod of Bishops for Africa also opened my eyes to what a rich resource for reflection and practical theology the synod process and documentation were. The library of the secretariat of the synod is chock-full of the documentation of all the past councils and synods of the church, as well as all the relevant documents of the magisterium. Every intervention made orally and/or in writing in each synod is nicely bound up in volumes and stacked up in the synod library. All the meetings of the preparatory commissions are carefully documented and stored. The various groups and committees of the synod have easy access to whatever they might need.

Synod documentation begins with the *Lineamenta* (Outline Document) which assembles all the teachings of the magisterium and current theological opinion on the matter at hand, with questions for discussion. It is sent out to all the particular churches the world over. The *Instrumentum Laboris* (Working Document) feeds in the responses, questions, and perplexities of the various particular churches on the topic chosen. It often happens that what is standard in one particular church is not at all sure tradition in another. Such is the fact of inculturation, one faith in a diversity of forms and expressions.

The synod itself begins with a *report* that outlines the reception of the last synod and the issues of the current one. Then participants may each address the synod for six to eight minutes each. Another report ties up the discussion, and then the participants move into language groups for further discussions and the minting of *propositions*. The work of a synod is done under great pressure. For example, the propositions are assembled from the various committees in the course of one night. For the first synod for Africa they went to the printer at 3 a.m. to surface as bound books in five languages by 9 a.m. when the synod assembled the same morning! To enable a long view that takes in the entire process, all the documents of the synod are entrusted to the pope, who produces a *post-synodal apostolic exhortation*. He works with a body of twelve bishops elected by the synod itself (and three more appointed by himself). It was not always so. The synod of 1974 could reach no agreement as to a final document, so entrusted all the documentation to Paul VI, who in 1975 brought out the acclaimed *Evangelii Nuntiandi*. In the post-synodal apostolic exhortation, the pope takes account of all the work of the synod and exhorts the whole church to give close attention to those of its directives and wishes that he upholds. The tendency in recent times has been for the pope to pay close attention to the propositions (those approved by vote in the synod) and actually cite some of them. As head of the college of bishops, the pope also brings to bear his own pastoral priorities and evaluations of the synod. His apostolic exhortation is the official result of the synod to be used for pastoral animation all over the church.

Naturally, the pope cannot in one document take up all the significant contributions that emerged in the entire synod process. The official documents (*Lineamenta*, *Instrumentum Laboris*, and Message to the People of God), reports (Report before the Discussion, Report after the Discussion), and especially the propositions are usually cited, but rarely or never the individual contributions on the floor of the synod (except for those of the pope himself or maybe of the ecumenical patriarch of Constantinople) nor the reports of the language groups. In this book, I have provided sidebars or reported on some outstanding contributions on the floor in order to give the reader some idea of the richness and flavor of the synod.

My research seeks to ground the papal exhortation within the *entire* synod process, something some scholars have done for the documents of Vatican II. Detailing the very process of the synod would be like a "state of the question" on the synod's topic. It would manifest the current consensus, indicate advances made by the synod and/or questions still being asked, thus showing the lay of the land within which the papal document is to be understood and interpreted. For the Synod on the Word of God, for example, the discussions in the assembly showed unease and perplexity about the theology of the word of God (revelation), how Scripture is related to the word of God. Knowing such background is, I consider, invaluable help toward understanding the apostolic exhortation on the analogy of the word of God (*Verbum Domini*, 7). This is more so the case as the exhortation is all that most people will ever have access to.

While the October 2008 synod was in session, the Department of Biblical Languages and Literature at Catholic Theological Union, Chicago, held a one-day seminar on the topic of the synod. The members of the department paired with faculty from the other departments in presenting aspects of the synod. I paired with a colleague from the Department of Word and Worship to speak on "Bible and Catechesis." Preparing for and delivering that seminar became an impulse to researching and writing this book.

This book focuses on the synod itself and the post-synodal exhortation. I have sought to present the work of the synod in historical progression, signaling issues and developments in the flow of ideas (see the contents page). Between the synod itself, and the papal exhortation, I have isolated certain issues that kept coming up in the discussions. For some of them I have briefly indicated (in an appendix) some lines of discussion in current theology. These appendixes serve the interests of students and informed readers, and may be skipped by other readers. Chapter 7, a brief survey of recent Catholic exegesis, highlights current issues surrounding Catholic interpretation of the Bible. It prepares readers for the apostolic exhortation particularly on the matter of the interpretation of the Bible (see chapter 10).

The *Lineamenta* (preface) noted its dependence on the Vatican II Dogmatic Constitution on Divine Revelation, *Dei Verbum*, which it sought to reread from the pastoral point of view and in relation to successive pronouncements of the magisterium. Proposition 2 noted the great benefits that *Dei Verbum* brought the church on the exegetical, spiritual, pastoral, and ecumenical levels. *Instrumentum Laboris*, 6, nevertheless noted "a lack of familiarity with *Dei verbum*" as among tasks to be taken up, while number 18 saw the synod as providing the occasion to rediscover *Dei Verbum* and later pontifical documents on the topic of the word of God. *Dei Verbum* being so foundational a reference for the synod, I have generally begun the treatment of each topic with its teaching.

A word about the title of this book. Scripture does not exhaust the word of God and the synod was not just about Scripture. It was also about tradition and God's continuing self-disclosure in history and in the religions and cultures of humankind. I have, nevertheless, titled the book *Scripture in the Church*. The fathers of the synod focused on Scripture and its function in the church's pastoral care and mission, even though they did not ignore other ways in which God is present and speaking to our world. Scripture is "like a mirror in which the pilgrim Church on earth looks at God" (*DV*, 7). Without being revelation itself, it is the normative and irreplaceable witness to the originating event of revelation.

I am very grateful to the vice president and academic dean of the Catholic Theological Union, Professor Barbara Reid, OP, for writing the foreword. I thank her sincerely also for her leadership and the gift of her scholarship. The book is dedicated to the students of the Catholic Theological Union, Chicago, who both come from and do mission in all parts of the globe. Wherever you are, know that you have been an inspiration and source of personal energy and mission to me. Thank you all.

Part of the research for this book was completed at the Collegeville Institute for Ecumenical and Cultural Research, an oasis of research and peace. Thanks to the director, Donald Ottenhoff, and the officials of this institution. Thanks also to Hans Christoffersen, editorial director of Liturgical Press, Collegeville, who promptly accepted the manuscript and expedited its publication.

I end with my favorite psalm. "Yahweh is my light and my salvation, whom should I fear? Yahweh is the fortress of my life, whom should I dread?" (Ps 27:1, New Jerusalem Bible). May the name of the Lord be praised, both now and forever. Amen. Amen.

James Chukwuma Okoye, CSSp
Carroll Stuhlmueller Professor of the Old Testament
Catholic Theological Union, Chicago
April 18, 2011

Chapter 1

Why the Synod on the Word of God? The Synod Process

The Synod of Bishops

The Second Vatican Ecumenical Council (1962–65) was a wonderful expression of the collegiality of Roman Catholic bishops with the pope in regard to church governance and pastoral care. For four sessions during four years, all Roman Catholic bishops of the world gathered in St. Peter's in Rome, with and under the pope. They prayed, they sang, they deliberated, and together made decisions about outstanding issues of church and mission. Under the guidance of the Holy Spirit, this council proved to be epoch-making, opening a new era of *aggiornamento* (updating) in the church.

Already during the council voices were heard expressing the desirability of a structure of collegiality that would keep alive that collegiality the bishops of the world experienced during the four sessions of Vatican Council II. On September 15, 1965, Paul VI announced his *Motu Proprio* (his personal initiative) *Apostolica Sollicitudo* (Apostolic Solicitude) to establish the synod of bishops as a permanent structure of governance in the church. The word "synod" comes from Greek *sunodos*, meaning a coming together, a meeting or assembly. The synod would be a kind of "council in miniature." Unlike the council, however, it would not consist of all the bishops of the world but rather of their elected representatives approved by the Holy Father. The synod would thus be "an assembly of bishops representing the Roman Catholic episcopate, having the task of helping the Pope in the governing of the universal Church by rendering their counsel."[1] Elected representatives of the union of superiors general would be ordinary members of the synod, that is, *ex officio* members. The Holy Father appoints some experts in the material under discussion and significant persons from the lay faithful and various ecumenical ecclesial bodies.

[1] General secretariat of the synod of bishops, Introduction to the Synod of Bishops, 1.

1

The synod of bishops is an expression of the collegiality of bishops with the pope, the head of the college. It is served by its own permanent general secretariat, which is not part of the Roman Curia but is "subject directly and solely to the Holy Father."[2] The synod of bishops functions only when convoked by the Holy Father. Its counsels or decisions require the fiat of the Holy Father to become ecclesial and collegial acts. Synods may be ordinary (expression of ordinary pastoral care) and extraordinary (called for a pressing problem or emergency). They may also be general or special. General synods are for the universal

> *The synod would be a kind of "council in miniature."*

church, special ones for distinct regions. Each general synod elects twelve bishops (joined by three papal appointees, hence fifteen in all) to form an ordinary advisory council of the general secretariat charged with preparing the following synod.

As a structure of church governance and pastoral care, the synod is, however, not totally new. Something similar obtained in an earlier period of the church. The bishops of various regions of the church would gather regularly as a synod to deliberate over matters of governance or faith and morals, especially in the face of heresies or doubts. For example, in 393 the Synod of Hippo (North Africa), in which Augustine was one of the forty-four bishops who appended their signatures, was among the first of church bodies to draw up a list of books to be accepted as the (Catholic) canon, adding the instruction, "but let church beyond sea (Rome) be consulted about confirming this canon."[3] Synodal governance has continued in the Orthodox churches but was discontinued in the Western church till Paul VI.

In Orthodox churches, synods are meetings of bishops within each autonomous church area and are the primary vehicle for the election of bishops and the establishment of interdiocesan ecclesiastical laws.[4] Some Protestant and Reform communities also hold some types of synods, but as more or less democratic institutions. They tend to consist of three sections, the bishops, the pastors, and the laity, and decisions are generally by deliberative vote in the three sections, a process aimed at promoting consensus. On the other hand, the synod experience in the Roman Catholic Church is hierarchical and collegial, not deliberative but consultative,

[2] Ibid., 2.
[3] Catholic Online: Catholic Encyclopedia, "African Synods," accessed March 21, 2009, http://www.catholic.org/encyclopedia/view.php?id=285.
[4] Wikipedia, "Synod," accessed March 22, 2009, http://en.wikipedia.org/wiki/Synod.

and the effective determinations as to the implementation of the synod belong uniquely to the pope.

Since 1965 there have been twelve ordinary general synods in the Roman Catholic Church, as follows:

1967, On Preserving and Strengthening the Catholic Faith

1971, The Ministerial Priesthood and Justice in the World

1974, On Evangelization in the Modern World

1977, Catechesis in Our Time

1980, On the Christian Family

1983, Penance and Reconciliation in the Mission of the Church

1987, The Vocation and Mission of the Lay Faithful in the Church and in the World

1990, The Formation of Priests in Circumstances of the Present Day

1994, The Consecrated Life and its Role in the Church and in the World

2001, The Bishop: Servant of the Gospel of Jesus Christ for the Hope of the World

2005, The Eucharist: Source and Summit of the Life and Mission of the Church[5]

2008, The Synod on the Word of God in the Life and Mission of the Church

There have been two extraordinary synods, as follows:

1969, Extraordinary Synod, On Cooperation between the Holy See and the Episcopal Conferences

1985, The Twentieth Anniversary of the Conclusion of the Second Vatican Council

There have also been special assemblies: Netherlands (1980), Europe, 1st Special Assembly (1991), Africa (1994), Lebanon (1995), America (1997), Asia (1998), Oceania (1998), Europe, 2nd Special Assembly (1999). On November 13, 2004, Pope John Paul II announced a Second Special Assembly for Africa; Pope Benedict XVI confirmed it on June 22, 2005. It was held in Rome in October 2009 under the theme "The Church in Africa in Service to Reconciliation, Justice and Peace."

---

[5] Much of the information here has culled from Introduction to the Synod of Bishops, 4 (see note 1), and from the Holy See Press Office, Synod of Bishops, accessed March 22, 2009, http://www.vatican.va/news_services/press/documentazione/documents/sinodo_indice_en.html.

Between one synod and the next the Holy Father initiates a universal consultation of the bishops of the Roman Catholic world as to the topic of the synod to follow. The resultant opinions are sorted out by the general secretariat of the synod of bishops helped by the ordinary advisory council (mentioned above) and presented to the Holy Father, who then decides the topic and fixes the date. The venue of the general assembly of the synod of bishops has always been Rome. The council of the general secretariat of the synod of bishops wheels into action to produce the *Lineamenta* (Outline Document). This is sent to all the particular churches for discussion and responses back to the general secretary. All the responses are collated in the next document to be sent out to all the particular churches, the *Instrumentum Laboris* (Working Document). This is the document that guides the actual discussions in the assembly of the synod. Every member of the synod receives a copy. The *Instrumentum Laboris* often repeats the exposition of the *Lineamenta*, sometimes word for word, before appending the responses and questions from the particular churches. Here and there, however, there may be interesting departures and restatements of views found in the *Lineamenta*.

The assembly begins with a *Relatio ante Disceptationem* (Report before the Discussion), which informs the synod of the reception of the preceding synod and the process of preparing the current one. Then begins the debate, in which each member may speak for six to eight minutes, having handed in the text (or a longer piece) to the general secretary of the synod of bishops. At the end of the speeches from the floor, there is a *Relatio post Disceptationem* (Report after the Discussion) by a rapporteur who summarizes the issues so far and focuses them in a number of questions for discussion. The synod then breaks into language groups to take up the discussion of this report. The groups elect a committee to draft the Message to the People of God. The results of the group discussions are collated and tabled into specific *propositions*, which are debated and then finalized in general assembly, by each member voting *placet* (yes) or *non placet* (no). The synod order of one bishop, one vote, irrespective of status in the hierarchy, is a telling illustration of the collegial responsibility of all the bishops under Peter for the care of the universal church. The propositions with the votes are then handed over to the Holy Father. In more recent synods, the fathers of the synod have also issued a Message to the People of God on the topic of the synod. It has been the practice since the 1974 (third ordinary) general assembly of the synod of bishops (on evangelization) for the Holy Father, and not the synod, to issue a *post-synodal apostolic exhortation* that takes account of the entire synod process, especially the propositions, and that gives determinations concerning the implementation throughout the church of the agenda and wishes of the synod.

Why the Synod on the Word of God?

"The Synod desires to give the Word of God as bread to the People of God."[6] Its underlying purpose and primary goal is "to fully encounter the Word of God in Jesus the Lord, present in the Sacred Scriptures and the Eucharist."[7] The very choice of the theme of the word of God was influenced by the fact that the preceding synod had been on the Eucharist. There was a manifest desire among the bishops of the world to show clearly the intrinsic link between the "one table of the Bread and Word."[8] The word "encounter," which appears in the very first pages of the *Lineamenta*, becomes increasingly dominant in both the *Lineamenta* and *Instrumentum Laboris*. This word speaks of event, a "speaking" and a "listening" between persons. Hence, word of God is understood in these documents within the category of dialogue between persons. Relating the word of God to both the Scripture and the Eucharist serves notice that "word of God" is meant in a very deep and theological sense, to be clarified in the course of the documents and in the discussions of the assembly.

The *Lineamenta* further delineates the purpose of the synod as primarily *pastoral* and *doctrinal*, namely, "spreading and strengthening encounters with the Word of God by thoroughly examining its doctrinal underpinnings."[9] Besides, the synod intends to encourage the widespread practice of *lectio divina* (in the discussion it became clear that this was no technique but refers to the prayerful reading of Scripture in such a manner that it permeates the whole of life, whatever the method). Another aim is to "assist in the proper application of hermeneutics in Scripture, well geared towards the process of evangelization and inculturation."[10] Ecumenical dialogue being closely bound up with the hearing of the word of God, the synod wishes to promote this, and especially Jewish-Christian dialogue.

---

[6] *Lineamenta*, 5.

[7] Ibid., 4.

[8] Ibid., "Preface."

[9] Ibid., 5. *Instrumentum Laboris*, 4, describes the purpose slightly differently as primarily *pastoral* and *missionary*: "to thoroughly examine the topic's doctrinal teaching and, in the process, spread and strengthen the practice of encountering the Word of God as the source of life in various arenas of experience, and thereby be able to hear God and speak with him in a real and proper manner."

[10] Ibid.

It is the sincere hope and prayer of the synod that by doing all this it will help the church "rejuvenate herself and experience a new springtime,"[11] which will occur through

> an *inspired* [emphasis mine] rediscovery of the Word of God as a *living, piercing* and *active* [emphasis original] force in the heart of the Church, in her liturgy, and in her prayer, in evangelization and in catechesis, in exegetical studies and in theology, in personal and communal life, and also in the cultures of humanity.[12]

An "inspired rediscovery" is one activated and led by the Holy Spirit, the same divine agent of the inspired word of God. In short, as in Hebrews 4:12, the word of God is "living, piercing and active," so also the fathers of the Synod on the Word of God hope that the word of God will permeate and transform every aspect of the church's life and mission, and through this the entire cultures of humankind.

For a new springtime of the church

[11] *Instrumentum Laboris*, "Preface."
[12] *Lineamenta*, "Preface."

Questions for Discussion

1. Describe the various types of "synod" mentioned in this chapter.

2. Describe the synod process.

3. Describe the juridical status of the synod in the Catholic Church and the theological basis for this.

4. Discuss the aims of the synod of bishops on the Word of God in the Life and Mission of the Church.

Chapter 2

The *Lineamenta*
and the *Instrumentum Laboris*

**This Synod desires to give the Word of God as bread to
the People of God.**

Lineamenta, 5

As explained in the preceding chapter, the *Lineamenta* (Outline Document) is the first document of a synod. It is sent out to all particular churches. Its function is to give an outline of the topic under discussion and to prompt responses through questions for discussion at the end of each chapter. The responses from the particular churches are collated and integrated into the *Instrumentum Laboris*, which is the Working Document of the synod sent to every delegate of the synod. For the Synod on the Word of God, these two documents needed in the first place to clarify the synod topic of "word of God," in continuity with Vatican II's Dogmatic Constitution on Divine Revelation, *Dei Verbum*.

The Word of God

Dei Verbum presented the topic in the language of revelation. From its very preface, it linked revelation and salvation: the purpose of revelation is "eternal life" (*DV*, 1). Revelation concerns "the summons to salvation, so that through hearing [the world] may believe; through belief it may hope, through hope it may come to love" (ibid.). By revelation, it pleased the invisible God "to reveal himself and to make known the mystery of his will" (*DV*, 2),[1] inviting humankind to fellowship with God. The human response of faith becomes an obedience by which "one freely commits

---

[1] Unless otherwise indicated, *Dei Verbum* and the documents of Vatican II are cited from Austin Flannery, OP, *Vatican Council II: The Basic Sixteen Documents* (New York: Costello, 1996).

oneself entirely to God" (*DV*, 5).[2] Revelation occurs through deeds and words having an inner unity.

Creation is God's first deed that gives human beings "an enduring witness to Himself" (*DV*, 3).[3] Human reason can come to the knowledge of God through creation, though revelation is needed so that all may attain such knowledge "with ease, with solid certitude, and with no trace of error" (*DV*, 6).[4] God has revealed God's self also in history, especially in the particular history of Israel, which prepared it "for the promised Savior" (*DV*, 3). Jesus Christ is the One "in whom the entire revelation of the Most High God is summed up" (*DV*, 7), and so he is the measure of all revelation. *Dei Verbum* seems to suggest that active revelation has come to an end, having been completed by the death of the last apostle: "we now await no further new revelation before the glorious manifestation of our Lord Jesus Christ" (no. 4). Revelation is now found, as a passive deposit, in Scripture and tradition, which form a unified source, with tradition representing "growth in insight into the realities and words that are being passed on" (*DV*, 8). The Council of Trent had spoken of traditions (in the plural); Vatican II spoke of tradition (in the singular).

> "This plan of revelation is realized by deeds and words having an inner unity: the deeds wrought by God in the history of salvation manifest and confirm the teaching and realities signified by the word, while the words proclaim the deeds and clarify the mystery contained in them" (DV, 2).

The *Lineamenta* and *Instrumentum Laboris* preferred the term "word of God" to revelation. Revelation is an abstract term; word of God is dynamic. The Hebrew word *dabar* means both word and event. God's word is portrayed as an agent that accomplishes the divine mission in the world (Isa 55:10-11). In the Old Testament, in 225 of 241 times (that is, 93 percent

---

[2] This formulation represents a slight shift from Vatican I, which saw revelation in terms of propositional truth and faith as intellectual assent "that what God has revealed is true, not because the intrinsic truth of things is recognized by the natural light of reason, but because of the authority of God himself who reveals them" (J. Neuner and Jaques Dupuis, eds., *The Christian Faith: Doctrinal Documents of the Catholic Church*, 5th revised and enlarged ed. [London: HarperCollins Religious, 1990] 42; DS 3008).

[3] Following the translation of Walter Abbott, *The Documents of Vatican II* (London and Dublin: Geoffrey Chapman, 1966). This is called "natural revelation" as opposed to "supernatural revelation," but *Dei Verbum* does not use these terms.

[4] Ibid.

of the time),[5] the word refers to "word of Yahweh" in the mouth of the prophet. It can be said, therefore, that the word is distinctive of prophetic experience; the prophet proclaims the design and will of Yahweh.

Focus on the word of God foregrounds address and response, encounter. God actively speaks, calls for encounter and the return of love (*Lineamenta*, 6). The primary goal of the synod is to promote a deep encounter with the word of God in the various ways in which God is addressing our world (ibid., 4). The reader is invited to reread the goals of the synod in the preceding chapter.

Lineamenta, 9, discusses the various uses of the term "word of God." It calls the word of God a symphony, while *Instrumentum Laboris*, 9, speaks of "a hymn with many voices." The various uses are outlined in *Lineamenta*, 9, as follows:

> The "Eternal Word of God" (John 1:1-3)
>
> The created world: "render[s] 'perennial witness to [God]'" (cf. *DV*, 3)
>
> Jesus Christ, the "ultimate and definitive Word"
>
> The "proclamation of the prophets and the apostles"
>
> The "Books of Sacred Scripture"
>
> "Spirited preaching and many other forms in service to the Gospel" (*Instrumentum Laboris*, 9, takes it to mean "preaching . . . under the power of the Holy Spirit")

All these diverse senses share in a unity, Christ-the-Word: "the person of Christ the Lord is at the core of the Word of God" (*Lineamenta*, 3). The eternal word of God is "the foundation of communication within and outside the Trinity."[6] God's speaking in love *ad intra* (within the life of the Trinity) is prolonged by the speaking *ad extra* (that happens outside the Trinity through the Word Incarnate).[7] *Instrumentum Laboris* (preface) sought to balance the christological concentration of the word of God by pointing out a pneumatological dimension, when it affirmed that "this Christological approach, linked by necessity to the pneumatological one, leads to the discovery of the Trinitarian dimension of revelation."

---

[5] John L. McKenzie, "The Word of God in the Old Testament," *Myths and Realities: Studies in Biblical Theology* (Milwaukee: Bruce, 1963) 44.

[6] *Instrumentum Laboris*, 9. The reference to the eternal word of God is new in relation to *Dei Verbum* (2), which speaks mostly of revelation in Christ, the Word made flesh.

[7] Cf. René Latourelle, *Theology of Revelation* (New York: Alba House, 1966) 449.

The task of the synod is to enable people to rediscover the Word of God-become-Incarnate, that is, Jesus Christ (*Instrumentum Laboris*, preface). Apparently for this reason, "Word of God" was always written with capital *W* in the *Lineamenta* and *Instrumentum Laboris*. This typographic peculiarity alerts the reader to the fact that word of God in whatever usage points to and participates in something of Christ. However, the typography induced much confusion, for it began to look as if word of God were a univocal concept. It was never very clear to a reader when reference was to the eternal Word, the Incarnate Word, or the word of God in Scripture and elsewhere. Many voices in the synod assembly demanded clarification of the uses of the word and particularly of the relationship of Scripture to the word of God. *Lineamenta*, 13, had this to say on the subject: "Scripture has the essential role of providing access to and being the authentic source of the Word, thus becoming a reference point in the proper understanding of Tradition."

Question 5 of chapter 2 of the *Lineamenta* gives an idea of the relevance of the word of God to all the church is and does:

> Is the word of God the soul of theology? Is its character as the Word-Revealed sufficiently understood and reverenced? Is scientific research of the Bible animated and sustained by a proper grounding in the faith? What is the customary method of approaching the biblical text? What role does the Bible play in theological study? Is the Bible sufficiently taken into consideration in the pastoral life of the community?

Instrumentum Laboris, 12, followed through with saying that "clearly, the primary mission of the Church is transmitting the divine word to everyone." Number 44 noted that "everywhere national catechisms and the directories inspired by them have the Bible as a distinctive feature, giving first place to the word of God drawn from Scripture." It noted a point that needed clarification: how to integrate into biblical catechesis a knowledge of the faith proposed by tradition and the magisterium.

The Old Testament

Dei Verbum, 14, gave a dense and positive doctrine of the Old Testament as word of God: "the plan of salvation, foretold, recounted and explained by the sacred authors, appears as the true word of God in the books of the Old Testament, which is why these books, divinely inspired, retain a lasting value" (*perennem valorem servant*, retain a permanent value). Unless I am mistaken, this is the first time that an affirmation of the permanent validity of the Old Testament is made in an official document of the magisterium. However, these books contain some things that are "imperfect and provisional" (*DV*, 15). For example, Hebrews 10:4 (New Jerusalem Bible) says that "bulls' blood and goats' blood are incapable of taking away sins," so Christ replaced them with the sacrifice of himself.

The *Lineamenta* cites some difficulties with the Old Testament. Some Old Testament passages appear difficult and run the risk of being set aside, considered arbitrarily or never read at all (no. 16). *Lineamenta*, 22, mentions particular problems, such as, ideas of God, man and woman, and moral conduct. The solution advanced is "a formation centered on a Christian reading of the Old Testament" (*Lineamenta*, 16). *Instrumentum Laboris*, 17, returned to the matter, declaring that "knowledge of the Old Testament as word of God seems to be a real problem among Catholics." Among difficulties that needed clarification were "its figurative character and its relationship to the scientific and historical mentality of our times" (no. 18). Other issues mentioned were "a certain view of history, science and the moral life, particularly ethical behavior and how God is portrayed" (no. 45). *Instrumentum Laboris*, 13, dutifully advanced solutions from the responses of the particular churches, as follows:

- to work out a programme which considers Jesus' own rapport with Sacred Scripture, how he read the Scriptures and how they assist in understanding him;
- to present simple criteria for reading the Bible with Christ in mind, thereby resolving difficulties in the Old Testament.

The editors themselves called for:

> a formation centred on *a reading of the Old Testament with Christ in mind*, which acknowledges the bond between the two testaments and the permanent value of the Old Testament. (*Instrumentum Laboris*, 17)

For the various ways in which these solutions may be applied, the reader may turn to chapter 9 (the "dark" passages of the Bible).

The Relation of the Old Testament to the New

Dei Verbum, 16, recalled the dictum of St. Augustine[8] on this matter that God, the inspirer and author of the books of both Testaments, brought it

---

[8] *Quaestiones in Heptateucum*, 2, 73: PL, 34, 623.

about that "the New should be hidden in the Old and that the Old should be made manifest in the New" (*novum in vetere latet, vetus in novo patet*). It added an important rider: the books of the Old Testament in turn shed light on the New Testament and explain it (*illudque vicissim illuminant et explicant*). So the relationship is somewhat reciprocal. The Old Testament enriches the New Testament understanding of certain themes. For example, Stanislaus Lyonnet[9] noted how the New Testament so presumes the Old Testament doctrine of God that it speaks of God only in rapid allusions, and how we require the Old Testament to complete the idea of faith as surrender and trust, not just intellectual assent. Others remark how "the Old Testament keeps Christianity from pursuing salvation (exclusively) in the individual 'soul' or in the hereafter."[10]

I now examine what the *Lineamenta* and *Instrumentum Laboris* say concerning the relationship of the Old Testament to the New in three areas: idea of fulfillment, mutual relations, and implications for interpretation and pastoral care.

Idea of fulfillment. "The Word of God capable of being heard in the Old Testament became visible in Christ."[11] The Old Testament is to be understood as a stage in the development of the faith and coming to know God.[12] Some texts suggest that the Old Testament is of value uniquely in bearing witness to Christ as Messiah.[13] The idea of fulfillment is mostly that of continuity.

Mutual relations. Both Testaments form a single economy of salvation and the one Christian Bible. The Old Testament announces the New; the New is the best commentary on the Old.[14] The Old Testament gives a greater depth to the reading and understanding of the New Testament.[15]

---

[9] Stanislaus Lyonnet, "A Word on Chapters IV and VI of *Dei verbum*," *Vatican II: Assessment and Perspectives: Twenty-Five Years After (1962–1987)*, vol. 1, ed. René Latourelle, 157–207, here 164–68 (New York: Paulist Press, 1988).

[10] Hans Ausloos and Bénédicte Lemmelijn, *The Book of Life: Biblical Answers to Existential Questions* (Grand Rapids: Wm. Eerdmans, 2010) 117.

[11] St. Bernard, *Super Missus est*, Homily IV, 11; PL, 183, 86 in *Lineamenta*, 8bis (there are two nos. 8).

[12] *Instrumentum Laboris*, 18.

[13] *Lineamenta*, 8: "Christ-the-Word is in the history of the people of God in the Old Testament, which bears witness to him as Messiah." *Instrumentum Laboris*, preface: "The books of the Old Testament record their inspired words which kept alive the hope of the coming of the Messiah . . ."

[14] *Lineamenta*, 16, citing Gregory the Great, *In Ezechielem*, I, 6, 15.

[15] *Instrumentum Laboris*, 18.

Liturgical practice always makes a reading of the Old Testament essential for a full understanding of the New Testament.[16]

Hermeneutical implications. As inspired Scripture, both Old and New Testaments teach firmly, faithfully, and without error "that truth which God, for the sake of our salvation, wished to see confided to the sacred Scriptures."[17] Both are like a mirror in which the pilgrim church on earth looks at God.[18] Both have a direct and concrete power of appeal not possessed by other texts or holy writings.[19] As such, they are never to be replaced in the liturgy by other readings.

The New Testament

Dei Verbum, 2, stated that revelation reached its apex in the event of Jesus Christ, crucified and risen, "who is himself both the mediator and the sum total of revelation." Jesus declared this himself when he said, "All things have been handed over to me by my Father; and no one knows the Son except the Father, and no one knows the Father except the Son and anyone to whom the Son chooses to reveal him" (Matt 11:27). And again, "I am the way, and the truth, and the life. No one comes to the Father except through me" (John 14:6). He reveals by his words; he reveals by his love. his mercy and pardon, his attitude toward sinners, and his gift of self even unto the sacrifice of self portray the very love of God.[20] Jesus took the apostles in trust, sharing with them intimate knowledge of the Father and of himself and entrusting this revelation to them for the world. The writings of the New Testament witness to Christ and to his work of manifesting God and saving humanity; they thus have preeminence among the Scriptures. Among the writings of the New Testament, the gospels have special revelatory power in that "they are our principal source for the life and teaching of the incarnate Word, our Savior" (*DV,* 18). The apostles "and others of the apostolic age" (ibid.) were led by the Holy Spirit "to interpret normatively and apply what they had directly experienced of the fullness of revelation in the person of Christ."[21] The fourfold gospel is

[16] *Lineamenta,* 16.

[17] *Dei Verbum,* 11; cf. *Lineamenta,* 14.

[18] *Lineamenta,* 13, citing *Dei Verbum,* 7.

[19] *Lineamenta,* 9e; *Instrumentum Laboris,* 18.

[20] Cf. René Latourelle, "Le Christ signe de la revelation selon la constitution *Dei Verbum,*" *Gregorianum* 47/4 (1966) 685–709, here 690.

[21] Gerald O'Collins, "Revelation Past and Present," *Vatican II: Assessment and Perspectives,* 125–37, here 136.

therefore "the foundation of faith" (ibid.). The addition of "others of the apostolic age" leaves open the question of the authorship of some gospels by people who were not apostles but who both lived in their generation and were close to them. The council left open the question of the order of production of the gospels and had nothing to say about either the priority of Matthew (ancient tradition going back to Papias in the second century and argued scientifically in the nineteenth century in the Gries-bach Hypothesis, the so-called Two Gospel Hypothesis) or the priority of Mark (the so-called Two Document Hypothesis), which still holds the field, albeit with increasing attacks from scholars. What this seems to say is that neither hypothesis endangers divine and Catholic faith. It is rather a question of discerning which best solves the issues raised and is more congruent with the other realities of the faith.

The historicity of the gospels became a burning issue in Vatican Council II: did they hand on the very words and deeds (*ipsissima verba et acta*) of Jesus? In what manner are they reliable "history" witnessing to Jesus and thus "the foundation of faith"? The answer is that "Holy Mother Church"[22] has "firmly and with absolute constancy maintained and continues to maintain" (the earlier drafts had *believed* and continues *to believe*) that the four gospels faithfully hand on what Jesus Christ, while living among humankind, really did and taught for their eternal salvation (*DV*, 19).

> *The gospels present four faces of the same Jesus.*

Some features of our gospels seem to fly in the face of historicity. Even the casual reader notices that Jesus presents himself and speaks in the Gospel of John differently than in the Synoptics (the three gospels of Matthew, Mark, and Luke, so called because they contain parallels that can be read together in one glance, so to speak). In John, the ministry of Jesus lasted perhaps three years and was mostly in Judea and Jerusalem; in the Synoptics, it lasted perhaps one year and was mostly in Galilee. There are divergences that cannot be true at the same time. For example, sending out his disciples, Jesus told them to take "no bag for your journey, or two tunics, *or sandals, or a staff*" (Matt 10:10; cf. Luke 9:3). Mark 6:8 has them taking "nothing for their journey *except a staff*; no bread, no bag, no money in their belts; but to *wear sandals.*" As Jesus left Jericho with a great crowd, he encountered blind Bartimaeus,

---

[22] *Sancta Mater Ecclesia*—these very words begin *DV*, 19, and began the Instruction Concerning the Historical Truth of the Gospels (see below), thus evincing the dependence of one on the other.

as explained in Mark 10:46 and Matthew 20:29. In Luke 20:35 this encounter was as he drew near to Jericho! In Mark 16:8, the women left the
tomb "and they said nothing to anyone, *for they were afraid.*"[23] Matthew
28:8 reports, "*Filled with awe and great joy* the women came quickly away
from the tomb and *ran to tell* his disciples."[24] These features show that the
gospels are by no means journals of the life of Jesus. Rather, they present
four faces of the same Jesus, while always telling us "the authentic truth
about Jesus" (*DV*, 19).

The council was helped by a document published in April 1964 by
the Pontifical Biblical Commission, *Sancta Mater Ecclesia* (Holy Mother
Church), Instruction Concerning the Historical Truth of the Gospels, before the third session of the council. The reader may consult chapter 7 of
this book for more on this document. The document condemned the false
idea that faith had nothing to do with historical truth, even though the
genre of gospel is preaching, proclamation. Preachers proclaimed Christ
according to various modes of speaking: catechesis, stories, *testimonia*,
hymns, doxologies, prayers, and other literary forms customary at the time.
In its preaching, the early church was attentive to Jesus' testimony about
himself but also availed of the increased understanding of his mystery they
gained after Pentecost. *Dei Verbum*, 19, summarized sections of number
ix of this Instruction as follows:

> The sacred authors, in writing the four Gospels, selected certain of
> the many elements which had been handed down, either orally or
> in written form; others they synthesized or explained with an eye
> to the situation of the churches. They retained the preaching style,
> but always in such fashion that they have told us the authentic truth
> about Jesus.

So, three levels of the tradition about Jesus are to be distinguished: the
context of the life and ministry of Jesus, the preaching of the event of Jesus
adapted to the needs of various early communities, and the writing of the
gospels by four evangelists, each of whom had particular perspectives and
addressed certain concerns of his community.[25]

---

[23] Mark 16:9-10, the very next verses, but that belong to what is usually called the "longer ending" of Mark, reports of Mary Magdalene, one of the women, that "she went out and
told those who had been with him."

[24] New Jerusalem Bible; by adding "joy" to the root for fear, Matthew turned the fear of
the women in Mark into "awe"!

[25] Cf. José Caba, "Historicity of the Gospels (*Dei Verbum*, 19): Genesis and Fruits of the
Conciliar Text," *Vatican II: Assessment and Perspectives*, 299–320, here 312.

Among the fruits of *Dei Verbum*, 19, have been multiple books on "the historical Jesus," among which is that of Benedict XVI, *Jesus of Nazareth*.[26] Criteria for doing such research have developed and are constantly being sharpened.[27] Increasingly, Catholic scholars are taking account of the theology and tendencies of each evangelist, what is called redaction criticism.

Instrumentum Laboris, 13, among other things, asks that in teaching and reading the Bible the priority of the gospels be emphasized, even if they must be read in conjunction with the other books of the Old and New Testaments and the documents of the church's magisterium. This is because, as it explains in number 21, the spiritual sense of Scripture comports the reading of it "under the influence of the Holy Spirit in the context of the paschal mystery of Christ and the new life which comes from it."[28]

Appendix: Pathways of the Theology of Revelation

The synod answered the question, is Scripture word of God? in two ways. Scripture *contains* the word of God and *is* the word of God. According to *Dei Verbum*, 24, "the sacred Scriptures contain the word of God, and, because they are inspired, they truly are the word of God." Pressing the point further, the synod several times affirmed that ultimately the word of God was a Person, Jesus Christ, the Word Incarnate. However, all we know of this Person derives from Scripture,[29] and even direct knowledge of him, perhaps through contemplation and personal enlightenment or through private revelation, has Scripture as norm.

Revelation closed with the death of the last apostle and is now enshrined in the one fount of Scripture and tradition. Yet active revelation has not ceased. God, through the action of the Holy Spirit, continues to reveal God's self to all humanity, not just to Christians. O'Collins asks the

---

[26] Benedict XVI, *Jesus of Nazareth: From the Baptism in the Jordan to the Transfiguration* (New York and London: Doubleday, 2007).

[27] John P. Meier, *A Marginal Jew: Rethinking the Historical Jesus: The Roots of the Problem and the Person*, vol. 1 (New York: Doubleday, 1991) 167–95, gives the following: multiple attestation, discontinuity or dissimilarity, coherence or consistency, embarrassment, sufficient grounds for rejection and execution of Jesus. Minor and not so clear criteria are Aramaic substratum, Palestinian environment, vividness of narration, the tendencies of the evangelists.

[28] Citing the Pontifical Biblical Commission, The Interpretation of the Bible in the Church, II, B, 2.

[29] "It is stated that Scripture is the Word of God consigned to writing. Tradition, however, is described only functionally, in terms of what it *does*: it hands on the word of God, but is not the word of God" (Joseph Ratzinger in *Commentary on the Documents of Vatican II*, vol. 3, ed. Herbert Vorgrimler [New York: Herder, 1969] 194).

question, "if revelation was definitively completed in the past, how can it happen today?"[30] Is it that present revelation is no revelation in the true sense, only a growth in collective understanding of the completed biblical revelation? He answered by drawing a distinction between *foundational* revelation and *dependent* revelation:

> Revelation continues to be an actual encounter, but this living dialogue adds nothing to "the divinely revealed realities" (which essentially amount to Jesus Christ crucified and risen from the dead).[31]

The various ways in which God continues to speak through the Holy Spirit have been outlined above. The synod wished to respond to the word of God in all these diverse ways and so to attain to a renewal of the church, of Christians, and of humanity at large. A definitive theology of revelation that embraces all its aspects in a dynamic synthesis still needs to be crafted. Here we give a summary of the attempts of various scholars.

Sandra Schneiders[32] considers the significance of Scripture as word of God in the church. "Word of God" is a metaphor. A metaphor "is an instrument of new meaning"; it both "is" and "is not" what its referent says.[33] Metaphor gives opening to a "realm of significance that cannot be expressed literally but engages the imagination in a cognitive and affective exploration of the subject."[34] To say that Sacred Scripture is word of God is to use a "root metaphor," that is, "one that, like the root system of a tree . . . draws together in a living synthesis numerous diverse cognitive and affective elements and nourishes ever new growth in meaning."[35] "Scripture as language consists of human words and only human words"; but these human words are the "symbolic locus of divine revelation."[36] For Schneiders, "the real referent of the metaphor 'word of God' is the entire mystery of divine revelation . . . in and through such symbols as creation, sacred history, Jesus himself, and the life of the believing community."[37] In this

---

[30] Gerald O'Collins, "Revelation Past and Present," *Vatican II: Assessment and Perspectives*, 125–37, here 128.

[31] Ibid., 130.

[32] Sandra M. Schneiders, *The Revelatory Text: Interpreting the New Testament as Sacred Scripture*, 2nd ed. (Collegeville, MN: Liturgical Press, 1999).

[33] Ibid., 29.

[34] Ibid., 31.

[35] Ibid., 32.

[36] Ibid., 33.

[37] Ibid., 41.

sense, "Sacred Scripture is the sacrament of the word of God."[38] However, it is sacrament in the "fully actualized sense of the word only when it is being read, when it is coming to event as meaning through interpretation" and homily.[39] Scripture grounds and governs the ongoing revelatory experience of Christians in succeeding ages. By witnessing to foundational revelation, Scripture constitutes a privileged possibility of revelation in the present, that is, of address by God and response by humans.

Raymond Brown began his essay "And the Lord Said? Biblical Reflections on Scripture as the Word of God"[40] by asking whether God internally supplied words to the recipient of revelation/inspiration. The answer was no. Ecclesiastes would definitely deny that he had received any word of God; he was writing out of collected human experience. Amos 9:8-15 uses the prophetic formula "thus says the Lord" to correct the pessimistic tone of other "thus says the Lord" in the whole of Amos! Diverse traditions of the words of Jesus showed that his disciples felt these words as time-conditioned and local-conditioned, needing adaptation in transmission. Brown thus arrived at the conclusion that "word of God" meant divine communication in human words. Only humans speak words; revelation by the word of God "really means divine revelation to which human beings have given expression in words."[41]

Karl Rahner reflected on revelation on the grounds of the human experience of God.[42] Human beings meet God freely in their encounter with the world and other persons. Active revelation is "the transcendental experience of the absolute and merciful closeness of God, even if this cannot be conceptually expressed at will by everyone."[43] Human history is a "supernatural existential" in which persons receive the free self-communication of God as the innermost center of their being and history (the reader may refer to Cardinal Ouellet's *dimension anthropoligique* in chapter 4, "The Synod in Session and *Verbum Domini*," and his definition there of the human being as *un être appelé à l'écoute de la parole*). *Transcendental revelation* ("categori-

---

[38] Ibid.

[39] Ibid., 43.

[40] *Theological Studies* 42 (1981) 3–19.

[41] Raymond Brown, "'And the Lord Said'? Biblical Reflections on Scripture as the Word of God," *TS* 42 (1981) 13.

[42] For this review of Rahner, I am indebted to John D. Morrison, "The Nature of Holy Scripture in Roman Catholic Discussion from Vatican II to the New Catechism," *Trinity Journal* 24/NS (2003) 259–82.

[43] "Revelation," *Encyclopedia of Theology: The Concise Sacramentum Mundi*, ed. Karl Rahner (New York: Seabury Press, 1975) 1453–73, here 1461.

cal" or real revelation) is universal, coextensive with human history, even though not identical with it. It occurs in history through events, symbols, and words, and is dialogical, in the sense that it draws persons to this "ever more intensely an explicitly religious self-interpretation of this supernatural, transcendental and revelatory experience of God."[44] Transcendental revelation is not to be narrowly identified with revelation in the Old and New Testaments (Scripture). Though these manifest a "successful" instance or full realization of the single history of revelation, they remain "brief and partial histories within this categorical history of revelation in which a part of this self-reflection and reflexive self-presence of universal revelation and its history is found in its purity."[45] Jesus Christ is the criterion for distinguishing legitimate understanding of the transcendental experience of God. Is the Scripture "word of God" and how? As the church's book, a product of categorical revelation and literary concretization of the testimony of the apostolic church, Scripture is the norm for the church's understanding of faith and can be called the "written word of God." Yet it is a "moment" in the process of God's turning to human beings in revelation as saving history. God is not the *literary* author of Scripture; God is author of Scripture only in the indirect sense that God founded the church by God's Spirit in Jesus Christ and the apostolic witness (now in Scripture) is the norm for the faith of the church.

Models of Revelation

As *doctrine*

As *history*

As *inner experience*

As *dialectical presence*

As *new awareness*

As *symbolic communication*

Avery Dulles reflected on the models of revelation.[46] He explored five ways in which people have understood revelation: as *doctrine*, as *history*, as *inner experience*, as *dialectical presence*, and as *new awareness*, and proposed his own, revelation as *symbolic communication*.[47] Revelation as *doctrine* (conservative evangelicalism and Catholic neoscholasticism) is propositional, hence a deposit of truths. The Bible consists of propositions that give information about God and God's dealings with humankind

---

[44] Karl Rahner, "The History of Salvation and Revelation," *Foundations of the Christian Faith* (New York: Seabury Press, 1978) 138–75, here 154.

[45] Rahner, *Foundations of the Christian Faith*, 155, 156.

[46] *Models of Revelation* (New York: Doubleday, 1983).

[47] He used seven criteria to assess each: faithfulness to Bible and Christian tradition, internal coherence, plausibility, adequate to experience, practical fruitfulness, theoretical fruitfulness, and value for dialogue.

and the world. As "utterances of God bearing witness to himself,"[48] it is inerrant. The events themselves are not revelation, only as clarified by word. Revelation as *history* (pp. 54–67) is revelation through deeds, not words. G. Ernest Wright wrote in this vein that "the primary means by which God communicates with man is by his acts which are the events of history."[49] The Bible becomes not the words of God but a record of the acts of God. For Wolfhart Pannenberg,[50] revelation never occurs except indirectly through history. It is not found in a segment of history but its totality. The events themselves are self-interpreting. The totality of God's activity in history indirectly discloses God himself. Revelation as *inner experience* (pp. 68–83) consists in an immediate experience of God who inwardly communicates with each believer (Friedrich Schleiermacher, H. Wheeler Robinson, Karl Rahner, Piet Fransen). The dichotomy between natural and supernatural is rejected; religion always arises out of some particular experience of the divine. Revelation as *dialectical presence* (pp. 84–97) sees the revealing God as the concealed God, who in Jesus turns to humans in forgiveness and judgment (Karl Barth, Emil Brunner, Rudolf Bultmann). Nature, religious experience, and non-Christian religious traditions are incapable of conveying revelation. Faith and revelation are correlatives: revelation is never so unless when it is occurring. The Bible becomes word of God for me in the very moment of revelation, when God's Spirit renders me capable of acknowledging what has happened in Christ. Finally, revelation as *new awareness* (pp. 94–114) posits an expansion of consciousness that projects a new perspective on self and world (Gregory Baum, Thomas O'Meara, Leslie Dewart). It is primarily a state of mind, not knowledge of an object. Faith is not new knowledge but new consciousness created by the Christian message. What does it mean to say that revelation closed with Jesus Christ? Divine revelation is fully given in the incarnation, but the incarnation continues to occur as the Body of Christ is built up (Teilhard de Chardin). It has to do with the transformation of humans now (Baum). Dulles himself saw revelation as *symbolic communication* (pp. 131–54). For him, it never occurs as a purely interior experience or unmediated encounter with God but rather revelatory symbols mediate and express God's self-communication. Revelation as symbol is not informative, only evocative. Its truth is its capacity to create

---

[48] *Models of Revelation*, 39, citing J. I. Parker, "Contemporary Views of Revelation," *Revelation and the Bible*, ed. C. F. H. Henry (Grand Rapids: Baker Book House, 1958) 90.

[49] *The God Who Acts: Biblical Theology as Recital* (London: SCM, 1952) 107.

[50] *Revelation as History: Basic Questions in Theology*, vol. 1 (Philadelphia: Fortress Press, 1970).

"a new vision of the world and new possibilities." This occurs within the formative, directive, and interpretive parameters of the community of faith, with Scripture, church tradition, revelatory events, and encounters serving as the lens by which God's revelation is apprehended. What, then, is the relation between Scripture and revelation (p. 201)? The actual content of God's self-disclosure is unknowable. "God is first and foremost author of his people" (p. 202). However, God's authorship of a community of faith involved the production of writings expressive of that faith, and so concomitantly God willed to be "author" of the religious writings (p. 202).

Questions for Discussion

1. "By deeds and words having an inner unity" (*DV*, 2). Explain and give some examples of this from the Bible.

2. Is God speaking actively to our world today? Discuss.

3. Discuss the relationship of the Old Testament to the New Testament as described in the *Lineamenta* and *Instrumentum Laboris*.

4. There are various senses of the "word of God." What are these senses and of what import are they for your Christian commitment and/or pastoral work?

5. Which of the positions on revelation in the appendix resonates with you and why? Trace some implications of the position you have chosen.

6. Discuss the historical truth of the gospels.

7. Discuss the criteria for the historical Jesus in John P. Meier, *A Marginal Jew*, vol. 1, 167–95 (see note 27 above).

Chapter 3

The Word of God
on the Five Continents

On October 6, 2008, various bishops reported on the word of God in their continents. They were the following:

Most Rev. John Onaiyekan, archbishop of Abuja, Nigeria, on Africa

Most Rev. Thomas Menamparampil, archbishop of Guwahati, India, on Asia

Oscar Cardinal Andres Rodriguez Maradiaga, archbishop of Tegucigalpa, Honduras, on the Americas

Most Rev. Michael Putney, bishop of Townsville, Australia, on Oceania

Josip Cardinal Bozanic, archbishop of Zagreb, Croatia, on Europe

This chapter outlines the salient points of the responses contained in the *Instrumentum Laboris,* and then presents those of the reports on the continents. To organize the material I developed three headings of *access, practice,* and *hermeneutics,* except for the last report (on Europe), where I use the rapporteur's own categories of *revelation, interpretation,* and *celebration.* There is some overlapping of the responses and reports. The reports are available on the web site of the synod of bishops.[1]

The Responses in the *Instrumentum Laboris*

Access. The Dogmatic Constitution on Divine Revelation, *Dei Verbum,* 22, called for giving Catholics wider access to Sacred Scripture. For as St. Jerome said, "ignorance of Scripture is ignorance of Christ."[2] The Catholic Biblical Apostolate has, in fact, advanced immensely since Paul VI instituted the World Catholic Biblical Federation in 1968, now operative in 129 countries.

---

[1] http://www.vatican.va/news_services/press/sinodo/documents/bollettino_22_xii
-ordinaria-2008/02_inglese/b05_02.html, accessed September 2, 2009. For the summary of these reports only the name of the rapporteur can be referenced.

[2] *Lineamenta,* 24. Jerome, *Commentary on Isaiah,* prologue.

Its goal is to distribute Bibles in various languages and provide people with assistance in knowing it and living its teaching through accurate translations.[3] Despite this effort and the extensive distribution of the Bible through the biblical apostolate and the endeavors of communities, groups, and ecclesial movements,[4] many Christians remain without any contact with the Bible.[5] In many parts of the world widespread illiteracy means that "learning depends primarily on seeing and hearing; as a result it is momentary and limited."[6] In other parts of the world, the prevailing religious culture does not allow immediate access to the Bible (ibid). In some parts of the world, there is a scarcity of Bible translations, such that many cannot access the word in their own language. Even where the Bible is fully accessible, too many of the faithful are reluctant to open it for various reasons, especially because they feel it might be too difficult to read. Some prefer to read easily understood spiritual books, edifying talks or writings, and various other works associated with popular piety. Some even hold that people encounter the word of God in a practical way by living it in their lives, more than by knowing its origin or reasoning.[7] Many of those who read the Bible lack either sufficient knowledge of the deposit of faith to which the Bible belongs or the suitable method of reading it necessary for real encounters with the Word.

Practice. Some new Christians are attributing magical powers to reading the Bible, without commitment and responsibility.[8] Numerous sects use the Bible for purposes and methods that are opposed to the church.[9] In the context of dialogue with other religions, the danger exists of reducing Christianity to a "religion of the Book" comparable to the sacred texts of other religions.[10] Yet the Bible is not exclusively for Christians; it is a treasure for all humanity.[11]

---

[3] Ibid., 26.

[4] *Instrumentum Laboris,* "Forward."

[5] *Lineamenta,* 4.

[6] *Instrumentum Laboris,* 46. While this may be true in part, it does seem to represent a certain cultural bias in favor of writing and reading, rather than speaking and hearing. Before the advent of writing, whole cultures transmitted knowledge orally. The word was first spoken and heard for centuries before being committed to writing. In parts of the world, experiments with oral exegesis and oral communication of the Word and dramatization have proven very successful. See the report on Africa below.

[7] *Instrumentum Laboris,* 18.

[8] Ibid., 23.

[9] Ibid.

[10] Cf. *Lineamenta,* chapter II, q. 1.

[11] *Instrumentum Laboris,* 56.

The faithful hunger for the word of God, but they are not always fed by the preaching of many pastors. The formation of some pastors did not make the word of God the center and source of all pastoral activity. The result is that the people of God have hardly been introduced to a theology of the word of God in the liturgy.[12] In the sacrament of reconciliation, the relation of the word to the sacrament appears to be given little value (ibid.). There is a general lack of familiarity with *Dei Verbum*, the Vatican II Dogmatic Constitution on Divine Revelation.[13] One of the results of such lack of familiarity is the apparent dichotomy between exegesis and the spiritual life of Catholics and between exegetical research and theological formulation. The remedy is to fully implement the instruction of *Dei Verbum*, 24, that "the study of the sacred page should be the very soul of sacred theology," also the recommendations of *Optatam Totius* (Vatican II Decree on Priestly Formation) on the subject of biblical exegesis and the teaching of theology.[14] Pastors in the particular churches are requesting better thematic coordination of the three readings in the liturgy (ibid).

Hermeneutics. Many question the meaning of inspiration and the truth of Scripture, and demand clarification of the historicity of the biblical narratives. Gnostic and esoteric forms of interpreting Sacred Scripture are on the rise. Fundamentalist attitudes are growing even in Catholic circles. Fundamentalism takes refuge in literalism and refuses to take into consideration the historical dimension of biblical revelation, thus showing itself unable to fully accept the incarnation.[15] Many of Christ's faithful do not understand in what sense Jesus is at the heart of the word of God.[16] Also, "knowledge of the Old Testament as the word of God seems to be a real problem among Catholics."[17] The listing of difficulties with the Old Testament includes ideas on God, man and woman, and moral conduct,[18] and also a certain view of history, science, and the moral life, particularly ethical behavior and how God is portrayed.[19] Present-day developments

---

[12] Ibid., 33.

[13] The person in the pew, and even some pastors, in the name of fidelity to faith, resist some approaches to the Word outlined in the council document.

[14] *Instrumentum Laboris*, 40.

[15] Ibid., 29.

[16] Ibid., 11.

[17] Ibid., 17.

[18] *Lineamenta*, 22b.

[19] *Instrumentum Laboris*, 45. During the group discussion phase, a Spanish group (report by Rev. Julien Carron, president of Communion and Liberation) noted that Catholics are unfamiliar with the Old Testament and are embarrassed with and resist divine and human

in bioethics and inculturation pose problems for Bible reading. Many are seeking a proper pastoral approach to the exegesis of the biblical text. It would seem that many exegetes adopt a merely historical approach and fail to achieve "an inner immersion into the presence of the word" that would make Scripture "an up-to-date Word of God."[20]

After the responses from the particular churches, I now present the reports on the various continents.

The Word of God in Africa (Archbishop Onaiyekan)

Introduction. Much of what is happening concerning the word of God in Africa remains undocumented. They take place on the local level and remain there, because of limited resources for publication. Nevertheless, one can take heart in the fact that the local level is where the action of the Spirit of the Lord is working. The *Instrumentum Laboris* well said that "in younger local churches, Bible usage among the faithful is more extensive than in other places."[21] This is the case for Africa. The word of God in the synod documents is a reality that goes beyond the text of Scripture: it is "the dialogue of God with the entire humanity, which reaches out to all human beings of every age and place" (I, 1). The Word, being "the true light, which enlightens everyone" (John 1:9), has touched also the practitioners of African Traditional Religion. This religion has been not just a *preparatio evangelica* (preparation for the gospel) "but indeed a welcoming environment and a fertile soil for the announcement of the Word of God, both in scripture and in the ministry of the church" (I, 1). In fact, followers of African Traditional Religion gladly listen to the stories of the Bible and even adopt much of what it says.

Access. Since Vatican II, large sections of the lay faithful have developed a strong thirst for the word of God in Sacred Scripture. However, with the weak economies of Africa, a Bible may cost as much as one month's wages in many places. The Protestants are to be commended for making access to the word of God a priority. In many places, the Catholic Church has teamed up with them within the context of the Bible Society. One must also mention the efforts of the Fathers and Daughters of St. Paul (the

---

violence in it. They also complain about the amorality of some biblical figures and the insufficiency of its views of the afterlife.

[20] *Lineamenta*, 15, citing Benedict XVI, Discourse to the Bishops of Switzerland, November 7, 2006, in *L'Osservatore Romano*, weekly edition in English (November 22, 2006) 5, 10.

[21] *Instrumentum Laboris*, 7b.

Paulines) and the SVD (Congregation of the Divine Word), who publish
many Bible texts and materials at more affordable prices. Many languages
do not have an adequate translation of the Bible, yet the Bible in the vernacular is absolutely essential. Since Vatican II, the Catholic Church has
joined Protestants to produce ecumenical translations. Hindrances in this
task are financing and the necessary expertise. African culture is largely an
oral culture; one cannot overemphasize the importance of listening to the
word of God. In fact, those who listen to the word of God may be even
more blessed than those who read it. Though Africa still lags behind in
the new communications technologies, cellular phones and the internet
are becoming available even in remote areas. These technologies are great
possibilities for the spread of the word of God, but there is "a crying need
for a world-wide solidarity and sharing of resources" if these possibilities
are to be adequately tapped in Africa (I, 3.4).

Practice. Being only 14 percent Catholic, Africa is still a continent of
primary evangelization. In accordance with the *General Directory for Catechesis* and following the example of the *Catechism of the Catholic Church*,
catechesis in Africa has become more and more deeply rooted in Sacred
Scripture. Greater familiarity with Scripture is bringing Catholics closer to
our brothers and sisters of other Christian traditions, for whom Scripture
is often the main source of guidance for Christian living. Problems exist
with groups who are both fundamentalist and anti-Catholic, but precisely
the greater familiarity with Scripture is enabling Catholics to stand their
ground when others attack their beliefs or the Catholic Church. Muslims
respect the sacred text and the Qur'an has many parallels with our Scriptures. However, because of Christian-Muslim rivalries in many places,
not much is being done by way of Christian-Muslim dialogue. Besides,
some Muslim fanatics assert that the Holy Qur'an is God's correction and
improvement on the Christian Scriptures.

Since Vatican II, *lectio divina* has been part of the Bible Apostolate in
Africa. Some of the methods for reading, meditating, and applying the
Scriptures to the lives of the people have come from the Lumko Pastoral
Center in South Africa and the Dzogbegan Monastery in North Togo, to
name a few, and these have been adapted in places around the world.

Almost every Episcopal conference has a commission on the Bible and
the direction of the Bible Apostolate. At the continental level, SECAM
(Symposium of the Episcopal Conferences of Africa and Madagascar) runs
a coordinating office called the Biblical Centre for Africa and Madagascar
(BICAM), now in Accra, Ghana. There is also PACE (Pan-African Associ-

ation of Catholic Exegetes), which holds congresses about once every two years.

Hermeneutics. The word of God is interpreted both at the scientific level and at the popular level. In Africa, a kind of popular "'spiritual instinct' for the right understanding of the Word of God . . . sometimes puts to shame the irresponsible speculations" of some critical exegetes (I, 3.3). But Africa does need more trained exegetes for the Catholic principles on Scripture to take root in clerics and religious in formation, in catechists and other ministers of the Word, and indeed among the lay faithful.

The Word of God in Asia (Archbishop Menamparampil)

Introduction. "It was in Asia that the Word became flesh. It was from there that His saving message was carried in all directions" (no. 1). Syrian monks carried God's word with great enthusiasm to Persia, Afghanistan, Central Asia, West China, and South India. Local faith expressions took shape. It was not long before Christians numbered over seventy million.

One hindrance to evangelization has been the bale of empire. When Christianity was declared the official religion of the Roman Empire, Persia's chief rival and enemy, Christianity tended to look to Persians like an alien loyalty. The advanced civilizations of Asia did not think they needed anything beyond the results of their own intellectual effort and religious search. The dominant classes resisted Christian evangelization, but marginal groups welcomed the liberative power of the Good News (Luke 4:18). Later missionaries, people like Francis Xavier, Matteo Ricci, Roberto de Nobili, and others who knew how to adapt to the culture, created great openings for the word. Missionaries put oral languages to writing, "pursued ethnological studies," "intervened on behalf of oppressed communities," and offered generous services in the fields of health and education. "They initiated theological reflection in different cultural contexts, with an edifying measure of self-criticism, that laid the foundation of today's missiological thinking" in Asia (no. 7). The word had persuasive power especially as it was translated into action, with people like Mother Teresa as a recent example. In recent times, missionaries have entered new areas: "illiteracy, unemployment, urban violence, gender and caste inequality, female feticide, and drug addiction" (no. 8).

Access. In many places, the word is better "whispered behind closed doors" than "proclaimed from the housetops" (Luke 12:3)—a strategic choice in places where freedom of religion is limited. Many new Asian

Catholics suffer harassment and Christian communities are persecuted. In the midst of all this, Vatican II's call for giving the faithful greater access to the word has been heeded. Bible translations, many as ecumenical efforts, have multiplied. Bibles and Bible-related materials are available in schools and hospitals and for people in various situations of life. Bible-related books keep growing in our libraries. The Amity Printing Company of Nanjing (China) printed six million Bibles in 2007, and is planning to increase its printing to twelve million Bibles per year.

Practice. The sacred Word is meaningful to Asians who have ancient books they consider sacred and authoritative and that deeply influence their lives and culture. Asians are open to God's word and even people who are unwilling to convert to Christianity are eager to hear the Word in their search for greater spiritual depth. Biblical studies are pursued through correspondence courses, even in the vernacular. Bible schools are an innovative service; weekend Bible courses are becoming popular. Study aids are produced on a large scale (audio visuals, paintings, art pieces, films, CDs, cassettes, lessons on the internet, etc.). Electronic media (Radio Veritas, Shalom TV) bring Catholic news and views to remote villages. Folk media (dances, dramas, storytelling, etc.) skillfully retell biblical stories.

> *"Catholics in Japan are 0.4% of the 120 million population. Yet the Bible is one of the most read books and appreciated by non-Christians, especially the cultured. For children, the Bible is available in cartoons, for lovers of music in a vast repertoire of excellent music"* (Sr. Appollinaris Yuriko, CSM, superior general, Sisters of Charity of Miyazaki, Japan, October 17, 2008).

Church attendance is encouragingly high in Asia. Bible Sundays are observed. Bible study groups are increasing in number. In remote villages where the Eucharist is not possible every Sunday, people gather with great devotion around the word of God. "People in large numbers flock to charismatic retreats that announce God's Word in all its power" (no. 15). Significant church growth is being recorded through direct interaction with and sharing of the word of God with some ethnic minorities in parts of China, Indonesian Islands, North Myanmar, Thailand, Northeast India, and other places. Asians seek the spiritual depth that comes from contemplation and God-experience. It is in this sense that contemplation of the word of God is very much the future of mission in Asia.[22] No wonder there is growing interest in *lectio divina*, people reading the Word, reflecting on it, praying, and applying it to their situation. Some follow the Lumko (developed in South Africa) and AsIPA (developed in Asia) methods. However, without guidance free interpretation often leads people to leave the church and join some fundamentalist groups. Homilies break open the word during the liturgy, though they generally need to be less academic and more relevant to Christian living.

People are turning to Christ in their search for meaning. Young adults turn to the biblical message to deepen their understanding of life and become sharers of the word. This is a very important development, seeing that Asia is 65 percent young. "Asian religions are showing signs of great vitality and a capacity for renewal. . . . Dialoguing with members of vibrant religions can be a stimulus to one's own faith" (no. 14).

Vocations are flourishing in Asia. Religious life is understood, for "there are native models of religious life" in the Asian religions and people have high regard for "religious values like renunciation, austerity, silence, prayer, contemplation, and celibacy" (no. 18). Formation houses for clergy and catechists multiply, creating a great need for trainers of these announcers of the word.

Hermeneutics. Reflection needs to deepen God's word in the Asian context of poverty, injustice, and plurality of religions. There is need for categories of thought, symbolism, and spiritual traditions that are meaningful to Asians. When this is done, inculturation of the word of God takes place at a deep level. "It is in order to further this effort that Asian theological journals keep offering a wide selection of indigenous theological reflection," seeking thus "to contribute to 'the growth of the word' (Acts 6:7; 12:24; 19:20)" (no. 21). Despite all this, the present style of teaching the Scriptures seems too academic and not adequately oriented to a spiritual and pastoral use of the Bible. (A synod father reported that plans were afoot to produce an Asian biblical commentary and to establish an Asian biblical institute.[23]) Beyond textbook presentation based on truth claims, however, ordinary human encounters have proven an occasion for interpreting the word of

[22] Citing John Paul II, *Redemptoris Missio*, 91: "my contact with representatives of the non-Christian spiritual traditions, particularly those of Asia, has confirmed me in the view that the future of mission depends to a greater extent on contemplation."

[23] Bishop Arturo Bastes, SVD, bishop of Sorsogon, Philippines, October 11, 2008. The Asian commentary series will combine the historical-critical method with comparative cultural hermeneutics.

God in human situations: "a message of peace to situations of conflict, of justice to oppressed communities, of probity to corruption-ridden societies, of equality to unfair situations," and also in the Christian community's dedication to the common good (no. 25).

The Word of God in the Americas
(Oscar Cardinal Rodriguez Maradiaga)

Introduction. The report covers Latin America, the Caribbean, the United States of America, and Canada. More than 50 percent of the world's Catholics are found on the continent, which also contains some of the poorer nations of the world. "Christopher Columbus carried with him the first exemplar of the text of the Bible, . . . and usually gave biblical names to the islands he discovered" ("Historical Introduction"[24]). The first to teach the gospel in the language of the natives was probably the Catalan monk Ramon Pane, who arrived with Columbus's second journey. He learned the language of the region of Macori and wrote the first American anthropological treatise. Unfortunately, "Christianity reached America at the time of Reformation, when the Bible lost its privileged place in the Catholic Church" ("Four Centuries of Biblical Hibernation"). The continent as a result suffered four centuries of biblical hibernation. Translations of the Bible into the local languages became difficult. The *Catechism* and doctrine replaced biblical texts. But Vatican II initiated a veritable renewal in the ministry of the word.

Access. A hunger for the word of God has spread throughout the continent, especially among the marginalized. The increasing use of the vernacular in celebrations calls even more urgently for translations of the Bible into the vernacular. There are four major languages and about two hundred minor ones—a daunting task for translations of the word!

The Fourth General Conference of Santo Domingo (1992) called for translations of the word into the native languages and the production of popular editions. Bibles still cost too much for the poor, so there is need for less expensive editions. Currently there are twenty-six versions or translations approved by the church, among which are two complete Bibles in English (for the United States of America, parts of Canada, and the Caribbean) and eight in French (for parts of Canada and the Caribbean). The first edition of the Latin American Bible has had, since 1972, a

---

[24] Since sections of the report are not numbered, the titles of his section headings are cited.

distribution of sixty million copies. The United Bible Societies have made an important contribution in translations in cooperation with Catholic biblicists and in new presentations of the Bible in support of pastoral work.

Practice. The Conference of Medellin (1968) gave an important place to the Bible in its deliberations. It called for the preparation of experts in Sacred Scripture. Catechesis is to transmit the word of God faithfully and it should pervade popular devotions. In Puebla (1979) CELAM (Episcopal Council of Latin America) called for rooting evangelization on the word of God. It declared Sacred Scripture "the soul of evangelization"[25] and the "fount of catechesis."[26] The Fourth General Conference of the Latin American bishops in Santo Domingo (1992) explicitly requested that the final document be "Christocentric in its content and biblical in its expression" ("Four Centuries of Biblical Hibernation"). The Conference of Aparecida (2007) had as its theme "disciples and missionaries of Jesus Christ so that our people may have life in Him." Its aim was to "make the word of God the source that animates all pastoral activities of the Church."[27] This conference insisted on the prayerful reading of the word, on pastoral care based on the Bible, and on the Bible's ecumenical import. In fact, the ecclesial originality of the Latin American church depends on meditation on the word. In 2004, CELAM opened the Biblical Pastoral for Latin America (CEBIPAL) for courses of pastoral biblical animation. This institute both promotes *lectio divina* and offers courses for the permanent formation of Bible teachers. It has trained *lectionautas*, young people formed in *lectio divina* through use of the internet. Today, the continent counts "a vast biblical bibliography in all the main languages, . . . a variety of editions of the *lectio divina*," and a great number of biblical journals and magazines that publish articles of a high quality and level of exegesis ("Study Institutes and Biblical Works"). Biblical formation through modern means of communication is on the increase. "Delegates of the Word" originated in Honduras in 1966. These are laypeople given a special biblical formation and authorized by the bishop to animate various ecclesial communities.[28] Among the shadows

---

[25] Echoing Leo XIII, *Providentissimus Deus*, 58, on Scripture as "soul of theology."

[26] In line with the teaching of Vatican II, for example, *Dei Verbum*, 24: "this ministry [of the Word] includes pastoral preaching, catechetics and all other Christian instruction, among which the liturgical homily should have an exceptional place."

[27] Inaugural speech of Pope Benedict XVI to the conference.

[28] Bishop Guido Plante of Choluteca, Honduras, October 11, 2008, gave their origin as follows. In March 1966 in the wake of Vatican II's Constitution on the Sacred Liturgy, Bishop Marcelo Gérin of Choluteca trained seventeen peasants and sent them to celebrate Holy Week in isolated communities without a priest. The enthusiasm was so great that the

emphasized by the Santo Domingo Conference were "the lack of biblical formation, homilies that are not very biblical, tendency to fundamentalism and biblicism, the lack of access to inexpensive editions for the poor" ("Four Centuries of Biblical Hibernation"). One may also mention readings that encourage passivity. It is a sobering fact that many who have passed through Catholic centers of formation and gone into public life seem to lack the requisite gospel orientation in their personal and public lives. "Did we help them encounter the God of the Word? Why, when inserted in public life . . . are the gospel values not the orientation of their lives?" ("Public Life. Christians Living According to the Word").

> "In my diocese . . . for example, all young priests were Delegates of the Word" (Bishop Guido Plante, Choluteca, Honduras, October 11, 2008).

Hermeneutics. There are more than thirty institutes in a network of biblical institutes. Latin America places hermeneutic understanding before exegesis. It identifies "fidelity to the message" with "fidelity to humankind." Puebla (1979) insisted on the importance of listening, studying, celebrating, and proclaiming the word of God. The church is to bear witness to the Word by denouncing situations of sin, carrying out the conversion it calls for, and contributing to building a new society. Interpretation is to be "not so much on the interpretation of the Bible as the interpretation of life in the light of the Bible" ("Four Centuries of Biblical Hibernation"). The Conference of Santo Domingo (1992) pointed the way when it spotlighted three texts as paradigmatic of the new evangelization: Hebrews 13:8, "Jesus Christ is the same today as he was yesterday and as he will be forever" (the motto of the conference), Luke 24:13-35 (Emmaus episode), and Luke 4:16-22 (Christ's programmatic preaching at Nazareth, foundational for the preferred option for the poor). These three texts emphasize the word of God, the central role of the laity, and the animation of the community. Aparecida (2007) adopted three moments of reflection on the word, as suggested by the Emmaus episode: "seeing through the eyes of the word (77), judging with the centrality of the word (134–40), and acting with the praying and reading community: *lectio divina* (331)" ("Four Centuries of Biblical Hibernation"). The kerygmatic

---

communities requested celebrations each Sunday. Thus arose the Delegates of the Word of God, now over ten thousand in Honduras and neighboring countries. The program has become a source of priestly vocation: "in my diocese of Choluteca, for example, all young priests were Delegates of the Word."

presentation of the word is to center on Christ the Savior, something that calls for five attitudes: the following of Jesus, witness of life, spirituality and prayer, poverty, and community life. The Catholic Biblical Federation of Latin America and the Caribbean has, among other themes, insisted on the profound spirituality that is rooted in the Bible for the building of a new society.

Nevertheless, there seems to be a divorce between exegesis and the interecclesial community, between exegesis and dogma, and between exegesis and pastoral care.

Conclusion. One may trace the continent's biblical journey in recent years as follows. "From 1965 to 1985 is the period of contact with the Bible text. These are the years of the translations and editions of the Bible, . . . the organization of biblical circles, of the reading and study of the sacred books on the part of the laity and the basic ecclesial communities" ("Tendencies in and Justification of Biblical Animation in the Whole of Pastoral Life"). The period from 1985 to 1993 is the stage of contact with the biblical message: indigenous biblical interpretation, structuring of methods of biblical pastoral activity, and the organization of study centers. From "1993 to 2007 is the period of contact with the person revealed in the Bible, Jesus Christ" (ibid.). It is the period of the centrality of the Bible in the life and mission of the church. From 2007 is the move to a reading that sets out from discipleship and *lectio divina* to produce its fruit in mission.[29]

The Word of God in Europe (Josip Cardinal Bozanic)

Introduction. There is an indissoluble bond between the Bible and Europe. Europe was born thanks to Christianity and thanks to the efforts of its patrons, Saint Benedict and Saints Cyril and Methodius. Christianity is both the founding principle that embraces and unifies Europe and "the privileged key for reading to understand our continent in its entirety" (no. 1). European culture is founded on the word of God. Christianization simply means a proclamation of the word of God capable of enlightening the different aspects of the life of people. Various themes of European culture find their origins in the Bible: human dignity, the recognition of

---

[29] It seems to this author that, except for the brief reference to versions of the Bible in the United States of America and Canada, this report centers mainly on Latin America and the Caribbean.

"Before Vatican II we had no Bibles in the vernacular. Under communism Bibles were forbidden and taken away. Only since 1990 have Bible and spiritual books begun to appear" (Sr. Janice Soluk, superior general, Handmaids of the Blessed Virgin Mary, the Immaculate, Rome, Italy, October 17, 2008).

human rights, separation of church and state, social justice and equitable law, to mention a few.[30]

Revelation. Revelation is not static but rather always accompanied by interpretation and celebration in an ongoing process. The word of God portrays a God who offers humankind the possibility of discovering God in the mystery of one's life. This word of God was proclaimed on European soil first to the Greco-Roman world in circumstances that often required the witness of martyrdom. This revelation transformed and "re-culturized" the mores of life. The process was repeated with the Franco-Germanic culture and with the Slavonic and other peoples. But now, Europeans are facing "the cultural marginalization of Christianity, the search for freedom outside the presence of God" (no. 3). Europe "wishes to run away from the revealed God and is looking for the source of its identity by closing itself into the *humanum* [the human dimension]" (no. 4). But life and identity come to Europe only through the interpreting word of God, without which Europe suffers a crisis of hope. "When humans do not listen to what God says, inevitably they will start speaking in God's place, but underlying this speaking is fear" and discouragement (ibid.). The word of God restores hope and joy.

Interpretation. Interpretation of the word of God is done in concert with a glance at humankind and at the world. In Europe, interpretation began already with the fathers of the church. With the Reformation important changes emerged and differences in method created disputes. Through the action of the Spirit and fruitful detachment from these disputes, European theology and pastoral ministry have been mutually enriched in their hermeneutic visions. The promotion of the knowledge of the Bible is necessary ever more today to avoid new fundamentalist readings and ideological drifting. In parts of Europe once under dictatorial regimes, the

---

[30] For this report, as said above, I have adopted the rapporteur's own scheme of *revelation, interpretation,* and *celebration,* which he centered on the dynamic divine-human exchange in *lectio divina.*

last of which was communism, "pastors and the faithful were able to resist the cruelty and horrors of ideology only because they trusted in the word of God" (no. 5). Europe rightly boasts its own development of theological thought. But more productive confrontation with scientific research and new ways of interpreting are called for, even if some of these ways seem to veer from the hermeneutical paradigms of Christian truth.

Celebration. The word of God interpreted becomes the celebrated Word and basis for the mission and action of the church. God's revelation is received, interpreted, and celebrated in *lectio divina*. By the latter is meant "not only the reading of the sacred text, which still always remains the essential reference for ecclesial discernment, nor . . . reading limited to restricting subjectivity. Rather, I think about listening to God which continuously acts upon history, unveiling his presence in every event" (no. 3). By such *lectio divina* we allow "God to read us." The life of the church in Europe becomes, then, the place where God is seen to reveal God's self. The differences of opinion in the church and conflicts between people are put in perspective. Celebration in such case makes the event of God present in the here and now (*re-praesentatio*). The prayerful and meditated reading of the word of God becomes the starting point for the most ordinary pastoral acts. To live as a Christian becomes "to be *lectio divina*," and this is an ongoing divine-human dynamic that transforms church and world.

The Word of God in Oceania (Most Rev. Michael Putney)

Access. European missionaries brought the word of God first to northeast Australia. The local population first rejected the offer of the word but then changed and embraced it, and it transformed their lives. During the nineteenth century, missionaries, Catholic and Protestant, carried the word from Australia and New Zealand to Oceania, which is inhabited by predominantly oral cultures. In these cultures, nevertheless, the Scriptures are treasured and read in homes. A challenge is the incredible number of languages in Oceania in which the word of God needs to be communicated and for whom Bible translations need to be prepared. For example, Papua New Guinea alone counts 843 languages; overall in Oceania there are as many as 1,200 distinct languages.

Practice. In Australia and New Zealand, which received the word of God first and in which churches grew and flourished, now, unfortunately, the word struggles to be heard. Australia (almost equally New Zealand) is one of the most secular countries in the world. Underneath the secularism, however, many Catholics live lives of deep faith in the word of God. The problem is that "the existence of God is not acknowledged in any way in the daily life of ordinary Australians and many New Zealanders." During his recent visit for the World Youth Day in Sydney, the Holy Father, Benedict XVI, spoke of a "spiritual desert" and the desperate search for meaning everywhere except where it can be found—in the word of God practiced in love. Many Australian youths returning from the World Youth Day and recognizing their ignorance of the teaching of the church are requesting opportunities for catechesis and for hearing the message of the gospel. The Pacific Islander people (in parts of New Zealand) tend to be more religious, though the new churches of the Pacific face the challenge of cultural transition from village to urban life. "Some Protestant groups have an approach to evangelization which ignores the cultural context and relies at times on a fundamentalist understanding of the word of God." Catholic evangelization is sometimes rejected because it is not distinguished from these.

Hermeneutics. The challenge confronting Australia and much of Oceania is to find new ways to enable the gift of the word of God to be heard. *Ecclesia in Oceania*[31] saw the word of God as the "inexhaustible wellspring of evangelization." Intense search continues as to how to translate this into practical terms, though there is as yet no one chosen method or even shared understanding. The recommendations of *Ecclesia in Oceania* as to the practice of *lectio divina* and the biblical formation of the people have only been partially acted upon.

Conclusion

I now point out some salient aspects of these reports. One result of Vatican II is that everywhere effort is being made to found the church's life and mission more and more on the word of God. *Lectio divina* seems to be practiced everywhere, though in different forms, but seems particularly emphasized in Asia, Africa, and the Americas. In Europe, *lectio divina* becomes the continuous listening to God who acts upon history and unveils the divine presence in every event. For more on *lectio divina* the reader should consult chapter 8 of this book.

Everywhere there is the danger of a fundamentalist biblical approach to the Bible. In some places the danger is more of sects who attack the church

[31] Apostolic exhortation, *Ecclesia in Oceania* (Vatican City, November 22, 2001) 10.

and even win over some Catholics. In others, the danger is within the church itself. Despite advances since Vatican II, a spirituality fully rooted in the word of God still needs to emerge among Catholics. Everywhere a dichotomy is noted between exegesis and theology, and between exegesis and the pastoral life of the church.

An urgent need for translations of the word of God into the vernacular is experienced particularly in Africa and Oceania, the latter with some 1,200 distinct languages. Another enormous task is the training of competent translators and exegetes. Ways must be found to make the word of God more affordable for people in the developing world. Urgently demanded by all is the correct blending of the historical-literal sense and the theological-spiritual sense.

"Over the past 40 years since Dei verbum *the United Bible Societies have completed 134 translations in collaboration with the Catholic Church. In only 438 of the world's 7,000 languages is there a translation of the complete Bible. Currently the United Bible Societies is involved in 646 translation projects worldwide" (Rev. Archibald Miller Milloy, secretary general of the United Bible Societies, Great Britain, October 14, 2008).*

Chapter 4

The Synod
in Session and *Verbum Domini*

We recounted to one another all that the Lord is doing in the midst of the People of God, and we shared our hopes and concerns. All this made us realize that we can deepen our relationship with the word of God only within the "we" of the Church, in mutual listening and acceptance.

Verbum Domini, 4

This chapter reflects on certain topics in the interventions in the assembly, the Report after the Discussion, the propositions, and the Message to the People of God. The theme of the word of God, already dealt with in chapter 2, is picked up and developed further.

The Word of God

The *Lineamenta* and *Instrumentum Laboris* spoke of the word of God as a symphony (see chapter 2). *Instrumentum Laboris* (preface) sought to balance the christological concentration of the word of God by pointing out a pneumatological dimension when it affirmed that "this Christological approach, linked by necessity to the pneumatological one, leads to the discovery of the Trinitarian dimension of revelation." Its number 30 alluded to the agency of the Holy Spirit in liturgical celebration, citing the preface of the Lectionary to the effect that "the working of the Holy Spirit is needed if the word of God is to make what we hear outwardly have its effect inwardly." However, a synod father felt the Holy Spirit largely absent from the interventions on the floor and queried, "where is the Holy Spirit in the *Instrumentum Laboris*? Hidden between the lines of casual statements? If, then like now, the word of God was made and is present in such a way and under every aspect through the Holy Spirit, then we should also state this in a clear way. The strategies for the proclamation should be illustrated and/or practiced in a specific way in the perspective of the Holy Spirit."[1]

The Report after the Discussion given by Cardinal Ouellet accentuated the role of Christ in relation to the word of God: all salvation history has a christological concentration (*une concentration christologique*, no. 6). The analogy of the Word means that there are diverse modes of the presence of the word of God. However, every presence of this word cannot be understood except with reference to the event of Christ. Scripture educates us to discern the diverse words of God in the voices of nature, history, and cultures, as also in our very existence (no. 5). Revelation is fully given in Christ, but this very fullness demands a deeper dialogue with all reality in an authentic search for truth. It demands attention to how God may be speaking in and through the religious traditions of humankind (no. 7). As a synod father said, the Bible gives us a "basic language course" for discovering "the sparks of the Word" in human culture, in interreligious dialogue, in our own life history.[2] The report carried to its logical conclusion the dynamic element of the word of God stressed by the *Lineamenta* and the *Instrumentum Laboris*. Whereas these others focused on the word of God in the church, the cardinal also stressed *la dimension anthropologique* (the anthropological dimension). The word of God is addressed to every human being and is the foundation for all reality that exists. In speaking God created humans for encounter with God. To encounter the word of God is to really understand creation and oneself (no. 1). The human being is *un être appelé à l'écoute de la parole* (a being whose vocation is to listen to the word); this hearing is not facultative but constitutive.[3] Human beings realize themselves by going out of self to embrace God's project for them (no. 10). It can be said that the Word brings humans "whatever is true, whatever is honorable, whatever is just, whatever is pure, whatever is pleasing, whatever is commendable . . . [and] worthy of praise" (Phil 4:8). The cardinal proposed, for the first time in the documents of this synod, the centrality of the church in relation to the word of God. For the

---

[1] Bishop Pöllitzer, OMI, bishop of Keetmanshoop, Namibia, October 14, 2008.

[2] Very Rev. Heinz Steckling, superior general of the Oblate Missionaries (OMI), October 8, 2008.

[3] One may see this in the submission of Bishop José Rodríguez, bishop of Líbano-Honda, Columbia, on October 7, 2008: "the ontological structure of human beings, of each human being, . . . is essentially dialogue . . . In the depth of our being we discover a dialogical dynamism that makes us different from other beings of our experience. And so our personal existence is, above all, as listeners. The human being is made such by his ability to listen to God."

self-gift of the Trinity, in Christ and in the Spirit, already had the church in mind as the Bride that responds to Christ. Hence, "ignorance of the Scriptures is ignorance of Christ" (St. Jerome) also comports the assertion that ignorance of the church is ignorance of Christ (*ignoscere Eccclesiam ignoscere Christum est*, no. 8).

The Message to the People of God calls the church "the house of the Word." It is true that *ecclesia semper reformanda est* (the church must always be in process of reforming itself). Yet in the designs of God it is said of her,

> *"Ignorance of the Scriptures is ignorance of Christ" (St. Jerome).*

"You are the light of the world. A city built on a hill cannot be hid. No one after lighting a lamp puts it under the bushel basket, but on the lampstand, and it gives light to all in the house" (Matt 5:14-15). From what has been said, it should be clear that the word of God is not reducible to the Sacred Scriptures (no. 9). The Scriptures present themselves as inspired witness, normative and irreplaceable, of the originating event.[4] The living character of the word of God is not exhausted by the letter. The word of God is a Person who offers himself to us in an encounter, becoming contemporary with all humans of all times and places (nos. 18–19).

God does not only speak; God also listens. In listening, God educates us to listen to the cry of those who seek peace, justice, and the truth (no. 13). The living word of God demands silence and prayer, a heart that prays and contemplates (no. 15). The word of God has an inherent sacramental dimension: in the liturgy, especially the eucharistic liturgy, it addresses the faithful here and now and makes them participate in it so as to be transformed more and more each day by its enduring efficacy (no. 9). Scripture and the voice that proclaims the word of God are "signs" that allow the Spirit to communicate inward grace (no. 25). There is need for greater connection between the study of Scripture and of the social doctrine of the church (no. 40).

The propositions. Proposition 5 addressed the issue of the Holy Spirit and the word of God, though restricting the attention somewhat to the role of the Spirit for understanding and interpreting Scripture. For the first time in the synod, there is treatment of natural law in its own right.[5] One of the

---

[4] Proposition 3 has it that "this word of God transcends the sacred Scriptures, even if they contain it in a very singular manner."

[5] Archbishop Raymond Leo Burke, prefect of the Supreme Tribunal of the Apostolic Signatura (October 15, 2008), had asked that "the scriptural teaching on the natural moral

questions for clarification from particular churches noted in *Instrumentum Laboris*, 10, concerned the natural law, the origin of the world and ecology. Proposition 13 affirms that the natural law written on the human heart (Rom 2:14-15) can be regarded as a type of word of God. Pastors are to train ministers of the Word to rediscover the role of the natural law in the formation of consciences.

The synod hopes that a theological reflection on the sacramentality of the Word can be promoted (proposition 7). Proposition 8 struck a new chord: the word of God is a word of reconciliation, with God reconciling all things to himself in Christ (2 Cor 5:18-20; Eph 1:10). The Word thus calls the church and Christians to engagement with the continuing work of reconciliation that God is accomplishing in Christ, especially in these days of conflict of every kind and interreligious tensions. The synod hopes that everyone of Christ's faithful will possess a personal copy of the Bible (proposition 9).

> *"To have a Bible is the right of all Christian people and it is the duty of the pastors to make access to the nourishment of the word of God possible"* (Bishop Venant Bacinoni, bishop of Bururi, Burundi, October 15, 2008).

The Message to the People of God strongly affirmed Jesus Christ as the "face of the Word": that the divine Word has put on a face is at the center of revelation (no. 6). The Word made flesh parallels the word made book (no. 5). The word of God "precedes and goes beyond the Bible, which itself is 'inspired by God' and contains the efficacious divine word (cf. 2 Tim 3:6)" (no. 3). As such, Christianity is no religion of the book; our faith is not only centered on a book but also on a history of salvation and on a person, Jesus Christ (ibid.). The divine Word was at the origin of human history, saving, judging, and penetrating its woven fabric with tales and events of the Word. Christians are thus to listen attentively to human history, discerning what in it makes for judgment or salvation, and what contains hidden appeals of the Word.

The contribution of the apostolic exhortation *Verbum Domini* can be read in chapter 10. Suffice it to mention here that its numbers 15–16 give a somewhat fuller outline of the "pneumatological horizon" of the Word.

---

law be presented as the common heritage of every human person," and that in this relationship of the word of God and law, it is important to underline the service of canon law in the church.

The Old Testament

Interventions in the synod assembly. The Latin patriarch of Jerusalem mentioned the particular difficulty of the Old Testament for Arab Christians
"because of the political and ideological interpretations."[6] The report of
a Spanish group[7] listed as difficulties with the Old Testament divine and
human violence and a theology that is insufficient concerning the afterworld. It is well known that much of the Old Testament either denies or
questions the afterlife. For example, Ecclesiastes 3:19 states:

> For the fate of humans and the fate of animals is the same; as one
> dies, so dies the other. They all have the same breath, and humans
> have no advantage over the animals; for all is vanity.

The propositions. Proposition 29 repeated the difficulties above (elements
of violence, injustice, immorality, and nonexemplary behavior on the
part of important biblical personalities) and called for adequate formation of the faithful so they can read the texts in their historical and literary
context, the central hermeneutical key being the gospel and the new commandment of Christ fulfilled in the paschal mystery. For interpretation in
general, proposition 6 mentioned the analogy of faith,[8] while proposition
52 pointed to the unity of the Testaments in Jesus, the Word made flesh.
The reader should consult chapter 9 of this book, where "dark" passages
of the Bible are discussed and criteria of interpretation given.

The apostolic exhortation *Verbum Domini,* 39, insisted on the unity of
all Scripture, though as Christians "we relate the New Testament and its
writings as a kind of hermeneutical key to Israel's Bible, thus interpreting
the latter as a path to Christ." Thus, "the person of Christ gives unity to
all the 'Scriptures' in relation to the one 'Word'" (ibid).

The Relationship of the Old Testament to the New

Interventions in the synod assembly. A synod father warned that "our
reading of the Old Testament should leave space for the Jewish reading."[9]
Another[10] wondered how the faith of believers of the Old Testament

[6] October 10, 2008.
[7] Spanish Group A, October 18, 2008.
[8] The intrinsic connection of the truth of faith among themselves and in their totality
in the design of revelation.
[9] Bishop Francis Deniau, bishop of Nevers, France, October 10, 2008.
[10] Cardinal Giovanni Lajolo, October 15, 2008.

period would have benefited from the later fulfillment of the prophecies, for such fulfillment would be *post fidem* (after their act of faith). They would have needed to have been shown *ante fidem* (before their act of faith), the Christian meaning of the prophecies realized in Jesus the Messiah. Four days earlier, Bishop Ramón Alfredo Dus,[11] commenting on the bond between the Testaments and the permanent value of the Old Testament as detailed in *Instrumentum Laboris*, 17, reminded the assembly of the words of *Dei Verbum*, 16, namely, that the Old Testament in turn shed light on the New Testament and explained it. If so, "the reading and interpretation of the Old Testament cannot be given up, in principle or in practice, in the understanding of the New Testament." He referred to Irenaeus, *Adversus Haereses*, IV, 33, 13,[12] which seemed to assert that "the salvation that the Trinitarian God realizes in each moment of history participates, on an ontological level, [in] all his salvific work, thus it is always complete." Irenaeus asked the question, "what then did the Lord bring to us by His advent?"[13] He answered, saying, "know that he brought all [possible] novelty, by bringing himself who had been announced." Bishop Dus then argued that the categories of *participation and analogy* offered better promise over the model of *promise-fulfillment* that has led to "a purported uselessness of the Old Testament."

Cardinal Vanhoye reported on the document of the Pontifical Biblical Commission, The Jewish People and Their Sacred Scriptures in the Christian Bible (2002). The document mentions three types of fulfillment, namely, *continuity*, *difference*, and a *surpassing* element (*Verbum Domini*, 40, took up these three types of relation of the Old Testament to the New). He said that the notion of fulfillment was very complex and easily falsified. Christian faith, he said,[14]

> does not understand this fulfillment as a literal one. Such a concept would be reductionist. In reality . . . fulfillment is brought about in a manner unforeseen. It includes transcendence. Jesus is not confined

---

[11] Bishop of Reconquista, Argentina, October 11, 2008.

[12] I believe the right reference to be rather IV, 33, 15, which posits the trinitarian participation in salvation from the beginning of time: the same Spirit of God descends "even from the creation of the world to its end upon the human race simply as such, from whom those who believe God and follow His word receive that salvation which flows from Him."

[13] *Against Heresies*, IV, 34, 1. Text from Alexander Roberts and William Rambaut, trans., *Ante-Nicene Fathers*, vol. 1, ed. Alexander Roberts, James Donaldson, and A. Cleveland Coxe (Buffalo, NY: Christian Literature, 1885), rev. and ed. for New Advent by Kevin Knight, accessed January 13, 2010, http://www.newadvent.org/fathers/0103434.htm.

[14] The Jewish People and Their Sacred Scriptures, 21.

to playing an already fixed role—that of Messiah—but he confers, on the notion of Messiah and salvation, a fullness which could not have been imagined in advance. . . . The Messiahship of Jesus has a meaning that is new and original.

Because Israelites are still loved by God (cf. Rom 11:29), "whoever wishes to be united to God, must also love them."[15] Commenting on number 7 of the document, the cardinal said,

> It [the Old Testament] is the base, the fundamental part. If the New Testament was established on another basis, it would have no real value. Without its conformity to the Sacred Scriptures of the Jewish people, it could not be presented as the accomplishment of God's project.

The New Testament takes for granted that the election of Israel is irrevocable, and preserves intact the prerogatives of this people (Rom 9:4). Far from being a substitution for Israel (which would be supersessionism), the church is in solidarity with it. One problem in all this is the epistle to the Hebrews that asserts the insufficiency and abrogation of the cultic institutions of the "first covenant" (Heb 7:18-19; 10:9). The Jewish People and their Sacred Scriptures did not fully consider this epistle, said the cardinal. However, the "new covenant" of which Christ is mediator is no mere renewal of the Sinai covenant but rather one founded on a new base: Christ's personal sacrificial offering.[16] Though the document did not fully reckon with the epistle to the Hebrews, the cardinal insisted that it remained true to the epistle in upholding the permanent validity, not of the covenant-law of Sinai (which was broken many times) but of the covenant-promise of Abraham.[17] One implication of the outlined relationship of Old and New Testaments would be that the Jewish and Christian readings of the Old Testament are both possible and both bound up with the vision of the respective faiths, "consequently both are irreducible" (ibid.).

> It cannot be said, therefore, that Jews do not see what has been proclaimed in the text, but that the Christian, in the light of Christ and in the Spirit, discovers in the text an additional meaning that was hidden there.[18]

[15] Ibid., 86.
[16] Ibid., 42.
[17] Ibid.
[18] Ibid., 21.

The Report after the Discussion emphasized *une concentration chris-tologique* (concentration on Christ) as key for reading the entire history of salvation (no. 6). In number 37 the report outlined concrete attitudes called for, namely, seeing that the word of God is the source of the dialogue between Christians and Jews: always to speak of the Jews in the present, holding the survival of the Jewish people as a spiritual fact,[19] accepting the universal reach of Judaism, avoiding every theology of substitution, allowing a place for Jewish interpretation in the Christian reading of the Old Testament, and finally sharing the eschatological hope with the Jews.

The propositions. The event of Christ is the culmination of revelation (proposition 4), though in regard to the actual text of the Old Testament fulfillment is far from literal. It is the dynamic movement of the Old Testament that finds fulfillment and completion in the New Testament, with aspects of continuity, discontinuity (proposition 52), and newness, for "Jesus' death and resurrection give to texts of the Old Testament a fullness of meaning which was previously inconceivable" (proposition 10). Awareness of the Old Testament is indispensable for anyone who believes in the Gospel of Jesus Christ (proposition 10).[20] The books of the Old Testament acquire full meaning in the New Testament, but they "in turn shed light on it and explain it" (cf. *DV*, 16). The Jewish understanding of the Bible can help Christians understand Scripture (proposition 52).[21] Paul VI called the Holy Land "the Fifth Gospel." It is the land of Jesus. The synod recommends pilgrimages, and if possible, the study of the Sacred Scriptures in the Holy Land and in the footsteps of St. Paul. Such will help understand better the physical and geographical environment of the Scriptures, and particularly the relationship between the two Testaments (proposition 51). A review of the Lectionary might avoid an overly restrictive bond between the Old Testament and the *pericopai* of the gospels or the exclusion of certain important passages (proposition 16).

The apostolic exhortation Verbum Domini. The fathers of the church used typological interpretation wherein the entire Old Testament is a path to Jesus Christ (no. 38). In no way an arbitrary procedure, typology "discerns in God's works of the Old Covenant prefigurations of what God accomplished in the fullness of time in the person of God's incarnate

---

[19] Cf. *Lineamenta*, 29, citing John Paul II.

[20] The *Catechism of the Catholic Church*, 121, says categorically that "the Old Testament is an indispensable part of Sacred Scripture."

[21] Cf. The Jewish People and Their Sacred Scriptures, 22.

Son" (no. 41).[22] The Old Testament is replete with tensions between its institutional and prophetic aspects; the paschal mystery of Christ is in full conformity, even if in an unexpected manner, with the prophetic aspects and foreshadowings of Scripture. Christians must not, however, forget that the Old Testament retains its own inherent value as revelation, as our Lord himself reaffirmed (cf. Mark 12:29-31). Early Christian catechesis made constant use of the Old Testament.[23] Thus, as the synod itself stated, "the Jewish understanding of the Bible can prove helpful to Christians for their own understanding and study of the Scriptures" (ibid.).[24]

Typology is to be distinguished from allegory. Allegory often discovers literary correspondences, whereas typology is firmly rooted in correspondences seen in the events, institutions, and persons of both Testaments in light of God's design seen in Scripture.[25] The Greek word *tupos* means a pattern, type, antitype. An example is Paul in 1 Corinthians 10:1-4:

> I do not want you to be unaware, brothers and sisters, that our ancestors were all under the cloud, and all passed through the sea, and all were baptized into Moses in the cloud and in the sea, and all ate the same spiritual food, and all drank the same spiritual drink. For they drank from the spiritual rock that followed them, and the rock was Christ.

Here Paul reads the pattern of Christian baptism in the Exodus experience of the Hebrews and actually identifies the rock from which they drank with Christ! He drew conclusions from the one to the other. Patristic and medieval exegeses have built on such use of typology. However, the Pontifical Biblical document The Jewish People and Their Sacred Scriptures in the Christian Bible, 20, raised an issue of such use, that of "detaching each detail from its context and severing the relationship between the biblical text and the concrete reality of salvation history. Interpretation then became arbitrary." The teaching given may have been animated by faith, "but such teaching was not based on the commented text. It was superimposed on

---

[22] Citing *Catechism of the Catholic Church,* 128.

[23] It is not clear whether this formulation is meant to bypass or approve what the synod stated in proposition 10, namely, "we hope that preaching and catechesis will take into proper account the pages of the Old Testament, explaining them adequately in the context of the history of salvation, and helping the People of God to appreciate them in light of faith in Jesus the Lord."

[24] Citing proposition 52.

[25] Cf. Bruce K. Waltke and James M. Houston, *The Psalms as Christian Worship: A Historical Commentary* (Grand Rapids: Wm. Eerdmans, 2010) 9.

it." Having acknowledged as much, the document upheld the legitimacy, even the necessity, of typology for Christians, as long they bear in mind that "this is a retrospective perception whose point of departure is not in the text as such, but in the events of the New Testament proclaimed by the apostolic preaching" (ibid., 21). For some criteria for discerning valid inference of typology, see chapter 10 of this book.

The New Testament

The very topic of the synod, the Word of God in the Life and Mission of the Church, "can be understood in its Christological sense, namely Jesus Christ in the Life and Mission of the Church" (*Instrumentum Laboris*, preface). This is not all. The christological approach is bound to the necessity of a pneumatological one, leading to the discovery of the trinitarian dimension of revelation (ibid.). The centrality of Jesus Christ in relation to the word comports the affirmation of the New Testament as preeminent among the Scriptures and the gospels as having special revelatory power. All this means that the word of God has a dynamic and *living* character; it calls for encounter with a Person. It means also that "Christ retrospectively sheds his light on the entire development of salvation history and reveals its coherence, meaning and direction" (Message to the People of God, 6). Creation itself is to be read in the light of the accomplishment of the history of salvation realized in the incarnation, death, and resurrection of Jesus and the definitive gift of the Holy Spirit (Report after the Discussion, 5).

Questions for Discussion

1. What, in your judgment, is the special contribution of Cardinal Ouellet's *Relatio post Disceptationem*?

2. Christianity is not a religion of the book. Discuss.

3. Discuss Cardinal Vanhoye's contribution.

4. Discuss the contributions of Cardinal Lajolo and Bishop Dus based on Irenaeus.

5. What is typology? Give some illustrations.

Chapter 5

Issue I:
The Inspiration and Truth
of Scripture

Sacred Scripture is the word of God inasmuch as it is consigned to writing under the inspiration of the divine Spirit.

Dei Verbum, **9**

The Inspiration of Scripture: *Dei Verbum*

The translator of Ben Sira tells us how his grandfather applied himself to the writing of that book:

> My grandfather, Jesus, having long devoted himself to the reading of the Law, the Prophets and other books of the fathers and having become very learned in them, himself decided to write something on the subjects of learning and wisdom, so that people who wanted to learn might, by themselves accepting these disciplines, learn how better to live according to the Law.[1]

Both the writer and his grandfather were not conscious of any divine assistance in their work. They were rather conscious of their own efforts in creating the work. That is, they were conscious of being authors in the full sense of the word.

Ecclesiastes spent much time debunking and/or questioning some of the beliefs of his community of faith. He too was conscious of having "acquired great wisdom, surpassing all who were over Jerusalem before me; and my mind has had great experience of wisdom and knowledge. And I applied my mind to know wisdom and to know madness and folly. I perceived that this also is but a chasing after wind" (Eccl 1:16-17). He

---

[1] Ben Sira, foreword, 7–14.

actually denied one of the emerging tenets of faith in his time when he said, "For the fate of humans and the fate of animals is the same; as one dies, so dies the other. They all have the same breath, and humans have no advantage over the animals; for all is vanity" (Eccl 3:19).

When dealing with a topic like the inspiration of Scripture, it is better to begin with the text as it is and with facts that ground it in the human experience of the authors.[2] We need to also factor in the fact that the Bible contains variant forms of the text and some obscure passages that defy interpretation.

Dei Verbum, 9, says that "sacred Scripture is the utterance of God put down as it is in writing under the inspiration of the Holy Spirit." This statement does not yet tell us the how of inspiration. *Dei Verbum*, 11, defined inspiration as follows:

> Holy Mother Church . . . accepts as sacred and canonical the books of both the Old and New Testament, whole and entire, with all their parts, on the grounds that, written under the inspiration of the holy Spirit (see John 20:31; 2 Tim 3:16; 2 Pet 1:19-21; 3:15-16) they have God as their author, and have been handed on as such to the Church itself.

The biblical texts cited above as basis for the doctrine of inspiration bear some examination. John 20:31 says that "these are written so that you may come to believe that Jesus is the Messiah, the Son of God, and that through believing you may have life in his name." Second Timothy 3:16: "All scripture is inspired by God and is useful for teaching, for reproof, for correction, and for training in righteousness." The word translated as "inspired by God" is the Greek *theo-pneustos*, a word that occurs only here in the New Testament and was never used in the Greek Septuagint. It suggests the sense of "God-breathed." An alternative translation would be "all inspired Scripture is useful for . . ." Second Peter 1:20-21 says that "no prophecy of scripture is a matter of one's own interpretation, because no prophecy ever came by human will, but men and women moved by the Holy Spirit spoke from God." God moves prophets to speak, so God must give the interpretation as well.[3] Second Peter 3:15-16 states that

---

[2] I here develop insights from Raymond E. Brown, "'And the Lord Said?' Biblical Reflections on Scripture as the Word of God," *TS* 42 (1981) 3–19, here 6.

[3] Cf. Paul J. Achtemeier, *Inspiration and Authority: The Nature and Function of Christian Scripture* (Peabody: Hendrickson, 1999) 95.

our beloved brother Paul wrote to you according to the wisdom given him, speaking of this as he does in all his letters. There are some things in them hard to understand, which the ignorant and unstable twist to their own destruction, as they do the other scriptures.

The above quotation shows that already by the time 2 Peter was written (about early second century CE) the letters of Paul were being venerated as inspired.

In the Old Testament, God is seen as speaking especially through Moses (Exod 20:18-20; Deut 5:5) and the prophets (see Luke 1:70). As such, the Torah of Moses can be called "Torah of Yahweh." In fact, the Ten Words (the Decalogue) were said to have been written by the very hands of God (Exod 34:1, 28). On the mountain Moses received from God the pattern of the tabernacle (Exod 25–31), just as the laws were portrayed as dictated by God to Moses. For this reason, nothing must be added to it and nothing taken from it (Deut 4:2).[4] Philo of Alexandria (circa 20 BCE–50 CE) seems to be the first to apply Greek ideas of ecstatic inspiration to the Scriptures of Israel, for example, in his *Life of Moses* and *The Migration of Abraham*.[5]

The definition of *Dei Verbum*, 11, ties together inspiration and the canon of Scripture (the list of books that the church regards as sacred and holy). As Achtemeier felicitously stated:

The canon is a key element in understanding the inspiration of Scripture, since it delimits the area within which inspiration is understood to have operated. God inspired the canonical books, with no exception, and no non-canonical books are inspired, with no exception.[6]

This neat phrasing, however, does not close the matter. The Protestant and Catholic canons differ. Accordingly, Protestants regard as apocrypha some books Catholics hold to be inspired.

The Magisterium

The Catholic canon of forty-six books of the Old Testament and twenty-seven books of the New Testament was definitively fixed at the Council of Trent, 1546.[7] Catholic doctrine does not accept that the judgment of the

---

[4] An injunction repeated in Revelation 22:18-19.

[5] See John R. Levison, "Spirit and Inspired Knowledge," *Filled with the Spirit* (Grand Rapids: Wm. Eerdmans, 2009) 178–201.

[6] Achtemeier, *Inspiration and Authority*, 105.

[7] For the Old Testament, the church took over the list of books in the Greek Septuagint, which included the Hebrew Scriptures and some books written in Greek. Until the second

church to include a certain book in the canon conferred on it the charism of inspiration. Rather, the same Spirit who was at the origin of the inspired book also led the church to discern and affirm its inspiration. Vatican Council I (1870) had this to say:

> These [books] the Church holds sacred and canonical, not because, having been carefully composed by mere human industry, they were afterwards approved by her authority, nor merely because they contain revelation with no admixture of error, but because, having been written by the inspiration of the Holy Spirit, they have God for their author and have been delivered as such to the Church herself.[8]

As to the how of inspiration, the Council of Trent (1546, First Decree) spoke of the Sacred Scriptures as coming "from the mouth of Christ himself, or from the apostles *by the dictation of the Holy Spirit.*"[9] The Vatican I constitution *Dei Filius*, On Revelation (1870), explained inspiration as follows:

> Hence, the fact that it was men whom the Holy Spirit took up as his instruments for writing does not mean that it was these inspired instruments—but not the primary author—who might have made an error. For, by supernatural power, he so moved and impelled them to write—he so assisted them when writing—that the things which he ordered, and those only, they, first, rightly understood, then willed faithfully to write down, and finally expressed in apt words and with infallible truth. Otherwise, it could not be said that he was the author of the entire Scripture.[10]

The Latin word *auctor* is broader in meaning than the English word author, and can mean "originator" (German *Urheber*) or literary author (German *Verfasser*).[11] It is not clear which of the two meanings Vatican I meant. Vatican I conceived the divine agency in inspiration on the pattern of a human

---

century CE "Scripture" for the church referred to these books of the Old Testament. In early second century, Christian writings began to be read and collected also as Scripture, beginning with the letters of Paul. There were disputes about certain books currently in the canon; other books that were at some time regarded as "Scripture" later did not make the cut. The first complete listing of books of the canon as we now have it was Athanasius's Thirty-Ninth Easter Letter in 367 CE.

[8] Cf. James J. Megivern, ed., *Official Catholic Teachings: Bible Interpretation* (Wilmington: McGrath, 1978) 191.

[9] Ibid., 179.

[10] Ibid., 216.

[11] Cf. Luis Alonso Schökel, *The Inspired Word: Scripture in the Light of Language and Literature* (New York: Herder and Herder, 1965) 78–82.

author using an instrument, for example, a pen. Any error whatsoever (including in the areas of science and history) would accrue to the principal agent, the Spirit. Leo XIII in the encyclical letter *Providentissimus Deus*, 1893,[12] upheld such teaching, and so did Benedict XV in the encyclical letter *Spiritus Paraclitus*, 1920. It is important to note that such teaching of the ordinary magisterium was not defined as matter of faith.

Pius XII's encyclical letter *Divino Afflante Spiritu*, 1943, was important in clarifying the human factor in inspiration. The Holy Spirit did not suppress the human faculties of the sacred writer. The human writers were authors in the full sense of the word even while being under the influence of the Holy Spirit. Furthermore, the different books show clearly "the special character of each one and, as it were, his personal traits."[13] Pius XII urged scholars to use all available means to study what are called *genres*, that is, "certain fixed ways of expounding and narrating, certain definite idioms"[14] used by ancient authors, citing St. Thomas Aquinas to the effect that "in Scripture divine things are presented to us in the manner which is in common use amongst men."[15] He added the following important comment:

> For as the substantial Word of God became like to men in all things, except sin (Heb 4:15), so the words of God, *expressed in human language*, are made like to human speech in every respect, except error [italics mine].[16]

Dei Verbum, 11, incorporated the teaching of *Divino Afflante Spiritu* when it stated:

> To compose the sacred books, God chose men who, all the while he employed them in this task, made full use of their powers and faculties, so that, though he acted in them and by them, it was as true authors that they consigned to writing whatever he wanted written, and no more.[17]

The theological problem is that of merging in a synthesis the inspiring action of the Holy Spirit and the full use of the human faculties of the sacred writer(s). Such synthesis still needs to be crafted.

---

[12] Only partly cited in *Dei Verbum*, 11.

[13] Megivern, *Official Catholic Teachings*, 331 (no. 33). A quotation from Benedict XV, *Spiritus Paraclitus*.

[14] Ibid., 333 (no. 37).

[15] Ibid., cf. St. Thomas Aquinas, *Commentary on Hebrews*, chapter 1, *lectio* 4.

[16] Megivern, *Official Catholic Teachings*, 333 (no. 37).

[17] Message to the People of God, 5, affirms that divine inspiration did not erase the historical identities and personalities of its human authors.

The Truth of Scripture: *Dei Verbum*

Earlier church documents tended to affirm the inerrancy of Scripture in all matters, religious and profane. A major contribution of *Dei Verbum*, 11, was the shift from inerrancy to the *truth* of Scripture. The first draft of the Constitution on Divine Revelation presented to Vatican II embraced the absolute inerrancy of Scripture in all matters, including science and history. In the course of the discussions an important shift occurred: the draft of 1964 replaced inerrancy with truth (*veritas*).[18] Saint Thomas Aquinas was quoted (still appears in the current footnotes to *DV*, 11) to the effect that "any knowledge which is profitable for salvation may be the object of prophetic inspiration. But things which cannot affect our salvation do not belong to inspiration." Eventually the fathers of the council struck upon this happy phrasing:

> We must acknowledge that the books of Scripture, firmly, faithfully, and without error, teach that truth which God, for the sake of our salvation, wished to see confided to the sacred Scriptures.

This qualification of truth by the phrase "for the sake of our salvation" is not quantitative but formal, for the section had already affirmed that the Scriptures "in their entirety, with all their parts" are inspired. What is made clear is that the truth of revelation is about "the full self-communication of God, his truthfulness and fidelity, but also the life of humans."[19] Aspects of history, geography, and the sciences enter into this formal aspect to the extent that they are bound up with the message of our salvation. For example, the historical fact that Christ "suffered under Pontius Pilate, was crucified and was buried" (the Creed) is intrinsically part of the statement of faith, "for us humans and for our salvation."

Inspiration and Truth of Scripture: *Lineamenta* and *Instrumentum Laboris*

Sacred Scripture, under divine inspiration, unites Jesus-the-Word to the words of the prophets and apostles and thus can truly be said to be word of God (*Lineamenta*, 8). Through inspiration the Holy Spirit has preserved in written form the unchanging character of the original and constitutive elements of the living tradition (cf. *Lineamenta*, 13; *Instrumentum*

---

[18] Cf. Alois Grillmeier in *Commentary on the Documents of Vatican II*, vol. 3, ed. Herbert Vorgrimler (New York: Herder and Herder, 1969) 204.

[19] Ibid., 209.

Laboris, 16).[20] Tradition guards past events and gives the community of faith its distinctiveness; it also aids in shaping the community's life according to these originating events. Hence, "biblical traditions . . . remember the past for the sake of the present and the future."[21] Just as the work of the Holy Spirit precedes, accompanies, and brings to completion the celebration of the liturgy, so it does the same for the production of the books of the Bible and their use in the church (cf. *Lineamenta*, 19). "Through the charism of divine inspiration, the books of Scripture have a direct, concrete power of appeal not possessed by other texts or holy writings" (*Lineamenta*, 9; *Instrumentum Laboris*, 9). As Benedict XVI wrote,[22] the Christian religion cannot be called a "religion of the book" in an absolute sense, for the inspired book has a vital link to the entire body of revelation (*Instrumentum Laboris*, 10). *Instrumentum Laboris*, 15,[23] in answering the queries from the particular churches, notes as follows:

> *Inspiration "leaves the freedom and personal capacity of the writer intact, while enlightening and inspiring both."*

— the charism of inspiration allows God to be the author of the Bible in a way that does not exclude humankind itself from being its true author. In fact, inspiration is different from dictation; it leaves the freedom and personal capacity of the writer intact, while enlightening and inspiring both;

—. . . inerrancy[24] applies only[25] to "that truth which God wanted put into sacred writings for the sake of salvation" (*DV* 11);

[20] Message to the People of God, 3: they memorialize the creative and saving event of revelation by way of canonical, historical, and literary means. Therefore, the word of God precedes and goes beyond the Bible, which itself is "inspired by God" and contains the efficacious divine word (cf. 2 Tim 3:16).

[21] Achtemeier, *Inspiration and Authority*, 110.

[22] *Deus Caritas Est* (God Is Love), 1.

[23] The Report after the Discussion, 31, also noted the demand to deepen doctrine on inspiration, hence on hermeneutics, inerrancy of Scripture, and the relation inspiration-Scripture-tradition-magisterium.

[24] Reverting to terminology rejected by the council, which replaced it with truth (see note 11 above).

[25] The word "only" is unfortunate and is not in the original. It could suggest a material limitation, whereas the council had in mind a formal one. See above.

— in virtue of the charism of inspiration, the Holy Spirit constitutes the books of the Bible as the Word of God and entrusts them to the Church, so that they might be received in the obedience of faith.

Inspiration and Truth of Scripture: The Propositions

Sacred Scripture is the inspired witness of revelation, which along with the living tradition of the church constitutes the supreme rule of the faith (proposition 2, citing *DV*, 21). Proposition 12 requested that "the Congregation for the Doctrine of the Faith clarify the concepts of inspiration and truth of the Bible, along with their reciprocal relationship, in order to better understand the teaching of *Dei verbum* 11."

Inspiration and Truth of Scripture: *Verbum Domini*

Benedict XVI treated the subject briefly (see chapter 10 of this book). The inspiration of the Holy Spirit makes the text of the Bible the locus where "we can hear the Lord himself speak and recognize his presence in history" (*Verbum Domini*, 19). It lets the human author act fully as such, while making God himself the true author. Scripture thus participates somewhat in the analogy of the incarnation: "the body of the Son is the Scripture which we have received"[26] (*Verbum Domini*, 18). The truth of Scripture is a consequence of its inspiration:

> [S]ince, therefore, all that the inspired authors, or sacred writers, affirm should be regarded as affirmed by the Holy Spirit, we must acknowledge that the books of Scripture firmly, faithfully and without error, teach that truth which God, for the sake of our salvation, wished to see confided to the sacred Scriptures.[27]

The pope went no further in explaining the doctrine of inspiration and truth of Scripture but rather acknowledged the need for a fuller and more adequate study of these realities. In fact, since 2009 the Pontifical Biblical Commission has taken up the study of "Inspiration and Truth of the Bible."

Some Questions

DV 11's linking of truth with the *intended* assertions of the sacred writers raises multiple questions.[28] How know when they intend to assert something or merely retail beliefs of their time? Is every such assertion covered by the charism of truth, seeing that inspiration left

---

[26] St. Ambrose, *Exposition of the Gospel according to Luke*, 6, 33.

[27] *DV*, 11: *Cum ergo omne id, quod auctores inspirati seu hagiographi asserunt* (assert).

[28] Most of *Letter & Spirit: For the Sake of Our Salvation; The Truth and Humility of God's Word* 6 (2010) discussed these questions. The volume arrived too late for comment here.

Scripture in the Church

56

intact the writers' full human identity, hence the limitations of history and culture? How is this truth related to the truth of interpretation which, in DV 12 (see next chapter), calls for attention to the unity of Scripture, the living tradition of the whole Church and the analogy of faith?

The texts above consistently link the inspiration of Scripture with the sacred *writers* or authors. To regard inspiration as the *impulse to write* coming from the Holy Spirit or the Holy Spirit's use of the biblical writer is to locate inspiration in the author(s), just as the medieval schools treated inspiration on the model of prophecy. Today, many would see inspiration as a charism of the text itself (see literary theories of inspiration below). We now know that many books of the Bible are compilations involving the community of faith and many individual hands. An adequate doctrine of inspiration would have to reckon with such features of the literary production of the biblical books. There is as yet no definitive Roman Catholic theology of the inspiration and truth of Scripture or the synod would not have requested a study of these. However, for the sake of students, I give a very brief summary of Raymond F. Collins's incisive input in *The New Jerome Biblical Commentary*.

Appendix: Raymond F. Collins, "Inspiration"[29]

Matthew 22:43 says that David was inspired by the Holy Spirit (cf. Mark 12:36). Luke 1:70 has God speaking through the prophets (see also the Creed). However, it is never said explicitly in the Old Testament that its writings are inspired. The early church cited the Old Testament as *hai graphai* (the Scriptures), which it considered inspired, hence it relied upon them to proclaim the event of Christ. During the second and third centuries after Christ, *hai graphai* (the Scriptures) came to be used also for the Christian writings that were also considered to have the same divine origin as the Old Testament writings (no. 1026).

Early Christian and Jewish Tradition

In conformity with Greek theories of inspiration, some fathers of the church considered inspiration an ecstatic phenomenon. For example, Athenagoras (second-century apologist) spoke of "Moses or of Isaiah and

---

[29] *The New Jerome Biblical Commentary*, ed. Raymond E. Brown, Joseph A. Fitzmyer, and Roland E. Murphy (New Jersey: Prentice Hall, 1990) 1023–33. Page numbers in this section refer to the pages of *The New Jerome Biblical Commentary*.

Jeremiah and the rest of the prophets who in the ecstasy of their thoughts, as the divine Spirit moved them, uttered what they had been inspired to say, the Spirit making use of them as a flautist might blow into a flute" (the Greek for Spirit is *pneuma* and the verb *pnein* means to blow) (no. 1026). Origen rejected this explanation. He rather saw the Holy Spirit illuminating the mind, will, and memory of the biblical writers, who freely and consciously collaborated with the word that came to them. He distinguished the "word of revelation" from the writers' commentary on that word, thus leaving some scope for error on the part of the writers. He shifted from the prophetic model of inspiration to the inspiration of the text itself, admitting levels and degrees of inspiration, something not common among the Eastern fathers (no. 1026).

Saint Augustine, while holding that the Scriptures were dictated by the Holy Spirit, nevertheless allowed the human authors a large role (no. 1027). These human authors used various forms of expression and could adapt the content in expressing it. They also may not be entirely successful in recalling the words they heard with the utmost accuracy.

Models of Inspiration among Catholics

The *prophetic model of inspiration* (psychological theory of inspiration) lasted from New Testament times till scholasticism in medieval times, and into our times (no. 1028). From this stream comes the language of God as "author" of the Scriptures. The scholastics spoke of God as the principal efficient cause and the biblical writers as the instrumental efficient cause. Think of a painter using a brush. They considered prophecy a habit of the soul, hence a permanent gift that conferred on the prophet a new nature connatural with what God revealed. Saint Thomas Aquinas, however, considered prophecy a *motio* (movement), a gift given on a temporary basis by which the prophet could judge that some knowledge received was the word of God. In more recent times M.-J. Lagrange (1855–1938) adopted the theory of intellectual enlightenment from St. Thomas Aquinas. For him, inspiration was totally the work of God and totally the work of the human authors (no. 1030). His thought has been revived and developed by Pierre Benoit, who likewise locates inspiration in the human psyche. Inspiration is for him the impulse to write and produce a work, and God is active throughout as the originating cause (no. 1032).

Literary approaches locate the influence of the Holy Spirit on the text as text. The Spirit is active in the long process of the production of the text within the believing community but also as the faith community reads and identifies with the text. This approach sees the Bible as a whole inspired and in all its parts. Lack of error is related to the total biblical view of a topic, avoiding concentrating inspiration on isolated texts, something that leads to fundamentalism. An attempt at sketching out a literary theory of inspiration, though written just before Vatican II, is the book of Alonso Schökel (see bibliography).

The *social theory of inspiration* was associated with John L. McKenzie (see bibliography). Among Protestants, one of the protagonists of this approach was James Barr (see bibliography). An excerpt from Barr suffices to characterize this approach (no. 1032):

> If there is inspiration at all, then it must extend over the entire process of production that has led to the final text. Inspiration therefore must attach not to a small number of exceptional persons. . . . It must extend over a larger number of anonymous persons . . . it must be considered to belong more to the community as a whole.[30]

Karl Rahner (see bibliography) proposed an *ecclesial approach* to inspiration. For him, inspiration is a charism of the written communication of the word of God insofar as a constitutive element of the church. God willed the Scriptures in willing the church as it came to be.

Cardinal Carlo Martini distinguishes the various senses of the term "word of God," which he considers an analogical concept (no. 1033). For him, "word of God" should not be used of the Scriptures without further ado. Some distance is to be maintained conceptually between the scriptural expression and the self-communication of God, even in the case of the prophets. Theologically it is better to say that the Scriptures *witness* to the word of God, rather than that they *are* the word of God. John Henry Newman in 1884 (when already forty years a Catholic) equally affirmed that the word of God was morally separable from the words of the human authors (no. 1030).

Models of Inspiration among Protestants

The *concursive theory* of inspiration states that the action of the Holy Spirit is concursive with human actions in the processes of writing (no. 1031).

Liberal Protestants often *deny inspiration* through silence, and sometimes explicitly. Among those who deny inspiration in the traditional sense is

---

[30] James Barr, *Holy Scripture: Canon, Authority, Criticism* (Oxford: Clarendon Press, 1983) 19, note 59.

Marcus J. Borg.[31] To the question whether a passage from Paul tells us what *God* says or how *Paul* saw things, he answered as follows:

> It is all a human product, though generated in response to God. As such, it contains ancient Israel's perceptions and misperceptions of what life with God involves, just as it contains the early Christian movement's perceptions and misperceptions. Thus it is we who must discern how to read and interpret, how to hear and value its various voices. The Bible does not come with footnotes that say, "This passage reflects the will of God; the next passage does not," or "This passage is valid for all time; the next passage does not . . ." Thus any and every claim about what a passage of scripture means involves interpretation.[32]

The following text from the Hanson[33] brothers is along similar lines, though more radical (no. 1033):

> The ancient doctrine of the inspiration and inerrancy of the Bible not only is impossible for intelligent people today, but represents a deviation in Christian doctrine, whatever salutary uses may have been made of it in the past by the Holy Spirit, who often turns human errors to good ends.

A variation on denying inspiration in the traditional sense is the theory of *consequent behavior*. As a teacher would so "inspire" students that they are led to consequent behavior, so here the Holy Spirit inspires the biblical authors.

Finally, Karl Barth affirms that "inspiration is not a quality of the Scripture text itself, but an affirmation of a divine ability to use Scripture to communicate revelation to human beings, individually or in groups" (no. 1033). Aligned with this is the view of Rudolf Bultmann that the Scriptures become "word of God" (a dynamic reality) only when they come alive in proclamation and preaching (ibid.).

Plenary Verbal Inspiration

Some Evangelicals, and those who hold a theory of God's dictation of every word of Scripture, believe in what is called *plenary verbal inspiration*

---

[31] *Reading the Bible Again for the First Time: Taking the Bible Seriously but Not Literally* (San Francisco: HarperSanFrancisco, 2001).

[32] Ibid., 27–28.

[33] A. T. Hanson and R. P. C. Hanson, *Reasonable Faith: A Survey of the Christian Faith* (Oxford: OUP, 1980) 42.

(no. 1028). The inerrancy of Scripture is for these the most basic of the fundamentals of faith (see chapter 9 on fundamentalism). Every word in Scripture must be inerrant since God who dictated it does not deceive, at least as far as the original manuscripts are concerned. Ultimately, the truth of the Bible is propositional. The unity of the Bible obviates any real contradictions among biblical texts. The Bible does not contain or bear witness to revelation; it is physically identical with the words God spoke. The reader may consult chapter 9 on the Chicago statement of 1978.

Questions for Discussion

1. What is inspiration?

2. What in your judgment are the implications of inspiration?

3. Look at the models of inspiration above. Which one appeals to you and why?

4. Discuss the truth of Sacred Scripture in relation to the accounts of the end of Judas in Matthew 27 and Acts 1.

5. Read and discuss Brown, "'And the Lord Said'" (see bibliography).

6. Discuss the views of Borg and the Hanson brothers.

Chapter 6

Issue II:
Interpreting the Word of God

It is important to remind ourselves from the very beginning of this chapter that the goal of interpretation, according to St. Augustine, is love of God and neighbor that leads us to communion with the Trinity. He stated it as follows:[1]

> And so people supported by faith, hope and charity, and retaining a firm grip on them, have no need of the Scriptures except for instructing others. And so there are many who live by these three even in the desert without books. This leads me to think that the text has already been fulfilled in them.

There are two ways of hearing and interpreting Sacred Scripture in faith, through study and *lectio divina*. *Lectio divina* will be treated in chapter 8. Interpreting Scripture through study is the subject of this chapter. One of the propositions of the synod is that the culture of reading, praying, and living Sacred Scripture must be promoted among Catholics, and especially that *Dei Verbum*, the Dogmatic Constitution on Divine Revelation, must be made better known among Christ's faithful.

Dei Verbum

A central principle of interpreting Scripture is that "in sacred Scripture, God speaks through human beings in human fashion" (*DV*, 12). This implies that we have to search out "the meaning which the sacred writers really had in mind, that meaning which God had thought well to manifest through the medium of their words" (ibid.). Because the sacred writers were moved by the Holy Spirit as fully human authors, their intention and background are also important to the sense. (In Catholic parlance the

[1] St. Augustine, *Teaching Christianity: De Doctrina Christiana*, trans. Edmund Hill, OP (New York: New City Press, 1996) 125.

divine sense, when not fully known to the human author, is called *sensus plenior* ["fuller sense," see later].)[2] The council fathers did not resolve the question of the extent of the coalescing of human and divine intentions; they left it open. The *human* element demands that we investigate the background, style, and conventions used by the sacred writer.[3] This is a very important principle. Even today we say that the sun rises in the east and sets in the west, although we know that it is the earth that circles around the sun. The council prescribes no particular method of interpretation, even though some of the aspects just mentioned belong to the historical-critical method. The *divine* element demands that "holy Scripture must be read and interpreted according to the same Spirit by whom it was written" (*DV*, 12).[4] The Holy Spirit makes the written word to become *living* word. The three principles of interpretation in the Spirit are the unity of the whole of Scripture, the living tradition of the whole church, and the harmony that exists between the elements of the faith (*analogia fidei*, analogy of faith). In other words, what happens in exegesis (biblical interpretation) is not unlike what happens with the incarnation. In both, we discern the divine in the human. *Dei Verbum*, 13, expresses this in words drawn almost verbatim from *Divino Afflante Spiritu* (no. 37):

> Indeed the words of God, expressed in human language, are in every way like human speech, just as the Word of the eternal Father, when he took on himself the weak flesh of human beings, became like them. (*DV*, 13)

The *"unity of the whole of Scripture"* demands that the interpreter is aware of rereadings and possible developments of thought throughout Scripture. For example, some psalms and Ecclesiastes 3:19-21 (among other texts) flatly deny the resurrection and the afterlife. When seen in light of the entire teaching of the Bible, such denial becomes a step in the development of the biblical doctrine of resurrection, which became clear only late in the Old Testament period (Dan 12:1-2; 2 Macc 7) and is professed all through the New Testament. The Interpretation of the Bible in the Church states as follows:

---

[2] However, note the contention of Carolyn Osiek in chapter 7 that the so-called fuller sense was not just "not fully known" to the sacred writer but not all in his mind, since it is a meaning that is theologically comprehensible only at a later point of the tradition.

[3] Cf. Pius XII, *Divino Afflante Spiritu*, 1943.

[4] Following the translation of Walter Abbott, *The Documents of Vatican II* (London and Dublin: Geoffrey Chapman, 1966).

Although each book of the Bible was written with its own particular end in view and has its own specific meaning, it takes on a deeper meaning when it becomes part of the *canon* as a whole.[5]

The *"living tradition of the whole church"* reminds the interpreter that Scripture is the book of the church and has a dialogical relationship with the faith of the church. It also recalls what was mentioned in *DV*, 10, that "the task of giving an authentic interpretation of the word of God, whether in its written form or in the form of tradition, has been entrusted to the living teaching office of the Church alone," although "this magisterium is not superior to the word of God, but is rather its servant." Another principle in the Catholic tradition of biblical interpretation is that no sense is accepted that goes against the unanimous agreement of the fathers of the church.[6] However, such common agreement is rare. Here belongs also the interpretation of Scripture in the liturgy and the prayers of the church (*lex orandi, lex credendi*, the rule of prayer is the rule of faith). Another element is the continuity of faith in the whole church, for the whole church also received the promise of indefectibility, that is, the whole church will never in any one period defect from Christ. Here enters the testimony of the saints, for saintly living is a particularized interpretation of the gospel.

Finally, there is *"the analogy of faith"* or coherence among the articles of faith. For example, because the God of Jesus Christ is the God of the Old Testament, one may not admit portrayals of the character of God in either testament that contradict the image of God as Jesus has taught us.

Lineamenta and *Instrumentum Laboris*

These documents of the synod reflect on the rich doctrine of *Dei Verbum*. They introduce new terminology, the "historical-literal" sense and the "theological-spiritual" sense,[7] borrowed from the *Catechism of the Catholic Church* (117). The *Catechism* also refers to the ancient four senses of patristic and medieval exegesis: the literal, allegorical, moral, and anagogical (*anagogë* means "leading," that is, to our final end). The last three make up the spiritual sense, leaving thus two senses, the *literal sense* and the *spiritual sense* (*Catechism*, 115). The literal sense is described as "the

---

[5] III, C, 1.

[6] Council of Trent, fourth session. See J. Neuner and Jacques Dupuis, *The Christian Faith: Doctrinal Documents of the Catholic Church*, 5th revised and enlarged ed. (London: HarperCollinsReligious, 1990) 79.

[7] *Lineamenta*, 15; *Instrumentum Laboris*, 21.

meaning conveyed by the words of Scripture and discovered by exegesis, following the rules of sound interpretation" (*Catechism*, 116). It is the foundation for all the other senses of Scripture. The allegorical sense gives "a more profound understanding of events by recognizing their significance in Christ"—for example, the Red Sea as a type of Christ's victory or sign of Christian baptism. (Here allegory seems identified with typology, but the reader should remember the distinction between the two made in chapter 4.) The moral sense instructs us how to act justly. The anagogical sense views realities and events in light of their eternal significance, leading us toward our true homeland, for example, the church on earth as sign of the heavenly Jerusalem (*Catechism*, 117).

Instrumentum Laboris, 21, follows rather The Interpretation of the Bible in the Church[8] in defining the spiritual sense:

> As a general rule, we can define the spiritual sense, as understood by Christian faith, as the meaning expressed by the biblical texts when read, under the influence of the Holy Spirit, in the context of the paschal mystery of Christ and of the new life which flows from it. This context truly exists. In it the New Testament recognizes the fulfillment of the Scriptures. It is therefore quite acceptable to re-read the Scriptures in the light of this new context, which is that of life in the Spirit.

It goes on to affirm that

> contrary to a current view, there is not necessarily a distinction be-tween the two senses. When a biblical text relates directly to the paschal mystery of Christ or to the new life which results from it, its literal sense is already a spiritual sense. Such is regularly the case in the New Testament. It follows that it is most often in dealing with the Old Testament that Christian exegesis speaks of the spiritual sense. But already in the Old Testament, there are many instances where texts have a religious or spiritual sense as their literal sense. Christian faith recognizes in such cases an anticipatory relationship to the new life brought by Christ.

This statement calls for analysis. First, it states that *generally* there is no dis-tinction between the literal and the spiritual sense. This is the case for the New Testament and many Old Testament texts (examples are not given). Old Testament texts that show unity of literal and spiritual senses are

[8] II, B, 2.

instances of "anticipatory relationship to the new life brought by Christ." That means that the distinction between literal and spiritual senses most often applies to the Old Testament, because many passages of the Old Testament do not attain the perfection of the paschal mystery and the new life in the Spirit.

Lineamenta, 15, outlines some dangers to authentic interpretation of the word of God. Some people view the Bible in ideological fashion or simply as human words apart from faith. The faithful generally lack clear knowledge of the rules of hermeneutics. But the greatest danger reported all over the church is that of *fundamentalism* or literalistic interpretation that totally ignores the human factor in inspiration. Chapter 9 will deal briefly with fundamentalism.

Report after the Discussion

Cardinal Ouellet stressed holiness as the goal of every exegesis of the Word. The dichotomy between spiritual and scientific reading of Scripture is to be bypassed through a hearing and believing reading of the word of God (no. 16). Each one is called to be a living gospel, a gospel that takes on flesh and blood. Authentic exegesis of the word is found in those who have listened to the Word in faith and produced the fruit of holy lives (no. 17). Along this line Benedict XVI called the charisms and diverse forms of the consecrated life "living exegeses of the word." True exegesis observes the circularity between word of God, written and transmitted, and the life of the church, for Scripture presupposes the church and depends on it for its authentic interpretation (nos. 19, 21). To the criteria already given for authentically interpreting the word, many in the assembly added the following: the liturgy, the witness of saints, canonical exegesis, the promotion of unity, docility, prayer, and humility. Exegetes must never forget that the meaning of Scripture is, by its nature, theological, and that the interpreting process should result in the fullness of the spiritual sense. There is a necessary connection between the literal/historical meaning and the spiritual/fuller meaning (no. 31).

The mention of the "fuller sense" calls for explanation. This sense was of fairly recent mintage in Catholic exegesis, being coined by A. Fernández in 1925.[9] It is "a deeper meaning of the text, intended by God but not

---

[9] *Institutiones Biblicae* (Rome: Biblical Institute, 1925) 305–7. This information is culled from Joseph A. Fitzmyer, *The Interpretation of Scripture: In Defense of the Historical-Critical Method* (New York: Paulist Press, 2008) 96.

clearly expressed by the human author."[10] Ordinarily this sense is found
in "the meaning that a subsequent biblical author attributes to an earlier
biblical text, taking it up in a context which confers upon it a new literal
sense, or else it is a question of the meaning that an authentic doctrinal
tradition or a Conciliar definition gives to a biblical text."[11] For example,
Matthew 1:23 gives a fuller sense to the prophecy of the young woman
(*'almah*) to conceive in Isaiah 7:14 by using the Greek LXX translation
parthenos (virgin). In the mind of the Pontifical Commission, it belongs
to no individual to ferret out "fuller senses" but rather "there is always
need of the control of further use of the text either in Scripture itself or in
the dogmatic Tradition of the Church."[12]

The Propositions

Interpretation of Scripture in the church must not overlook patristic
exegesis, which distinguishes two senses: the literal (through critical exegesis) and the spiritual (the reality of the events of which Scripture speaks,
taking account of the living tradition of the whole church and the analogy
of faith) (proposition 6). Interpretation has as model what reading and
hearing the Bible has produced in the fathers of the church, the saints
and doctors, and the masters of the spiritual life (proposition 32). New
emphasis needs to be put on the characteristic dimensions of the Catholic
interpretation of the Bible, as outlined in The Interpretation of the Bible
in the Church (propositions 12, 28).

What the synod fathers say about Catholic exegesis calls for some explanation. In essence, what characterizes Catholic exegesis (this topic is
treated more fully in the next chapter) is that it deliberately places itself
within the living tradition of the church, holding together modern scientific culture and the religious tradition emanating from Israel and the early
Christian community, hence faith and reason. In this, it holds on to the
"incarnational principle," which, in the words of John Paul II,[13]

> reject a split between the human and the divine, between scientific
> research and respect for the faith, between the literal sense and the

[10] Interpretation of the Bible in the Church, II, B, 3.
[11] Ibid.
[12] Fitzmyer, *The Interpretation of Scripture*, 97.
[13] Address on the Interpretation of the Bible in the Church (April 23, 1993), 5, on the
occasion of the presentation of the document of the Pontifical Biblical Commission, Interpretation of the Bible in the Church.

spiritual sense. They thus appear to be in perfect harmony with the mystery of the incarnation.

Because the Bible itself is a repository of many ways of interpreting the same events and reflecting upon the same problems, the Catholic exegete pays attention to "rereadings" within the Bible, whereby "certain aspects of the received interpretation be set aside and a new interpretation adopted."[14] Catholic exegetes look toward the living *magisterium* of the church that has the sole responsibility of authentically interpreting the word of God. They never forget that interpretation is an *ecclesial* task and that what they are interpreting is the word of God. They reach the true goal of their work when they have explained the meaning of the biblical text as God's word for today.

An aspect of interpretation that the synod fathers drew attention to is pilgrimage to the Holy Land:

> Paul VI called the Holy Land "the Fifth Gospel." The Synod recom-
> mends pilgrimages, and, if possible, the study of the sacred Scriptures
> in the Holy Land and in the footsteps of St. Paul. Pilgrims and stu-
> dents can, by means of this experience, understand better the physical
> and geographical environment of the Scriptures, and particularly the
> relationship between the two testaments. (proposition 51)

Some Outstanding Issues

Both *Dei Verbum* and the documents of the synod refer to the "intention of the author" as a factor in interpretation, an intention that can be discerned through exegetical methods. Already in 1946 Wimsatt and Beardsley[15] addressed the question of "the intentional fallacy." In recent times, most critics of literature, and of the Bible, do not believe that the intention of the author determines the meaning of texts. That would seem to ignore the role of the reader in creating meaning. Schneiders states it as follows: "meaning is not *in* texts but mediated *by* texts."[16] The Interpretation of the

---

[14] Interpretation of the Bible in the Church, III, A, 2.

[15] William K. Wimsatt, and Monroe C. Beardsley, "The Intentional Fallacy," *Sewanee Review* 54 (1946) 468–88. Revised and republished in *The Verbal Icon: Studies in the Meaning of Poetry* (Lexington, KY: University of Kentucky Press, 1954) 3–18.

[16] Sandra M. Schneiders, *The Revelatory Text: Interpreting the New Testament as Sacred Scripture*, 2nd ed. (Collegeville, MN: Liturgical Press, 1999) xxxii. She posits a Platonic-like "ideal meaning," that is, a certain dynamic structure in the text that can be made concrete in

Bible in the Church[17] notes that ancient exegesis attributed to every text of Scripture several levels of meaning. The quest for *the* precise sense came in the late nineteenth century with the historical-critical method, which saw this sense in the past, "but this thesis has now run aground on the conclusions of theories of language and of philosophical hermeneutics, both of which affirm that written texts are open to a plurality of meaning."[18]

Is there any closure to such plurality of meaning? Fitzmyer insists that any meaning must retain a link to the original author's intention:

> Such a "meaning" that goes beyond that of the historical biblical author can never be understood as losing all homogeneity with the original meaning of the author.[19]

In light of the above, the "literal sense" seems more complex than meets the eye. Luke Timothy Johnson questions the identification of the literal sense and the historical sense or the original meaning of the text, one determined only by historical exegesis.[20] The reader may consult the section "The Unity of the Literal Sense and the Spiritual Sense" in chapter 10. Briefly, the pope holds that one may not oppose or merely juxtapose these two senses, since they exist in reciprocity. The historical-critical and the theological are merely two *dimensions*, two methodological *levels* of the one hermeneutic of faith.

Chapter 10 discusses interpretation in the pope's apostolic exhortation, *Verbum Domini*.

---

the here and now in a number of interpretations that will vary according to the interpreter, the situation of the interpretation, and other factors (p. xxiii).

[17] II, B.

[18] Schneiders, *Revelatory Text*, xxiii.

[19] Fitzmyer, *The Interpretation of Scripture*, 72.

[20] Luke Timothy Johnson, "What's Catholic about Catholic Biblical Scholarship?," in *The Future of Catholic Biblical Scholarship: A Constructive Conversation*, Luke Timothy Johnson and William S. Kurz (Grand Rapids: Wm. Eerdmans, 2002) 15.

Questions for Discussion

1. Explain the two aspects of the interpretation of a text of the Bible.

2. Select any text of the Bible and apply to it the three principles of "theological" exegesis.

3. What is the "fuller sense"? Give examples.

4. Give some principles of Catholic exegesis.

5. From what you read in this chapter, what should one expect as one of the results of the synod on interpreting the word of God?

Chapter 7

Issue III:
Recent Catholic Exegesis,
a Brief Survey

This chapter gives a brief survey of recent Catholic exegesis. As explained in the introduction, it has the needs of students and advanced inquirers in mind. It is also an important background to issues raised in the synod itself and in the pope's post-synodal apostolic exhortation. In the nature of the case it cannot be exhaustive or one would need a whole book. It can only be a very succinct summary of trends in important documents of the magisterium and in the work of noted scholars. Some readers may miss certain names they believe should feature. My apologies in advance if a reader misses someone he/she considers should feature. It is my hope that groups or classes discussing this chapter will complete the list.

Divino Afflante Spiritu (September 30, 1943)

A survey of recent Catholic exegesis will have to start with the encyclical letter of Pius XII, *Divino Afflante Spiritu*, 1943.[1] Written to commemorate the fiftieth anniversary of Leo XIII's *Providentissimus Deus*, 1893, it became the Magna Carta of modern Catholic biblical studies. It officially ended the inquisition against modernism rolled out by Pius X at the beginning of the twentieth century. Putting to rest attacks against scientific exegesis by groups sponsoring what they called "mystical" exegesis, it opened the door to Catholics to share in the recent advances in biblical research, especially the various aspects of the historical-critical method. The following are a summary of some of the highlights.

Since the publication of *Providentissimus Deus*, excavations in the lands of the Bible have uncovered papyri, tablets, and texts that give a better view of

---

[1] Unless otherwise stated, the citations of the texts of the magisterium on the Bible are from *Official Catholic Teachings: Bible Interpretation*, ed. James J. Megivern (Wilmington: McGrath, 1978).

the manner of speaking, relating, and writing in use among those ancients. Catholic exegetes must neglect none of the discoveries, whether in the domain of archaeology or in ancient history or literature, which serve to make better known the mentality of the ancient writers, as well as their manner and art of reasoning, narrating, and writing (no. 39). The knowledge of Hebrew and other oriental languages has also grown apace. Catholic exegetes must use these and all other means with a view to critically establishing the text of the Bible. The authenticity of the Latin Vulgate, as declared by the Council of Trent, was primarily juridical, not critical (no. 21). So Catholics should have no qualms about preparing and publishing new Catholic editions of the Bible from the original languages. (Hitherto Catholic translations of the Bible had been made from the Vulgate.) They are to discern the various "forms" and conventions of the literature of the times. Pius XII was the first to establish the "incarnational principle" that has since become the anchor of Catholic exegesis.

> In Scripture divine things are presented to us in the manner which is in common use amongst men. For as the substantial Word of God became like to men in all things, "except sin," so the words of God, expressed in human language, are made like to human speech in every respect, except error. (no. 37)

This being the case, it is the task of the exegete to search out and expound the *literal* meaning of the words, intended and expressed by the sacred writer, as also the *spiritual* sense, provided it is clearly intended by God (no. 26).

> Let the interpreter then, with all care and without neglecting any light derived from recent research, endeavor to determine the peculiar character and circumstances of the sacred writer, the age in which he lived, the sources written and oral to which he had recourse and the forms of expression he employed. (no. 33)

Quite a few biblical scholars had been under attack. The pope pleaded for charity for biblical scholars, calling them devoted sons and daughters of the church. He reminded all that few texts have had their sense defined by the authority of the church and few texts have met the unanimous teaching of the fathers of the church. The encyclical was a seismic shift in light of the fact that as recently as June 26, 1912, the Pontifical Biblical Commission had rejected the hypothesis of "the two sources" of the gospels, the foundation for modern historical-critical study of the gospels that Pius XII was now advocating!

Lateran University versus
Pontifical Biblical Institute (1960–61)

In the wake of *Divino Afflante Spiritu*,[2] a professor at the Pontifical Biblical Institute (Rome), Luis Alonso Schökel, wrote an article titled "Where is Catholic Exegesis Headed?"[3] Before Pius XII, scholars (for example, L. Billot) tended to assert a singular and transcendent biblical genre. Now Pius XII had acknowledged diverse and linguistic genres in Scripture. Some had been of the opinion, for example, L. Murillo, that a unanimous consent of the fathers made an opinion *de fide* (of faith). If so, that Moses wrote the Pentateuch would be of faith for it attained the common consent of the fathers! Pius XII had quietly debunked this view. Was it true that interpreters were misconstruing what Pius XII wrote, especially in light of the fact that in *Humani Generis* (1950) the same pope had to proscribe certain deviations from doctrine? Schökel's answer was that most of the "errors" proscribed were less exegetical (interpretation of individual texts) than theological (on inspiration and hermeneutics). A few exegetes may have been rash in pronouncing on the historicity of texts with insufficiently grounded arguments. As a whole, however, Catholic exegesis was proceeding well along the "new direction" stimulated by *Divino Afflante Spiritu*.

Monsignor Antonio Romeo, professor of Scripture at the Lateran University in Rome, responded with a vitriolic article.[4] Romeo was so well placed that many thought that he was voicing an official view. Romeo denied any "new direction" but rather the so-called new direction was actually opposed to the directives of the magisterium and constituted a danger to the faith. Schökel's article was only an illustration of the rationalism and modern Catholic progressivism that threatened to subvert the foundations of Catholic doctrine, evidence of which could be found in some articles of *Theological Studies* and the *Catholic Biblical Quarterly*.[5] Romeo found "tremendously upsetting" Jean Levie's *The Bible, Word of God in Words of Men*—a book that has since become a classic! He was attacking not only individual professors but also the Pontifical Biblical Institute itself as not being "Catholic"

---

[2] Information here is indebted to Joseph A. Fitzmyer, "A Roman Scripture Controversy," in *The Interpretation of Scripture: In Defense of the Historical-Critical Method*, 17–36 (New York: Paulist Press, 2008); and Maurice Gilbert, "New Horizons and Present Needs: Exegesis since Vatican II," in *Vatican II: Assessment and Perspectives: Twenty-Five Years After (1962–1987)*, vol. 1, ed. René Latourelle, 321–43 (New York: Paulist Press, 1988).

[3] "The Encyclical 'Divino afflante spiritu' and the 'New Opinions,'" *Civiltà Cattolica* 111, no. 2645 (September 3, 1960) 449–60.

[4] "L'Enciclica '*Divino afflante Spiritu*' e le 'opiniones novae,'" *Divinitas* 4/3 (1960) 385–456.

[5] Cf. Fitzmyer, *The Interpretation of Scripture*, 26.

enough. When a request for retraction went unheeded, the Biblical Institute published its rejoinder in *Verbum Domini*, 39 (1961), 3–17.[6] In February 1961, the prefect of the Sacred Congregation of Studies and Universities let it be known that Romeo's article in no way represented the opinions of the congregation. On March 2, E. Vogt, the rector of the Biblical Institute, was named consultor to the Pontifical Theological Commission of the coming Second Vatican Council. Finally, a letter of the secretary of the Pontifical Biblical Commission, A. Miller, to the rector of the Biblical Institute deprecated the attacks of Msgr. Romeo and reaffirmed trust in the Biblical Institute.[7]

Sancta Mater Ecclesia,
Instruction Concerning the Historical Truth of the Gospels

Issued toward the last stages of Vatican II, this document[8] had a powerful effect on the final editing of *Dei Verbum* (the Dogmatic Constitution on Divine Revelation). *DV*, 19, on the gospels and history, is practically a summary of this Instruction. This is the first time the church explicitly accepted and formally incorporated the results of form critical and redaction studies on the gospels. The document traces three stages of tradition by which the doctrine and life of Jesus have come down to us. First is *Christ our Lord*, who impressed upon his chosen disciples his teaching and his very identity. Then the *stage of the apostles*, who pro-

Three Levels of the Tradition
  Christ our Lord
  The Apostles
  The Evangelists

claimed his ministry, above all his death and resurrection, and who faithfully explained his life and words while adapting them to various communities of faith. Finally, the *four evangelists*, who each wrote from a particular perspective and in response to the situation of their churches. The exegete needs to "seek out the meaning intended by the evangelist in narrating a saying or a deed in a certain way or in placing it in a certain context" (no. 9). The evangelists did not report the events and doctrines of the Lord for the sole purpose that people remember them but rather they "preached" these so as to offer the church a basis of faith and morals. The interpreter may use literary criticism

[6] The Pontifical Biblical Institute and a Recent Booklet of Msgr A. Romeo.
[7] However, a *monitum* (warning) of the Sacred Congregation of the Holy Office appeared on June 20, 1961, against opinions calling into doubt the genuine historical and objective truth of Sacred Scripture. The battle was still engaged. See Megivern, *Official Catholic Teachings*, 385.
[8] Pontifical Biblical Commission, April 21, 1964.

(then = source criticism) and other tools of exegetical method, always, how-ever, showing how these contribute to the theological teaching of the text.

Dei Verbum,
Vatican II's Dogmatic Constitution on Divine Revelation

The reader is by now familiar with this document.[9] Here we highlight three of its many contributions. The first is the clear assertion that "God speaks in sacred Scripture through humans in human fashion" (*DV*, 12). This calls for methods ordinarily used for the investigation of human language. The second is the delineation of the dimensions of interpreta-tion, the human element and the divine element, both forming a unity. The third are the criteria for Spirit-led meaning: the unity of the whole of Scripture, the living tradition of the whole church, and the harmony that exists between the elements of the faith (*analogia fidei*, analogy of faith). Further information on this is in chapters 6 and 10.

In Search of Spiritual Exegesis

The French original of de Lubac's[10] work appeared between 1959–64, but it was not till the '90s that the English translation appeared. Through a history of interpretation in the patristic and medieval periods, de Lubac advanced his views that interpretation of the Bible should integrate the *spiritual* exegesis (the four senses) so beloved by the ancients. "The spiritual sense of the Old Testament is the New Testament" (vol. 1, xv). Allegorical interpretation, as schematized in the doctrine of the four senses,[11] was no Greek invention but rather enabled patristic and medieval exegesis to be "animated by an extraordinarily powerful sense of synthesis" (ibid., xx). Such exegesis

> contains, as one might say today, a whole theology of Scripture. It organizes all of revelation around a concrete center, which is fixed in time and space by the Cross of Jesus Christ. It is itself a complete and completely unified dogmatic and spiritual theology. (ibid., xix)

It was this "synthesis" that de Lubac found lacking in much of modern exegesis. Because Jesus Christ is the end point and fullness of Scripture,

---

[9] November 18, 1965.

[10] Henri de Lubac, *Medieval Exegesis: The Four Senses of Scripture*, 3 vols. (Grand Rapids: Wm. Eerdmans, 1998). French original in four volumes, 1959–64.

[11] Literal, allegorical, moral, and anagogical (the last three being aspects of the "spiri-tual" sense).

"everything in it is related to him . . . Consequently, he is, so to speak, its whole exegesis" (I, 237). Christian exegesis is an exegesis in faith, an act of faith in the great historical Act that has never had and never will have its equal, for the incarnation is unique (I, 260). Scriptural allegory should not be confused with what in recent times is called typology. As defined, typology does not have its own intrinsic foundations nor says anything intrinsically about the *dialectical opposition between the two Testaments*, the "contrasting parallelism" underlined by the first Christian generation, or the conditions of the unity of the Testaments. (Obviously, de Lubac's use of the term "typology" reflects the usage and argument of his time. On typology, with a different take, the reader may consult chapters 4 and 10 of this book.)

De Lubac handled objections to the "spiritual" sense on the part of some "moderns" (I, 263–67). Some denounced it as equivocal, others as novel. Still others, concerned for the scientific method, tried to reclaim it as a literal sense, albeit the "full" literal sense. But, to de Lubac, such "fullness" is no object of a dead scientific knowledge but rather of a living understanding. An examination of the texts may put one on the track of the spiritual sense, but it is not a matter of pure technique or pure intellectuality. Not acquired without the gospel received in faith, it depended, like mysticism, on illumination, which can only be given from on high (I, 265).[12] De Lubac has had some influence, though it is not clear whether such influence extended to the *Catechism of the Catholic Church*. In numbers 115–19 the *Catechism* included a relatively long treatment of the patristic and medieval four senses of Scripture,[13] which did not feature in *Dei Verbum*.[14] The *Catechism* (no. 115) sees the "four senses" as "[guaranteeing] all its richness to the living reading of Scripture in the Church."

An Attack on the Historical-Critical Method

In 1989, then-Cardinal Ratzinger attacked the historical-critical method for its shortcomings. He incisively pointed out that in Wladimir Solowjew's *History of the Antichrist*, the Antichrist received his doctorate in Bible from

---

[12] In chapter 10 of this book, the section on "The Unity of the Literal Sense and the Spiritual Sense" will decry any dichotomy between scientific exegesis and spiritual interpretation.

[13] For Thomas Aquinas, *ST* I, 1, 10, ad. 1, the spiritual sense was necessarily based on the literal sense.

[14] They, however, featured in The Interpretation of the Bible in the Church, II, B, which gave them a qualified acceptance.

Tübingen![15] The historical-critical method has become a fence that blocks access to the Bible for the uninitiated. It discountenances faith and does not reckon with God in historical events. Very often it fashions a "real history" in place of the one in the text. One no longer learns what the text *says* but what it *should* have said. Certain forms of exegesis are appearing, for example, materialist and feminist exegesis, that no longer claim to be an understanding of the text itself. Historical method can serve such agendas by dissecting the Bible into discontinuous pieces that are then reassembled in a new montage altogether different from the original biblical context. A self-criticism of the historical method is needed.

The method claims pure objectivity, when even in the natural sciences the *Heisenberg principle* has established the relevance of the questions and point of view of the observer. Interest is always a requirement for the possibility of coming to know. The issue then becomes how interest may engender knowing without drowning out the voice of the other but rather developing an inner understanding for things of the past so they speak to us today.

Martin Dibelius and Rudolph Bultmann both sought to establish strict literary criteria to clarify the growth of the tradition. Both gave priority to the kerygma over the event itself. Both adopted the criterion of discontinuity between the pre-Easter Jesus and the church. Both regarded what is more simple as more original, what is more complex as later development. They thus transferred science's evolutionary model to spiritual history. To find the "simple," both authors look at standards of form and content, for Dibelius the *paradigm* (example narrative in oral tradition), for Bultmann the *apothegm*. Everything not corresponding to this form is attributed to later development, but this is arbitrary. Jesus must be conceived in strongly "Judaic" terms, with no admixture of anything Hellenistic. Whatever derives from cult or mystery must be rejected as later development. How, then, explain the transition from the unmessianic, unapocalyptic, prophetic Jesus to the apocalyptic community that worshiped him as Messiah? A collective "community" is posited. To connect the original message of Jesus to Christian life today, Bultmann posits the theory of demythologization. Here is where the self-critique of the historical method must pass into a self-criticism of historical reason. Bultmann attributed a kind of

---

[15] Joseph Cardinal Ratzinger, "Biblical Interpretation in Crisis: On the Question of the Foundations and Approaches of Exegesis Today," in *Biblical Interpretation in Crisis: The Ratzinger Conference on Bible and Church*, ed. Richard John Neuhaus, 1–23 (Grand Rapids: Wm. Eerdmans, 1989). It had been delivered as the Erasmus Lecture, at St. Peter's Lutheran church in New York City, January 27, 1988.

dogmatic character to the scientific worldview, so miracle stories cannot be historical. He embraced the presupposition of Kant that the voice of being-in-itself cannot be heard; humans can only indirectly hear the postulates of practical reason. Restriction to the purely empirical excludes the real appearance of what is "Wholly Other." God becomes inexpressible reality. The apparent voice of this "Other" in the Bible becomes merely myth. In its core, the debate is not really among historians; it is rather a philosophical debate. What is needed is to match the historical-critical method with a philosophy that has fewer drawbacks foreign to the text. We need a readiness to learn something new and not determine in advance what may or may not be. Dibelius and Bultmann see the event as no bearer of meaning; meaning lies only in the word. But, the event itself can be a "word"; *dabar* means both word and event. Both have to be considered equally original. To abolish the continuity between event and word is to gainsay the unity in Scripture between the Old and New Testaments: "a New Testament cut off from the Old is automatically abolished since it exists, as its very title suggests, because of the unity of both."[16] We need a return to the text, and also a distinction between those hypotheses that are helpful and those that are not.

A Defense of the Historical-Critical Method

The response to Cardinal Ratzinger was given by Raymond E. Brown.[17] Here, however, we summarize another equally spirited defense of the historical-critical approach, that of Joseph Fitzmyer.[18]

Historical criticism is being accused of "dismantling traditional Roman Catholic theology" (for example, by Thomas Sheehan), of paying attention to the human element and not sufficiently to the Bible as word of God, and of preoccupying itself with the prehistory of the text and not the text in its final form. The origins of this method date to "getting back to the sources" and the study of the Bible in its original languages initiated by the Renaissance. The incident of Galileo in this period still serves a timely warning. The Reformation abandoned allegorical interpretation for the literal sense. The Enlightenment, especially the influence of Leopold von

[16] *Biblical Interpretation in Crisis*, 20.

[17] "The Contribution of Historical Biblical Criticism to Ecumenical Discussion," *Biblical Interpretation in Crisis*, 24–49.

[18] Joseph Fitzmyer, "Historical Criticism: Its Role in Biblical Interpretation and Church Life," *Theological Studies* 50 (1989) 246–59; now also in Fitzmyer, *The Interpretation of Scripture*, 59–73.

Ranke, led to the search for history, "how it really was." In recent times there have been many discoveries of papyri and tablets that afford literary parallels for the literature of both the Old and New Testaments. Pius XII's *Divino Afflante Spiritu*, 1943, finally endorsed the historical approach to the Bible. This approach avails of various refinements, textual criticism, source criticism, literary and form criticism, and redaction criticism. It is true that some practitioners operate with presuppositions that are not necessarily part of the historical method. For example, Bultmann linked the method with Luther's justification by faith alone. That led to lack of interest in what Jesus said and did (the events) for what the gospel proclaims and how the preached word affects the individual believer of today. For him any quest for the historical basis of the kerygma was a betrayal of *sola fide* (faith alone). Hence his *New Testament Theology* begins with the primitive kerygma, not before it. In itself, however, the historical method is neutral. Used with faith presuppositions it becomes a properly oriented method of biblical interpretation. True exegesis draws out the meaning of a passage as intended by the inspired writer—the *textual meaning*, the *contextual meaning*, and the *relational meaning* (the sense in relation to the book or corpus as a whole). The relational meaning is sometimes called the biblical theological meaning. All combined give us the religious and theological meaning, that is, the meaning of the text as word of God couched in ancient human language. The historical method presupposes that God's word is set forth in human words. It is properly expounded in relation to the tradition that has grown out of it. Approaches like canonical criticism, sociological criticism, and structuralist analysis can be used to refine the historical-critical method but cannot replace it; it is basic to scriptural research. Nor can there be any true *spiritual sense* that is not based on the *literal* sense as intended and expressed by the biblical author. The 1964 Instruction of the Pontifical Biblical Commission presupposes the historical method when it refers to three stages of the gospel tradition: the stage of Jesus, the stage of the apostles and apostolic communities, and the viewpoint of the evangelist. It mentions the form critical method as among the "laudable achievements" of recent research. *Dei Verbum* of Vatican II incorporated parts of the Instruction.

There is some truth in the assertion of some today that meaning goes beyond the original author's intention. However, "such a meaning that goes 'beyond' that of the historical biblical author can never be understood as losing all homogeneity with the meaning of the original author."[19] The

---

[19] Fitzmyer, "Historical Criticism," 258.

use of the historical method by Catholics since *Divino Afflante Spiritu* prepared for the advances of Vatican II. It has aided ecumenism. The bilateral
ecumenical commissions after Vatican II have been greatly aided by the
fact of a method common between Catholics and Protestants.

Principles of Catholic Exegesis

The Interpretation of the Bible in the Church[20] was issued to celebrate
the centenary of *Providentissimus Deus* and the fiftieth anniversary of *Divino
Afflante Spiritu*. Attacks on the historical-critical method had intensified.
In fact, many expected the document to condemn it roundly. Surprisingly,
it asserted that Catholic exegesis did not have its own proper method but
rather uses whatever method that is not inherently against the faith. It
endorsed the historical-critical method as a necessary and foundational
tool for exegesis:[21]

> The historical-critical method is the indispensable method for the sci-
> entific study of the meaning of ancient texts. Holy Scripture, inasmuch
> as it is the "Word of God in human language," has been composed
> by human authors in all its various parts and in all the sources that
> lie behind them. Because of this, its proper understanding not only
> admits the use of this method but actually requires it.

However, like the other methods examined, it too received a few caveats
and needs to be complemented by other methods. Thirteen methods were
evaluated and were placed in groups.

A. Historical-Critical Method

Method	What it Does	Evaluation
1. Historical-Critical	Diachronic, uses historical criteria	Focus on what the text meant, sometimes ignores what it means
	Linguistic and semantic analysis	Insufficient attention to final form of the text and its message
	Textual, source, literary, and redaction criticism	
	Focus on the literal sense	Almost exclusive focus on the human author, not the divine

[20] Pontifical Biblical Commission (Vatican City: Libreria Editrice Vaticana, 1993).
[21] I, A.

B. New Method of Literary Analysis

Method	What it Does	Evaluation
2. Rhetorical Criticism	Analyzes techniques used to convince and persuade Three approaches: Based on Greco-Roman rhetoric Focus on Semitic ways of composing (e.g., parallelism) "new rhetoric": persuasive ability of texts in context	Sometimes merely describes, concern only for style Synchronic, hence cannot stand alone Not always clear what kind of rhetoric the text demands
3. Narrative Analysis	Text as story, story of salvation Not just a "window" but a "mirror"—projects a narrative world Attentive to plot, character, point of view, narrative world Concepts of "implied author," "implied reader" Two approaches: Methods of analysis Methods of theological reflection	Sometimes imposes preestablished models on the text Some rule out the doctrinal elaboration of the text Needs to be supplemented with diachronic aspect World of the text analyzed does not exhaust the full faith
4. Semiotic Analysis Structuralism	Immanence: each text a unit of meaning complete in itself Meaning lies in relationships (opposition, confirmation . . .) Each text has a grammar (certain rules or structures): *Narrative level:* roles played by actants	Attention to the text as a coherent whole Allows discovery of Bible without need of great knowledge of history But, needs to attend to history and extra-textual reference beyond the text Meaning often only at the formal level, fails to draw out the message

Continued from page 79

Method	What it Does	Evaluation
	Discourse level: operations concerning figures *Deep level:* analyzes binary oppositions (black/not black . . .)	

C. Approaches Based on Tradition

Method	What it Does	Evaluation
5. Canonical Approach	Considers each text in light of the whole Two strands: 　Final form is normative (Childs) 　"canonical process"— progressive development of Scripture (Sanders)	Supplements historical method, not a substitute The believing community is context for interpretation Original and early meaning not the whole or authentic meaning Event of Christ gives further meanings to the Old Testament
6. Jewish Traditions of Interpretation	Midrashic approach appears in the Bible itself E.g., Chr in relation to Sam and Kgs, some arguments of Paul	Dating necessary before material can be used for comparison Jews start from Torah, Christians from event of Christ
7. History of Reception of the Text	What meanings has this text had over time? E.g., readings of the Song of Songs, including its use in the church	Need to discern wrong interpretations No stage to be privileged

D. Approaches that Use the Human Sciences

Method	What it Does	Evaluation
8. Sociological Approach	Uses models from social contexts E.g., comparing Decalogue and ancient Eastern law	Caveat: society pays more attention to economic and institutional factors than the personal and religious

Method	What it Does	Evaluation
9. Cultural Anthropology	Sets up models based on cultural specifics E.g., "Mediterranean values" of honor/shame	Careful to distinguish what is permanent in the message and what is particular to context Caveat: not competent to determine the specific content of revelation
10. Psychological and Psycho-analytical	Religion and the Unconscious Symbols can convey religious experience not easily accessible to reasoning Examines how mystery is revealed in imagery, ritual . . .	Caveat: do not eliminate notions of sin and salvation Do not dismiss the historical character of the message of the Bible Biblical revelation must not be confused with spontaneous religiosity

E. Contextual Approaches

Method	What it Does	Evaluation
11. Liberationist Approach	Reading oriented to needs of people Reading for change, unites interpretation and praxis Starts from the social and political situation Foundational for this approach: exodus and passion and resurrection of Jesus	Tendency to focus only on narrative and prophetic texts (situations of oppression) Exegesis cannot be neutral, but this is one-sided Some use Marxist exegesis of class struggle, which is in tension with the faith

Continued from page 81

Method	What it Does	Evaluation
		This-earthly eschatology tends to eclipse scriptural eschatology

12. Feminist Approach	A variety of approaches with common theme as the liberation of women
	
	Three forms:
	  radical: Bible has no authority (irremediably androcentric)
	  neoorthodox: "canon within canon"
	  critical: rediscover role of women disciples in Jesus movement and Pauline churches; analysis of the text as to how it impacts on the lives of women
	
	Three criteria:
	  hermeneutics of suspicion
	  study societal stratification in communities of Bible
	  discover the power dynamics both in past and now
		Greater consciousness of female images of God
		
		Has raised question of power in the church
		
		But must not dismiss the gospel teaching of power as service
		
		Tends to construct hypotheses based on silence of the text or fleeting indications in it

F. Fundamentalist Interpretation

Method	What it Does	Evaluation
13. Fundamentalism	Verbal inerrancy—Bible is word of God, hence free from error in all its words and details	Rejects the historical and human aspect of revelation Does not reckon with figurative meaning or rereadings of certain texts within Scripture itself Danger of inviting people to intellectual suicide

Part III of the document deals with "Characteristics of Catholic Interpretation." In essence, what characterizes Catholic exegesis is that it is exegesis in faith that deliberately places itself within the living tradition of the church and holds together reason and faith, modern scientific culture and the religious tradition emanating from Israel and the early Christian community. In this, it holds on to the "incarnational principle," which, in the words of John Paul II,

> reject[s] a split between the human and the divine, between scientific research and respect for the faith, between the literal sense and the spiritual sense. They thus appear to be in perfect harmony with the mystery of the incarnation.[22]

Because the Bible itself is a repository of many ways of interpreting the same events and reflecting upon the same problems, the Catholic exegete pays attention to "rereadings" within the Bible, whereby "certain aspects of the received interpretation [are] set aside and a new interpretation adopted."[23] Catholic exegetes emulate the fathers of the church who read the Bible theologically, without adhering to some concrete aspects of their exegesis. They look to the living magisterium of the church that has the sole responsibility of authentically interpreting the word of God, whether in tradition or Scripture. They carry on their study and research as an *ecclesial* task, never forgetting that what they are interpreting is the word *of God*.

---

[22] Address on the Interpretation of the Bible in the Church, no. 5 (April 23, 1993), on the occasion of the presentation of the document of the Pontifical Biblical Commission, Interpretation of the Bible in the Church.

[23] III, A, 2.

Hence they reach the true goal of their work when they have explained the meaning of the biblical text as God's word for today. A good summary of Catholic principles for exegesis is found in twenty propositions by Peter Williamson.[24]

What Is "Catholic" about Catholic Exegesis?

Luke Timothy Johnson[25] found the scholarship of Catholics using the historical method as beyond doubt but asked in what sense it was any longer "Catholic." To be Catholic is to think inclusively ("both/and") rather than exclusively ("either/or"). For example, Catholics value both Scripture and tradition, hence they acknowledge the connections between Scripture and liturgy, Scripture and theology, and Scripture and the history of interpretation.

Recent Catholic engagement with the Bible can be divided into three generations. The *first generation* is the period before *Divino Afflante Spiritu* of Pius XII. Biblical scholarship has been nourished by a long tradition of patristic, medieval, and scholastic interpretation. Over the course of centuries, tradition tended to swallow up Scripture; Scripture lost its capacity to challenge rather than simply confirm tradition. The "both/and" of Scripture and tradition collapsed into *sola traditio* (tradition alone).[26] The *second generation* entered the arena with Pius XII's *Divino Afflante Spiritu*. Catholics joined a game that was already well advanced and freely used the methods of history to locate the specific circumstances of each biblical voice. It was hoped that the church could be renewed through the use of history to recover some of Scripture's "otherness." Catholics could contribute more positively toward ecumenism, for "the retrieval of the literal sense would help overcome accretions of dogmatic and polemical interpretations."[27] The historical method was supposed to be neutral and objective. The *third generation* is the current stream of Catholic scholars.

---

[24] "Catholic Principles for Interpreting Scripture," *CBQ* 65/3 (2003) 327–49. This article is a summary of the author's thesis, *Catholic Principles for Interpreting Scripture: A Study of the Pontifical Biblical Commission's "The Interpretation of the Bible in the Church,"* Subsidia Biblica 22 (Rome: Pontifical Biblical Institute, 2001).

[25] "What's Catholic about Catholic Biblical Scholarship?" First delivered at the Catholic Biblical Association meeting in Seattle, 1997. Revised and published in Luke Timothy Johnson and William S. Kurz, *The Future of Catholic Biblical Scholarship: A Constructive Conversation* (Grand Rapids: Wm. Eerdmans, 2002) 3–34.

[26] *The Future of Catholic Biblical Scholarship*, 8.

[27] Ibid., 9.

The first generation grew to maturity in the "old world" of Catholic piety and traditional theological education. The exercise of the historical method was for it a positive addition to its secure identity. It wrote popularizing books and treated theological top-ics, like the inspiration of Scripture. *What is Catholic in Catholic* The second generation accepted the *exegesis?* historical method unquestioningly and wrote mainly for other schol-ars. However, some were now being trained in secular universities, not Catholic institutions. There began a shift from seminaries to universities as locus for study of the Bible. The main conversation partners became not the church or theology but other disciplines in the social sciences and humanities. The third generation studied or did not study theology in the period of upheaval after Vatican II. They received their doctorates at Yale, Harvard, or Chicago. Now in late career and midlife, this genera-tion is asking whether the losses have not been as great as the gains. It is realizing that the historical-critical approach is not a method but rather "a model or paradigm for the study of the Bible."[28] This is evident in the fact of the various versions of "the historical Jesus" and "early Christian-ity" undergirded by the various historical reconstructions. There is ongo-ing literary dismemberment of the Bible through the reconstruction of putative histories of hypothetical communities. The hypothetical source Q is sliced into layers Q1, Q2, and Q3, which are then thought to yield the history of the "Q community."[29] The method has shown itself inca-pable of feeding the life of faith in a positive manner. The literal sense, as determined by historical exegesis, has become a limiting control to all other interpretations. Some even hold that "the literal sense of Scripture must be *opposed* to figurative interpretations."[30] It has become clear that the historical approach is not theologically neutral. Its theological pre-suppositions derive from the Protestant form of "either/or" Christianity from which it derived, that is, Scripture alone as guide of Christian life (discountenancing tradition). An example is the interpretation of parables from A. Jülicher to Joachim Jeremias and Dominic Crossan. The aim is a historical reconstruction that weeds out church tradition in distinction from the original teaching of Jesus, not the search for "the parables of the church." The approach is again "either/or." "For Jeremias, the Church

[28] Ibid., 14.
[29] Ibid., 29–30.
[30] Ibid., 16.

betrays Jesus' message through allegory."[31] Paul's perceptions are deemed as merely flattened, not deepened by Ephesians; 1 and 2 Peter, James, and the Pastorals are lumped together (revealingly) as "early Catholicism." The acorn may be distinguished from the oak, but which botanist will hold that the acorn, not the oak, is the point of perfection, or fail to see the continuity in identity between the two? History is an important aspect of biblical study, but Catholic scholars need to consider their relationship to the Catholic tradition. It is Catholic to look for organic growth, from Judaism to the New Testament, and from early Christianity to the patristic period and today. It is Catholic to reckon with the entire sweep of the history of interpretation. Interpretation did not begin with the Enlightenment and the nineteenth century! We ought also to pay closer attention to the variants and versions as a form of the history of aftereffects of the text. They show how the text has been understood and how it *can* also be understood. Rather than position biblical scholarship against the church, Scripture should be taught for the life of the church. Unfortunately, an increasing number of professors of Bible are lay and lacking a theological background. The study of the Bible (not understood as "Scripture") is increasingly a purely academic activity, often located within the scientific study of religion. Scholars need to know and declare their loyalties: loyalty to tradition *and* criticism but with tradition as the starting point of any inquiry. Catholic scholars need to rediscover dimensions of critical inquiry broader than the historical, for history is only one voice in the process of faith discernment. Commentaries need to interpret Scripture in ways that are translatable to the act of preaching. Catholic tradition has always embraced polyvalent interpretation, the literal sense and figurative senses. For even with the literal sense, polyvalence is unavoidable because of the multiple perspectives of readers and the diverse kinds of questions put to the text. Catholic scholars need to participate in shaping a pedagogy that will empower lay readership of the Bible. We need to renew the conversation between so-called precritical and critical scholarship, and recover a sense of how Scripture might play a role in theology.

Where and What Is Meaning?

Sandra M. Schneiders[32] sees criticism as having passed through three phases in recent times, "each yielding a different kind of criticism."[33] The

[31] Ibid., 17.

[32] *The Revelatory Text: Interpreting the New Testament as Sacred Scripture*, 2nd ed. (Collegeville, MN: Liturgical Press, 1999).

[33] Ibid., 170.

first phase, which began with the birth of higher criticism and continues to be developed, uses various approaches of the historical and literary methods to interrogate the text as witness (includes sociological and psychological approaches). Rudolph Bultmann launched the second stage with his demythologization. He examined the mythological worldview of the text in contrast to the modern scientific mind. Acceptance of the text does not have to include the underlying worldview. Upon the heels of Bultmann and in direct descent from him emerged the critique of the ideology of the text. An example would be conscious or unconscious assertion of patriarchy. This laid bare the

> *"Meaning is not in texts but mediated by texts."*

fact that presuppositionless understanding does not exist. Scholars like Jürgen Habermas and Elisabeth Schüssler Fiorenza used a "hermeneutics of suspicion" to unmask the distorting effects of ideology on the process and production of interpretation.[34] With all this, the Cartesian ideal of a single method modeled on mathematics that would afford reliable knowledge based on clear and distinct ideas in all spheres collapsed. The hegemony of the historical-critical approach was broken; other approaches began to emerge. Some of these added a richness and depth unknown to the historical method. The plethora of methods and diversity of results raised the question of what meaning is and what the criteria for a valid interpretation might be. The attention of biblical scholars was drawn to the role of the reader in the process of interpretation. Interpretation under the historical approach sought the "author's intention" as norm for the "literal meaning" of the text. Theoretically all exegetes using the right method on a particular text would arrive at the same interpretation. Now awareness arose that "meaning is not *in* texts but mediated *by* texts."[35] It arises in the interaction between texts and readers. In this new scenario, "textual meaning" should replace what had been called the "literal meaning."[36] The goal of interpretation, using Platonic notions of the ideal and real, would be the search for the "ideal meaning" of the text.[37] This meaning reposes in an inner governing structure of the text and acts as a norm of valid interpretation. It governs, without suppressing, a range of possibilities of multiple interpretations. The textual meaning is "made real" or concrete (realized)

[34] Ibid., 20.
[35] Ibid., xxxii.
[36] Ibid., 162.
[37] Ibid., 163.

in the here and now by a number of interpretations that vary according to interpreter, situation, and other factors.[38] Just as each rendition of a symphony realizes the ideal structure inscribed in the score and yet every rendition is unique and original, so "the biblical scholar both 'creates' the interpretation of the text, which may be very original, and submits to the text's own dynamics, which the interpreter did not invent."[39]

What is the relation of faith and biblical scholarship? "Word of God" is a "root metaphor" (one that generates and holds together multiple meanings) that integrates all manners of divine self-giving and self-disclosure,[40] that is, revelation. The Bible is not purely and simply revelation (word of God) but rather is *potentially* revelatory:[41]

> Sacred Scripture is the sacrament of the word of God . . . the entire mystery of divine revelation . . . this mystery here comes to articulation with a clarity and transparency that focuses our attention on the mystery of divine revelation and thus fosters our attentiveness to the word of God whenever we encounter it.

The biblical text mediates encounter with God when it is heard or read with faith. So its purpose is not information but transformative encounter. There is no adequate interpretation of the biblical text without attending to its truth claims. Meaning ultimately involves appropriation (Ricoeur) or "transformative understanding" (Schneiders). Understanding is the characteristic mode of being of humans; it expands the existential reality of the knower. The ultimate goal of interpretation, the existential augmentation of the reader, takes place in her or his participation, through the text, in the world before the text.[42] If faith is understood as fundamental, nonthematized openness to the transcendent, then faith is necessary for any adequate interpretation of the Bible, because this text's truth claims bear upon religious reality, that is, the transcendent.[43]

---

[38] Ibid., xxxiii.
[39] Ibid., xxxiv.
[40] Ibid., 39.
[41] Ibid., 41–42.
[42] Ibid., 167.
[43] Ibid., 60.

Catholic or catholic?

Carolyn Osiek gave the Presidential Address at the 2005 Society of Biblical Literature.[44] She addressed the question of "what is Catholic in Catholic exegesis" by reflecting on the interplay of Catholic with a capital *C* and catholic with a small *c*, namely, "biblical scholarship that arises from the traditions of the capital *C* but is at the service of the small *c*" (no. 6). "Catholic" means "universal" or "general"; used with capital *C* it refers to the Roman Catholic Church. Is interpretation Catholic (with capital *C*) because it is done by someone who professes adherence to the Roman Catholic Church and its teachings? By someone who has grown up with a Catholic cultural heritage? By someone who expressly and consciously holds in mind the major church documents of the last two centuries on biblical interpretation? By someone who simply interprets out of one's own academic and religious identity the unarticulated "preunderstanding"? The fact is, Roman Catholic biblical scholarship is founded on the rich tradition of patristic and medieval exegesis yet also embraces historical criticism (no. 7). The Interpretation of the Bible in the Church has become widely recognized as a modern manifesto of the significant contributions of the historical-critical method and the ways in which newer methods can be seen as complements to it rather than threats (no. 14), even if historical criticism is not the fool-proof method for reaching the literal level of the text that it was presented to be (no. 18). Being Catholic means learning to think in centuries (ibid.); it also means thinking universally as well as in the local particular (no. 15). Catholic preunderstanding holds closely together modern scientific culture and the religious tradition of Israel and the early church. This is the "both/and" spoken of by Johnson and Kurz, rather than the "either/or." From this center point, Catholic biblical scholarship can contribute to the common enterprise of interpretation, to the catholic endeavor with small *c*. The "four senses" of patristic and medieval exegesis tried to capture the various levels of meaning but imperfectly. *Allegoria* was supposed to teach what to believe, but Roland Murphy[45] has shown that sometimes the literal sense teaches what we are to believe or even hope for, and the spiritual meaning cannot be limited to allegory. It is doubtful that an adequate moral or spiritual sense could be retrieved today, for example, from prescriptions that slaves obey their masters, as found in the

---

[44] Carolyn Osiek, "Catholic or catholic? Biblical Scholarship at the Center," *JBL* 125/1 (2006) 5–22.

[45] Roland E. Murphy, "What Is Catholic about Catholic Biblical Scholarship—Revisited," *BTB* 28 (1998) 112–19.

Household Codes of the New Testament. Allegory was the patristic and medieval way of avoiding literalism and fundamentalism. Today, historical criticism plays that role in part. The mistake of some misuses of historical criticism was an assumption that a text can have only one meaning, but contemporary language theory recalls us to the reality that in fact all human communication is open to many possible levels of meaning (no. 19).

The Interpretation of the Bible in the Church suggests a threefold sense: literal, spiritual, and fuller sense. It describes the "spiritual sense" as "the meaning expressed by the biblical texts when read, under the influence of the Holy Spirit, in the context of the paschal mystery of Christ and of the new life that flows from it" (II, B, 2). The fact is, this new life did not cease at the end of the biblical period but continues to flow through the patristic, medieval, and modern eras into our own age. In light of this, one needs to expand on the understanding of the "spiritual sense" to include many newer methods and perspectives that are informed by the desire to have us live more authentically the new life that flows from the paschal mystery. Think of methods born out of the hermeneutic of suspicion, for example, liberation, feminist/womanist/*mujerista*, and postcolonial interpretation, which probe the implications of the paschal mystery in ways not envisioned in previous centuries (no. 20). They may challenge established power bases, yet are new manifestations of the same inspiration that led earlier interpreters to ask of the biblical text the question, What does this have to do with life today? If the paschal mystery is about deliverance from death to life, then without the hermeneutic of suspicion we risk being diminished, not by the text but by earlier preunderstandings that are not yet open to a wider and more inclusive way of living and loving (ibid.). There is some parallel between the suspicion with which historical criticism was first received and the suspicion of the newer hermeneutical methods now. For example, feminist hermeneutics is the only method that receives a caveat in The Interpretation of the Bible in the Church! The Interpretation of the Bible in the Church stresses that spiritual interpretation holds together three levels of reality: the biblical text, the paschal mystery, and the present circumstances of life in the Spirit. This is where the newer methods fit into the common endeavor, as part of the expanded spiritual sense in which we bring our own new understandings to the task, out of our own new questions, and discover new levels of meaning as participants in the ongoing flow of interpretive tradition (ibid.).

One eye of the Roman Catholic biblical scholar must be kept on the good of the community and this will sometimes lead to dissent from consensus in the interest of that new life that flows from the paschal mystery (no. 21). The so-called fuller sense is not just "not clearly expressed by the human author" but not at all in the mind of the human author and is a meaning that is theologically comprehensible at a later point in the unfolding of tradition (ibid.). It is unlikely that any of the sacred writers intended to write in the context of the whole biblical canon, be it Hebrew or Greek, as we have it today. Yet when their writings are read today in light of the canonical process and context, new theological insights emerge and new and richer meanings are acquired by the text (no. 22). Psychological interpretation also helps. Though biblical writers wrote with conscious intent to portray not psychological dynamics and relationships but rather social and theological ones, yet in light of modern understandings of the dynamics of unconscious forces, the symbols and relationships in the biblical text can be reread to give expanded meanings to profound human experiences. So what is the relation of Catholic to catholic? Roman Catholic biblical scholarship makes its contribution to universal exegesis precisely through the challenge of holding together ancient text, ongoing history of interpretation, modern science, and postmodern insights, within a conscious participation in a living tradition (ibid.).

Questions for Discussion

1. What, in your judgment, has been the impact of *Divino Afflante Spiritu* and *Dei Verbum*?

2. What is the importance to Catholic exegesis of the "incarnational principle"?

3. Select any pericope of the gospels and apply to it the main principles of *Mater Ecclesia*.

4. Discuss the arguments against and for the historical-critical method (Ratzinger versus Fitzmyer).

5. Which of the thirteen methods outlined by The Interpretation of the Bible in the Church do you espouse? Give reasons.

6. If your background is feminist or liberative exegesis, engage The Interpretation of the Bible in the Church on these.

   a. How did Osiek counter this document's condemnation of such novel exegesis?

7. Discuss the main issues in the debate concerning Catholic exegesis.

8. Analyze the concerns of Luke Timothy Johnson and respond to them.

9. What are the issues of interpretation in your culture or part of the world?

Chapter 8

Issue IV: *Lectio Divina*

Your prayer is the word you speak to God. When you read the Bible, God speaks to you; when you pray, you speak to God.

Verbum Domini, 86, citing St. Augustine,
Enarrationes in Psalmos, 85.7

Dei Verbum

The term *lectio divina* occurs expressly only once in the documents of Vatican II, in *Presbyterorum Ordinis*, Decree on the Ministry and Life of Priests, number 18. It says that "with the light of a faith nourished by spiritual reading [*lectione divina*], priests can carefully detect the signs of God's will and the impulses of His grace in the various happenings of life."[1] The *lectio divina* referred to includes both spiritual reading and the reading of Scripture. The closest *Dei Verbum* came to the technical term was when, in number 25, it urged on the Christian faithful "the frequent reading of the divine Scriptures [*ut frequenti divinarum Scripturarm lectione*] . . . whether in the sacred liturgy, which is full of the divine words, or in devout reading [*sive per piam lectionem*]." *Pia lectio* (pious reading) gave rise after the council to the recovery and flowering of *lectio divina* (literally, divine reading), an ancient monastic form of reading and praying Scripture. However, *Dei Verbum* in some places enunciates the substance of *lectio divina* without using the term. For example, it speaks of the church receiving her spiritual nourishment "from the one table of the word of God and the body of Christ" (no. 21). It also recommends that prayer should accompany the reading of Sacred Scripture "so that it becomes a dialogue

[1] Following the translation of Walter Abbott, *The Documents of Vatican II* (London and Dublin: Geoffrey Chapman, 1966).

between God and human reader. For, 'we speak to him when we pray; we listen to him when we hear the divine oracles'"[2] (no. 25).

Lineamenta and Instrumentum Laboris

A sign of the diffusion of biblical spirituality after the council is that the term *lectio divina* occurs fully ten times in the text of the *Lineamenta*.[3] The approach to the word of God all through this document is one of prayerful reading. Hebrews 4:12, placed at the very beginning (preface), warns as much when it says, "Indeed, the word of God is living and active, sharper than any two-edged sword, piercing until it divides soul from spirit, joints from marrow; it is able to judge the thoughts and intentions of the heart." *Lineamenta*, 22, cites the *General Directory for Catechesis*, 127, that "in concrete terms, catechesis should be 'an authentic introduction to *lectio divina*, that is, to a reading of the sacred Scriptures, done according to the Spirit who dwells in the Church.'" The initiate is thus to be inducted into a prayerful reading of Scripture as light to his or her path by drawing "from the biblical text the living word which questions, directs and shapes our lives" (no. 24). The same number of the *Lineamenta* mentions for the first time the four stages of *lectio divina*: *lectio, meditatio, oratio, contemplatio* (reading, meditation, prayer, contemplation). Saint Cyprian's advice is cited to "diligently practice prayer and *lectio divina*. When you pray, you speak with God; when you read, God speaks with you."[4] The saint stresses the initiative of God in *lectio divina*: this sacred reading is very much a listening to the living voice of God through the words of the text. The latter point is stressed by Benedict XVI, cited in *Lineamenta*, 27, when he showed how *lectio divina* in common can aid the unity of Christians:

> The Church does not make herself or live of herself, but from the creative word that comes from the mouth of God. To listen to the word of God together; to practice the *lectio divina* of the Bible, that is, reading linked with prayer . . . in order to achieve unity in the faith as a response to listening to the Word.[5]

The *Instrumentum Laboris* contains thirty references to *lectio divina*, and for the first time it has a number to itself, number 38 (with 16 of the 30

---

[2] St. Ambrose, *On the Duties of Ministers*, I, 20, 88: PL, 16, 50.

[3] A further two times in the questions that followed the chapters.

[4] *To Donatus*, 15. In some editions, this letter appears among the treatises of St. Cyprian. Augustine repeats a form of this saying (see caption of this chapter).

[5] Homily, "Our World Awaits the Common Witness of Christians" (January 25, 2007), in *L'Osservatore Romano: Weekly Edition in English* (January 31, 2007) 5.

references). One of the goals of the synod is "to encourage a widespread practice of *lectio divina* which is duly adapted to various circumstances" (no. 4). The document notes that among the fruits of Vatican II has been "a growing, fruitful practice of *lectio divina* in its various forms" (no. 5). In fact, *lectio divina* can be seen as "the privileged manner of approaching the Bible with faith" (no. 26). The rosary is a form of *lectio divina*, with Mary providing a universally applicable model of prayerfully hearing the word. In *lectio divina* the hearing of the word in faith becomes *understanding, meditation, communion, sharing,* and *fulfillment*—five moments, of which the last two were not mentioned in *Lineamenta,* 24. The idea of prayer sharing is singled out when number 27 speaks of two possibilities of *lectio divina,* individual and communal. Then number 38 gives a definition of *lectio divina*:

> A reading, on an individual or communal level, of a more or less lengthy passage of Scripture, received as the word of God and leading, at the prompting of the Spirit, to meditation, prayer and contemplation.[6]

This practice was kept alive in the monasteries, but today the magisterium is proposing it to all the faithful as an effective pastoral instrument and a valuable tool in the church for the spiritual formation of all. Our secularized world needs contemplative, attentive, critical, and courageous people who must, at times, make totally new, untried choices. Various particular churches call *lectio divina* different names, like "School of the Word" or "Reading in Prayer." Programs vary, for example, the Seven Steps are practiced in Africa.

The Synod Assembly

References to *lectio divina* blossomed on the assembly floor. In Latin America a variety of programs of *lectio divina* exist and are adapted for the use of monks, religious, and the lay faithful.[7] A notable initiative is that of CEBIPAL (Center of Biblical Pastoral for Latin America), founded in 2004 by CELAM (Episcopal Council of Latin America) for the permanent formation of Bible professors. With other institutes, this center promotes *lectio divina* and forms young people in it through the internet. When formed,

---

[6] Citing Pontifical Biblical Commission, The Interpretation of the Bible in the Church (Vatican City: Libreria Editrice Vaticana, 1993) IV, C, 2.

[7] Cardinal Oscar Maradiaga, president of the Episcopal Conference of Honduras, Report on the Word of God in the Americas, October 6, 2008.

these young people are called *lectionautas*. On December 7, 2006, Zenit reported on a project by CEBIPAL in cooperation with the United Bible

> "To learn the heart of God through the words of God" (St. Gregory the Great).

Societies to form ten thousand "missionaries of *lectio divina*" for Latin America.[8] *Lectio divina* is said to appeal especially to youth and the uneducated; it has become an integral part of the pastoral plan of many dioceses in Latin America. In these speeches *lectio divina* did not always have a precise sense beyond that of prayerful reading of the Bible. Some referred to the ancient four steps method,[9] others to a seven-stage approach,[10] while still others mentioned the Lumko Seven Steps explicitly (see appendix in this chapter for this). A few spoke of the AsIPA[11] method.

The tendency to propose *lectio divina* as a panacea for all the ills of the reception and interpretation of the Bible gave rise to words of caution. A synod father, remarking that *lectio divina* alone was not enough, asked for a book to be published explaining current methods of Bible sharing, with evaluations to allow people to choose according to their condition of life.[12] Remarking that in the last years a great emphasis had been placed in France on *lectio divina*, and that nevertheless few still practice it, a synod father cautioned about the obstacles of discouragement and subjectivism.[13] In the discussion groups, a French-speaking group noted that there should be several approaches to Scripture and *lectio divina* should not crowd out exegesis.[14] N. T. Wright, an Anglican bishop and famous biblical scholar, proposed a fourfold reading of Scripture as love of God where each part is balanced against others: heart (*lectio divina*, liturgical reading), mind (historical-critical study), soul (church life, tradition, teaching), and strength (mission, kingdom of God). In short, the contemplative regard

[8] "Missionaries of 'Lectio Divina' Being Formed," Zenit.org, accessed January 9, 2010, http://www.zenit.org/article-18392?l=english.

[9] Bishop Nestor Herrera Heredia of Machala, Ecuador: "a privileged way is the *lectio divina* that, with its four moments: reading, meditation, prayer and contemplation, enhances the personal encounter with Christ," October 10, 2008.

[10] For example, Archbishop Anthony Sablan Apuron of Guam spoke of a daily opportunity to scrutinize the word of God through *lectio divina* or the Seven Steps to Gospel Sharing, October 11, 2008.

[11] AsIPA stands for the Asian Integral Pastoral Approach developed by the Federation of Asian Bishops' Conferences.

[12] Archbishop Joseph Takami of Nagasaki, Japan, October 10, 2008.

[13] Archbishop Pierre-Marie Carr of Albi, October 7, 2008.

[14] October 17, 2008.

on Scripture embraces the entire church life and mission.

On October 14, 2008, Bishop Retamales of Valparaiso (Chile) gave an Explanatory Exposition of *Lectio Divina*. He dealt with the spirituality of *lectio divina*, the iden-tity and function of Holy Scripture in the church, and finally *lectio divina* as lived in his diocese, where they call it "Encounters with the Word." Scripture and *lectio divina* are located within the dynamism of encounter and dialogue. Primacy in the encounter be-longs to God. As Stephen J. Binz writes, "*lectio divina* continues the conver-sation that God has begun."[15] God's self-offer is through Jesus who "leads us to ourselves" and "recreates" us (personality, history, motivations). Bishop Retamales gave this definition of *lectio divina*:

Lectio
Meditatio
Oratio
Contemplatio

> *Lectio divina* is the practice of the prayerful reading of Holy Scripture, individually or in community, in order to "learn the heart of God through the words of God." (Saint Gregory the Great)

He outlined five steps,[16] namely, reading, meditation, prayer, contempla-tion, and practice. Be seated; clear the heart (attend to the setting, external and internal). Invoke the Holy Spirit and select the passage. *Reading* asks, what does the text say? Proclaim the text, with silences and repetitions. Put a question mark on what you do not understand; underline what seems to be the main message. *Meditation* personalizes the message, asking, what does the Lord say in his word? Put an exclamation point at passages that touch you. In group lectio, continue reading the passage and putting the marks, asterisks for prayer when the passage helps to pray. *Prayer* asks, what do we say to the Lord, motivated by his word? *Contemplation* may be aided by music, images, and location. *Practice*: at the edges of the text write a word that shows the path to be followed. Conclude with final sharing.

I comment on the above. The phases of *lectio divina* weave in and out of each other; they are like intertwined circles, not like a ladder. The entire movement is prayer right from the start, because it is all response to the God who speaks. Prayer masters thus advise that there should be no rush to move from one stage to the other but rather the individual or group

---

[15] Stephen J. Binz, *Conversing with God in Scripture: A Contemporary Approach to Lectio Divina* (Ijamsville, MD: The Word Among Us Press, 2008) 11.

[16] These steps are very compressed because only Bishop Retamales's summary was avail-able to the author.

responds as the Spirit moves them. "Study and *lectio divina* are not opposed; rather we must integrate them."[17] Initial approaches to the text vary.

> Some people ground their experience of *lectio* first by doing a thorough study of the sacred text. This usually involves the literal sense of the text. For others, the study of *lectio divina* is primarily about the prayer experience itself. They approach *lectio* more as a way of life than a way of thinking and learning. All forms of *lectio* bring us into a direct encounter with God's word and have the potential to lead us to a more intimate relationship with God and life.[18]

The danger of making the Spirit say whatever the person or group wants to hear can be obviated by some minimal study of the text. Meditation is not "head work" but "heart work,"[19] that is, attending to where and how the word of God has touched or wounded one. The fathers of the church constantly used the images of chewing and savoring for this. Here is how Paintner and Wynkoop describe it: "*meditatio* is not a process of analyzing or thinking about the words of the text, but rather a way of being with all that is stirred within you. It is the act of moving into relationship with the Scripture passage."[20]

Cardinal Bozanic[21] gave the Report on the Word of God in Europe (see chapter 3). His approach to *lectio divina* was rather novel. He saw *lectio divina* as a total response to the revealing God:

> I not only think about the reading of the sacred text, which still always remains the essential reference for ecclesial discernment, nor do I think about reading limited to restricting subjectivity. Rather I think about listening to God [who] continuously acts upon history, unveiling his presence in every event. This will allow reading the life of the Church in Europe as a place where God reveals God's self. (no. 3)

In speaking of "reading limited to restricting subjectivity" the cardinal warns of individualistic forms of *lectio divina*. In other words, *lectio divina* is a contemplative attentiveness to the word of God as God speaks through events that englobe individuals and communities. God's self-disclosure is

---

[17] Binz, *Conversing with God in Scripture*, 50–51.

[18] Christine Valters Paintner and Lucy Wynkoop, *Lectio Divina: Contemplative Awakening and Awareness* (New York: Paulist Press, 2008) 68.

[19] Ibid., 28.

[20] Ibid., 34.

[21] Report on the Word of God in Europe, October 6, 2008.

not only in Scripture but also in history and creation. Transformation is
the goal of all *lectio divina*, "taking our prayer into our everyday lives and
responding to our lives from that experience of prayer."[22] Our experience
of prayer transforms both our personal lives and the world in which God's
purposes are still being worked out.

Cardinal Marc Ouellet in the Report after the Discussion noted how
Benedict XVI had proposed *lectio divina* as decisive for the renewal of the
faith but remarked that, nevertheless, *la lectio divina n'est pas facile* (*lectio
divina* is not easy). There is need for a pedagogy of initiation into it, and
for clarification of what *lectio divina* really is, the diverse steps and the
manner of their application.[23]

The Propositions

Six of the fifty-five propositions handed to the Holy Father mention
lectio divina in some form. The synod invites all the faithful to "attend
assiduously to prayer and to *lectio divina*. When you pray you speak with
God, when you read, God speaks with you" (proposition 9).[24] The formation of candidates to holy orders must include multiple approaches to
Scripture, among which should feature prayerful reading of Scripture, in
particular *lectio divina*, as much personal as communitarian (proposition
32). Practicing *lectio divina* together should be seen as a path to Christian
unity (proposition 36). Warning against fundamentalist interpretations
that ignore the human mediation of the inspired text and the literary
forms, proposition 46 affirmed that to use *lectio divina* fruitfully the believer
must be educated to not "unconsciously confuse the human limits of the
biblical message with the divine substance of that message."[25]

Message to the People of God

The Message to the People of God dealt with *lectio divina* in part IV, "The
House of the Word: the Church" (nos. 7–10). The church of Acts 2:42 had
four pillars: *didache*/preaching the Word, breaking of bread, prayers, and
koinonia/fellowship of love. *Prayers* are actuated in the liturgy, psalms, celebrations of the Word, and *lectio divina*. The Message gave its own fourfold
phasing of *lectio divina* as follows:

---

[22] Paintner and Wynkoop, *Lectio Divina*, 8.
[23] Report after the Discussion, 32.
[24] Citing St. Cyprian, *To Donatus*, 15.
[25] Citing Pontifical Biblical Commission, Interpretation of the Bible in the Church, I, F.

This begins with the reading (*lectio*) of the text, which provokes the question of true knowledge of its real content: what does the biblical text say in itself? Then follows meditation (*meditatio*) where the question is: what does the Biblical text say to us? In this manner, one arrives at prayer (*oratio*), which presupposes this other question: what do we say to the Lord in answer to his word? And one ends with contemplation (*contemplatio*) during which we assume, as God's gift, the same gaze in judging reality and ask ourselves: what conversion of the mind, the heart and life does the Lord ask of us?

Verbum Domini

The post-synodal apostolic exhortation treated the topic in numbers 86–87. By comparison with the *Instrumentum Laboris* and the interventions in the assembly of the synod, it seems to have fewer references to *lectio divina*;[26] besides, it always distinguishes it as *one form* of the prayerful reading of Scripture. The apparent paucity of references is deceptive, for in the pope's mind biblical exegesis should already be a form of prayerful attentiveness to the word of God. Faith-filled study of Scripture leads naturally to the response of prayer. There is thus a close relationship between *lectio divina* and a true hermeneutic of faith (*Verbum Domini*, 82). His Holiness warned against an individualistic approach to *lectio divina* that would forget that God's word is given to us precisely to build communion (no. 86). He detailed and explained the basic steps of *lectio divina*—reading, meditation, prayer, contemplation, ending in action.

Postface

This discussion of *lectio divina* at the Synod on the Word of God cannot end without reference to one of the foremost current practitioners, Cardinal Carlo Martini, emeritus archbishop of Milan. He had great success with youths, having as many as fifteen thousand of them flock to his cathedral for his regular sessions of *lectio divina*. He described his method in an article in 1989.[27] His approach combines scientific exegesis with prayer on the text. With youth he uses a simple three-phase approach: *lectio, meditatio, contemplatio*. However, in the 1989 article he associated

---

[26] Outside numbers 86–87, which treats *lectio divina* expressly, *Verbum Domini* mentions it only four times (nos. 35, 46, 82, and 83).

[27] Cardinal Carlo M. Martini, "Lectio divina," *Bulletin Dei Verbum* 10 (1989) 16–18.

lectio divina with the Exercises of St. Ignatius, of which he is a master, to produce eight phases, as follows:

Lectio. Repeated reading of passage, with pen in hand, marking words that strike you, indicating with special markings verbs, actions, people, feelings expressed, key words. Of course, one puts the passage into the larger context, the book or the Bible as a whole. At this stage one assumes the historical, geographical, and cultural elements of the text.

Meditatio. "Reflection on the lasting values of the text." Here one asks, "What does this text say to me? What message for today is expressed in this passage, as the word of the living God?" What is the challenge of the values that underlie the actions, words, and persons?

Contemplatio. "Adoration, praise, and silence before Him, who is the ultimate object of my prayer: Christ, the Lord, conqueror of death, revealer of the Father."

Oratio. "Lord, make me understand the lasting values of the text, those which I do not have. Grant that I may know what your message is for my life." This stage may focus on the mystery of Jesus or the "face" of God; it may also be a request for forgiveness and enlightenment or in sacrifice.

Consolatio. The joy of praying, intimately feeling the "taste" of God, the "things" of Christ. This is a gift ordinarily produced in the context of *lectio divina*, though the Spirit is always free. From *consolatio* "spring the courageous choices of poverty, chastity, obedience, faithfulness, forgiveness, because it provides the place, the proper atmosphere for these interior options." What is not of this gift of the Spirit is fruit of a moralism we impose on ourselves and which lasts only a short time.

Discretio. Our "taste" becomes a sort of spiritual radar, sensitive to everything in line with Christ and the gospel, and what is not. "We are not called only to observe the commandments in general, but also to *follow* Jesus Christ." This latter becomes apparent in our everyday choices only if we have the mind of Jesus ("tasted" his poverty, cross, humility of the crib, his forgiveness).

Deliberatio. Discernment using the interior experience of *consolation* and *desolation*, consequently deciding as God wills. In fact, the choice of vocations follows these processes unconsciously. "A vocation is, in effect, a decision taken on the basis of what God has made one hear, and on the basis of one's own experience of the gospel requirements."

Actio. Fruit of the whole process. Bible reading and action go together: we read and meditate on it not to give us strength to put into practice what we have decided but "so that correct decisions are made and the comforting power of the Spirit helps us put them into practice." Not praying more so that I can act better but "so that I can better understand what I must do and how, through interior choice, I can do it."[28]

Appendix: The Lumko Method

The seven stages approach developed and spread by the Lumko Pastoral Institute,[29] Delmenville, South Africa, was often mentioned in the synod assembly. Here is a summary (the reader is encouraged to read the original itself).

Introduction

The method is communal in the sense that it helps the participants encounter God and one another, and advert to the presence and the workings of God in their everyday lives. The Bible is made to touch deeply the lives of those sharing it as prayer, and they are enabled to share this experience with others. The Bible is not only prayer; it needs to be studied also, for it comes to us from a different time and culture.

"Bible discussion and Bible meditation groups should not be too large. The ideal size is four to eight participants so that everyone may have the opportunity to talk. An atmosphere of quiet and calm is necessary."

First Step: Invite the Lord

The facilitator asks someone to voluntarily "invite the Lord." *Lectio divina* is founded on belief in the living presence of the Risen Christ in the group praying.

Second Step: Read the Text

The chosen text is announced and read. Then a moment of silence follows.

[28] Ibid.

[29] Lumko Institute, "The Lumko 'Seven Step' Method," Catholic Biblical Federation, accessed January 6, 2010, http://www.c-b-f.org/start.php?CONTID=11_01_02_00&LANG=en.

Third Step: Dwell on the Text

"The participants spontaneously read aloud the word or words that have impressed them. Whole verses are not read, only short phrases or individual words." A moment of silence after each one has spoken allows the words to sink in.

Fourth Step: Be Quiet

The entire passage is read again slowly and there follows a time of silence, during which people may repeat some words to themselves.

Fifth Step: Share What You Have Heard in Your Heart

There follows a moment of sharing what one has experienced.

Sixth Step: Search Together

Now is the time "for the participants to examine their lives in the light of the Gospel." The problems or issues that come up may not be direct responses to the text but have been facilitated by the reconciliation and communion engendered by the shared reading of the Bible. It could be something as mundane as getting the street lamp repaired.

Seventh Step: Pray Together

"The words of Scripture, the various experiences of God's Word, the daily problems—these all become fuel for prayer."

Questions for Discussion

1. What is *lectio divina*? Choose a short passage of Scripture and practice *lectio divina* on it.

2. What are the theological foundations of *lectio divina*?

3. Compare *lectio divina* and the study of Scripture. What do they share? Where may they differ?

4. Explain the various stages of *lectio divina*.

   a. Traditional four stage approach

   b. Lumko seven stage approach or other seven stage approach you know

   c. Cardinal Martini's eight stage approach

5. Compare and contrast the Lumko method and Cardinal Martini's.

6. Outline what you feel are the pastoral implications of the material you have just studied.

7. Why is Cardinal Bozanic's approach called "a novel approach"? Discuss its implications for the theology of revelation and pastoral care.

Chapter 9

Issue V:
Dark Sayings of Scripture
and Fundamentalism

*Biblical revelation is deeply rooted in history. **God's plan is
manifested progressively and it is accomplished slowly, in
successive stages and despite human resistance. God chose
a people and patiently worked to guide and educate
them. Revelation is suited to the cultural and moral level
of distant times and thus describes acts and customs,
such as cheating and trickery, and acts of violence and
massacre, without explicitly denouncing the immorality
of such things.***

Verbum Domini, **42**

Dark Sayings of Scripture

The pope here gives us a criterion for dealing with what he called "the 'dark' passages of the Bible." He cautioned that it is a mistake to neglect such passages that strike us as problematic. Rather, scholars and pastors are to help the faithful approach those passages through an interpretation that enables their meaning to emerge in the light of the mystery of Christ (no. 42). Here I examine sections of the Bible that the synod fathers found problematic and needing clarification. I shall briefly lay out the problem as encountered by the synod, present any solutions the synod fathers gave, and then try to show how such passages can be handled within a more refined understanding of the inspiration and truth of Scripture.

Dei Verbum

Dei Verbum, 15, says of the books of the Old Testament that "though they also contain some things which are *incomplete and temporary*, [they] nevertheless show us true divine pedagogy."[1] That some things in it were provisional is clear from the fact that the New Testament, and Judaism since the final ruin of the temple in 70 CE, have not taken up certain prescriptions of the Old Testament. Hebrews 10:4 (New Jerusalem Bible) says of the order of sacrifices that "bulls' blood and goats' blood are incapable of taking away sins," so Christ replaced them with the sacrifice of himself. Currently Judaism substitutes the reading of the Torah to temple worship and has not followed through with kingship as a political arrangement. Nor has the church itself followed through with the ministry of prophets within the liturgy as obtained in some early Christian communities, nor with church order as found, for example, in 1 Corinthians. Through the march of time the people of God discover certain things to be temporary that it before held to be absolute. *Dei Verbum* speaks of pedagogy; pedagogy is the patient training of a minor toward adulthood by which a trainer accommodates to the learning curve of the minor. It suggests that God did not force issues but has been patient enough to allow God's people move toward deeper transformation through their historical experience of God, gradually coming to a more refined knowledge of God. The principle of divine patience in dealing with human imperfection in an imperfect world is an important presupposition for addressing many of the issues to be discussed in this chapter.

Israel was not alone in being the focus of divine pedagogy. In the New Testament, there are texts like 1 Corinthians 14:34-35, which reads, "women should be silent in the churches. For they are not permitted to speak, but should be subordinate, as the law also says. If there is anything they desire to know, let them ask their husbands at home. For it is shameful for a woman to speak in church." This text raised no eyebrows in other times and places, but today many Christians see it as out of tune with the equality of man and woman in Christ and with elements of the "new life" of the Spirit as they now understand it.[2] In other words, such texts may

---

[1] Following the translation of Walter Abbott, *The Documents of Vatican II* (London and Dublin: Geoffrey Chapman, 1966), italics mine. Flannery has "even though they contain matters which are imperfect and provisional, nevertheless contain authentic divine teaching." The original has "*quamvis etiam imperfecta et temporaria contineant, veram tamen paedagogiam divinam demonstrant.*"

[2] Elisabeth Schüssler Fiorenza (*In Memory of Her: A Feminist Theological Reconstruction of Christian Origins* [New York: Crossroad, 1983] 230–42) believes that Paul prohibited the liturgical leadership of married women but allowed that of unmarried women. Anthony Thiselton (*Hermeneutics: An Introduction* [Grand Rapids: Wm. Eerdmans, 2009] 281)

have served an important function in the particular cultural context but may not claim universal application.

Lineamenta

The *Lineamenta* noted that some passages of the Old Testament that appear difficult run the risk of being set aside, considered arbitrarily, or never read at all (no. 16).[3] Particular areas that cause such problems are mentioned in number 22: Old Testament ideas of God, man and woman, and moral conduct. The document concluded by saying that "this situation urgently requires a formation centered on a Christian reading of the Old Testament" (no. 16).

Instrumentum Laboris

The *Instrumentum Laboris* declared that "knowledge of the Old Testament as word of God seems to be a real problem among Catholics" (no. 17). It added to the list of difficulties, among which are "its figurative character and its relationship to the scientific and historical mentality of our times" (no. 18). The term "figurative" suggests that the Old Testament is adumbration and shadow, while the New Testament is reality, the Old Testament is type, and the New Testament anti-type, hence the use of typology connects the two. Other issues noted are "a certain view of history, science and the moral life, particularly ethical behavior and how God is portrayed" (no. 45). For the first time, the character of God as portrayed in the Old Testament came under review. Two different pieces of advice from the responses of the particular churches are given (no. 13):

> to present simple criteria for reading the Bible with Christ in mind, thereby resolving difficulties in the Old Testament;
>
> to work out a program which considers Jesus' own rapport with sacred Scripture, how he read the Scriptures and how they assist in understanding him.

The editors of the *Instrumentum Laboris* (no. 17) gave their own suggestion for dealing with these "dark passages," namely,

---

suggests that wives may have been assessing their husbands' claim to be prophets in light of their conduct at home.

[3] Some of these difficulties with the Old Testament have been mentioned in chapter 4.

a formation centered on a reading of the Old Testament with Christ in mind, which acknowledges the bond between the two testaments and the permanent value of the Old Testament.

In saying this, they place in creative tension the bond between the Testaments and the permanent value of the Old Testament.

Interventions in the Assembly

Further difficulties with the Old Testament appeared in the report of a Spanish group,[4] namely, divine and human violence and a theology that is insufficient concerning the afterworld. It is well known that much of the Old Testament either denies or questions the afterlife. For example, Ecclesiastes 3:19 states:

> For the fate of human and the fate of animal is the same: as one dies, so the other dies; both have the selfsame breath. Human is in no way better than animal—since all is futile.

Part of the poignancy of the psalmist's lament was that this world was considered the only place for God to show God's redemptive power, "for in death there is no remembrance of you; in Sheol who can give you praise?" (Ps 6:5). The book of Job played out against the same background: another world as an aspect of God's justice did not come into view. Sirach 14:11-19 counseled making the best of today, for "there are no pleasures to be found in Sheol. Like clothes, every body will wear out, the age-old law is, 'everyone must die.'" Sheol is the abode of the dead, the furthest point down from the abode of God in heaven. No moral distinction between the good and the evil or punishment of one and reward of the other obtains there.

The desire for an afterlife did not arise early for various reasons. For one, early Hebrew thought did not distinguish soul from body; a person was an enlivened body. Neither soul nor body was held to survive independently. The first sparks of a longing for the afterlife emerged in prayer. The psalmist experienced God as the delight of his soul. He somehow hoped that "my body too will rest secure, for you will not abandon me to Sheol, you cannot allow your faithful servant to see the abyss" (Ps 16:9-10, New Jerusalem Bible).[5] In Psalm 73, the psalmist, faced with a crisis

---

[4] Spanish Group A, October 18, 2008.

[5] This text was cited by Peter on Pentecost to confirm the resurrection of Jesus, using the LXX text, which has "or allow your holy one to see *corruption*" (Acts 2:27).

of divine retribution, almost tripped over, were it not for the experience that his happiness was to be near God: "You guide me with your counsel, and afterward you will receive me with honor" (v. 24).[6] Prophecy of the postexilic period (fifth century BCE) projected a hope of resurrection from the dead: "Your dead shall live, their corpses shall rise. O dwellers in the dust, awake and sing for joy!" (Isa 26:19). Like Ezekiel 37, this may refer to the resurrection of *the nation* to new life. Isaiah 25:6-8 is a later text that promises the destruction of death, for "the LORD of hosts will . . . destroy on this mountain the shroud that is cast over all peoples, the sheet that is spread over all nations; he will swallow up death forever."

Eventually, the emergence of the individual in Jeremiah 32:29-30 and Ezekiel 18, the advent of Hellenistic culture and philosophy and its dichotomy of body and soul, and persecution and martyrdom for the sake of Yahweh all combined to generate belief in an imminent judgment that would end the present age dominated by evil powers and usher in a new age beyond death marked by God's victory. This idea first appeared haltingly in 1 Enoch 22 (third century BCE, extrabiblical), though in this work it is *the spirits* (not bodies) that are raised for judgment.[7] Daniel 12:2-3 was the first explicit biblical text to posit resurrection of *the body* in the context of the persecution by Antiochus Epiphanes IV (167 BCE). The text speaks of "some": the best and the worst are raised to confront themselves, while the rest of the people remain in the dust.[8] Only later did faith in a universal resurrection arise (2 Macc 7:9, 11-12), though by the time of Jesus resurrection faith was still not universal among Jews, for the Sadducees rejected it as novel and not proven from the Torah (Mark 12:18-27: the woman who had seven husbands). By the second century CE the resurrection of the body had become an article of Jewish faith. So there can be development of doctrine even in revelation. Seen in this manner, the apparent denials of the resurrection in Ecclesiastes, Job, and other texts become stages within a growing understanding of God's word.

I continue the interventions in the assembly. The Latin patriarch of Jerusalem mentioned the particular difficulty the Old Testament has for

---

[6] NIV: "and afterward you will take me into glory." *Kabod* means glory or honor; NRSV margin has "glory" as variant reading.

[7] Cf. George W. E. Nickelsburg, *Resurrection, Immortality, and Eternal Life in Intertestamental Judaism and Early Christianity*, expanded ed. (Cambridge, MA: Harvard University Press, 2006) 171.

[8] Robert Martin-Achard, *From Death to Life: A Study of the Development of the Doctrine of the Resurrection in the Old Testament* (London and Edinburgh: Oliver and Boyd, 1960) 146.

Arab Christians "because of the political and ideological interpretations."[9] A synod father[10] related how the faithful of his diocese were scandalized by "the humility of the word of God," passages full of violence, bigotry, cruelty, duplicity, and all other contradictions characteristic of all other sons and daughters of Adam. He noted wryly that

> we have in this canon texts that deny the resurrection and afterlife and texts that affirm them. We have texts that regard Satan as part of the heavenly court with a specific task and texts that present him as a fallen angel. We have texts that declare evil as a consequence of human sin and insist on human culpability and texts that present evil as a disease and human beings as mere victims that can only rely on God's forgiveness. We have texts that emphasize divine grace, and texts that put a prime on human effort.

In fact, as John Goldingay wrote, "from either Testament you can justify male headship or slavery or war because much of the Bible is written 'because of your hardness of heart' (Mark 10:5)."[11] The "eternal ideal" is clear in these texts, but they are also full of "timely compromise." Our texts witness to the "tension between what was designed from creation and what is possible given the obduracy of the human will, and with the same tension between what will be at the end and what is possible now given that obduracy."[12] Yet, through it all God's commitment to humanity and creation is never in doubt, nor God's ability to use human decisions, imperfect as they often are, for God's own plan of salvation.

In relation to the morality of biblical characters, the principle enunciated by James A. Sanders is worth remembering, namely, that "most biblical texts must be read, not by looking in them for models for morality, but by looking in them for mirrors for identity."[13] Except for Almighty God and Jesus, most characters in the Bible mirror for us the struggle between human sinfulness and the grace and faithfulness of God. Sometimes, the Bible itself contains a sort of dramatic justice. Jacob, who tricked his elder

---

[9] October 10, 2008.

[10] Bishop Pablo Virgilio S. David, auxiliary bishop of San Fernando, Philippines, October 10, 2008.

[11] John Goldingay, "Is Leadership Biblical?," *Key Questions about Christian Faith: Old Testament Answers* (Grand Rapids: Baker Academic, 2010) 266–71, here 268.

[12] Goldingay, "Is Election Fair?," *Key Questions about Christian Faith*, 211–23, here 222.

[13] James A. Sanders, "Hermeneutics," *Interpreters' Dictionary of the Bible*, vol. 5, supplementary vol., ed. George A. Buttrick and Keith Crim, 402–7, here 406 (Nashville: Abingdon Press, 1976).

brother and stole that brother's blessing, had to quickly flee from home to Mesopotamia. There he worked seven years for Rachel only to find Leah in bed on the night of his wedding. He said to Laban, "Did I not work for you for Rachel? Why then have you tricked me?" Laban's words to him were apposite: "This is not done *in our country*—giving the younger before the firstborn. Complete the week of this one, and we will give you the other also in return for serving me another seven years" (Gen 29:26-27). The trick and stolen blessing set in motion negative energies that pursued Jacob until he met his match when someone wrestled with him (Gen 32:23-33) and dislocated his hip—just before he finally met Esau face-to-face and reconciled with him. However, as His Holiness noted (see epigraph at the beginning of this chapter), Scripture does not always explicitly denounce immorality or show the evil actions of the wicked punished, though the ethos of the believing community, its traditions of faith, and the teaching of the whole of Scripture leave no doubt as to what God intends and what is evil before God.

Sometimes the very texts themselves reflect the moral qualms of the editors. In both Egypt (Gen 12) and Gerar (Gen 20), Abraham, and in Genesis 26 Isaac, thought to save their skins by passing their wives off as sisters. Pharaoh, the innocent victim of the ruse by Abraham, was inflicted with a plague from Yahweh, and the king of Gerar was struck with infertility and the barrenness of his wives and maids. What we have in the three stories is what narrative critics call "type-scenes."[14] The motif here can be termed "wife in danger." Looking closely at the three stories of the patriarchs, one notices some progression. In the first case, Pharaoh definitely touched Sarai, and Abraham enriched himself through his ruse. In Genesis 20, God made the king impotent so he could not touch Sarah. What Abraham received in this case was only a sort of "honor" money for Sarah to vindicate her in the eyes of all. In the third and last case, there was no question of Rebekah being taken into the king's harem and Isaac got nothing at all from the king. In other words, moral considerations have been factored into each retelling of the story. In passing we also learn that God and the peoples concerned abhorred wife snatching and adultery.

---

[14] Robert Alter, *The Art of Biblical Narrative* (New York: Basic Books, 1981) 50. They are certain "fixed situations which a poet is expected to include in his narrative and which he must perform according to a set order of motifs."

The Propositions

Proposition 29 repeated the difficulties already met above (elements of violence, injustice, immorality, and nonexemplary behavior on the part of important biblical personalities). It called for adequate formation of the faithful so they can read the texts in their historical and literary context, with the central hermeneutical key being the gospel and the new commandment of Christ fulfilled in the paschal mystery. Proposition 6 added the analogy of faith,[15] and proposition 52 the unity of the Testaments in Jesus, the Word made flesh.

Formation in reading the historical and literary context implies that believers take to heart that "in Scripture, divine things are presented to us in the manner which is in common use among humans."[16] The reader needs to determine "to what extent the manner of expression or the literary mode adopted by the sacred writer may lead to a correct and genuine interpretation."[17] *Dei Verbum*, 12, puts it as follows:

> Rightly to understand what the sacred authors wanted to affirm in their work, due attention must be paid both to the customary and characteristic patterns of perception, speech and narrative which prevailed in their time, and to the conventions which people then observed in their dealings with one another. (*DV*, 12)

Take Genesis 3:1: "Now the serpent was more crafty than any other wild animal that the LORD God had made. He said to the woman, 'Did God say, "You shall not eat from any tree in the garden"?'" Is this actual history or an ancient way of representing profound existential truths called myth? In critical theory, myth is not a synonym for fiction as in ordinary parlance but rather a way of expressing human experiences of the world and of realities in dramatic form, a way of conveying deeper truths in narrative form.[18] The snake in Genesis 3 had not yet metamorphosed into the devil or Satan, God's rival, as in Revelation 12, but was only one of the animals God created. The figure of the snake was a dramatic means of suggesting the appeal of temptation and originating evil from below, not from God. The responsibility for what happened was not attributed to the snake but rather to the human

---

[15] The intrinsic connection of the truths of faith among themselves and in their totality in the design of revelation.

[16] St. Thomas Aquinas, *Commentary on Hebrews*, chapter 1, *lectio* 4.

[17] Ibid.

[18] Cf. Sigmund Mowinckel, *The Old Testament as Word of God* (New York and Nashville: Abingdon Press, 1959) 101.

actors, who "saw that the tree was good for food, and that it was a delight to the eyes, and that the tree was to be desired to make one wise" (Gen 3:6). This is an example of applying the *literary genre* spoken of in chapter 6.

We briefly take up the topic of violence and the character of God in the text of the Old Testament. We can only consider sample texts. In Deuteronomy 7:1-6, among others, Yahweh is presented as ordering the slaughter of the native populations of Canaan, the land promised to Israel. In Genesis 9:25-27, Noah curses Ham and relegates his descendants to slavery forever.

We deal first with Genesis 9:25-27 and its effective history. Since the fifteenth century Christian Europe found the key justification for the enslavement of colored peoples in the "curse of Ham." The apartheid system in South Africa used Genesis 9:18-27 with Joshua 9:27 (Joshua decreed that the Gibeonites should forever be hewers of wood and drawers of water) to justify both job reservation to the whites and oppressive policies against the indigenous African population.[19] The American slave trade associated the curse of Ham with the discredited theory of the racial inferiority of Negroes.[20] That was then; now the current forty-fourth president of the United States of America, Barack Hussein Obama, is African American. Although both Testaments countenanced slavery as a social system, they nevertheless contain lofty liberation principles and mandates that have served for the liberation of slaves and eventually the abolition of slavery itself!

Deuteronomy 7:1-6 is in line with the rules of war as outlined in Deuteronomy 20 concerning all the nations within Canaan. Nations outside of Canaan may be offered a treaty but not those within. These are subject to the ban (in Hebrew *ḥerem*): no treaties, no intermarriage, and their altars are to be razed and their *asherah* (wooden poles representing a god or goddess) burnt. Because these resident peoples pose a risk of apostasy from Yahweh, they are to be entirely destroyed and all their religious symbols razed to the ground. In this text, Yahweh appears as a *national God* fighting on the side of Israel, just as Chemosh, the god of Moab, was deemed to fight on the side of Moab. The ban was an ancient practice of war followed by peoples of the ancient Near East, including Israel. To modern ears the command looks like the authorization of genocide for reasons of religious purity. At a certain point in her history, Israel did not see such as conflicting with her faith, but she later saw it so (clash of faith

---

[19] Cf. Gunther Wittenberg, "'. . . Let Canaan be his slave' (Gen 9:26). Is Ham also Cursed?" *Journal of Theology for Southern Africa* 74 (1991) 46–56.

[20] L. Richard Bradley, "The Curse of Canaan and the American Negro," *Concordia Theological Monthly* 42 (1971) 100–110, here 109.

and culture). For in due course, Israel transcended the notion of a national god and professed Yahweh as the God and Creator of all. Besides, many of Israel's texts portray the other side of Yahweh: "The LORD is gracious and merciful, slow to anger and abounding in steadfast love. The LORD is good to all, and his compassion is over all that he has made" (Ps 145:8-9). A much fuller characterization of this side of Yahweh is Wisdom 11:23-26, which deserves to be cited in full:

> But you are merciful to all, for you can do all things, and you overlook people's sins, so that they may repent. For you love all things that exist, and detest none of the things that you have made, for you would not have made anything if you had hated it. How would anything have endured if you had not willed it? Or how would anything not called forth by you have been preserved? You spare all things, for they are yours, O Lord, you who love the living.

If Yahweh is to be consistent, the real Yahweh cannot invalidate the right of some of Yahweh's creatures. On the other hand, Yahweh has chosen not to micromanage the world order, constantly intervening in human affairs to set things right. God's rule of the world order factors in human freedom and human responsibility. The discerning reader notices that not all texts speak of killing off the nations of Canaan. Exodus 34:11 says, "I will drive out [*garesh*] before you the Amorites, the Canaanites, the Hittites, the Perizzites, the Hivites, and the Jebusites." Important in such cases is to distinguish the "textual god" from the "actual god."[21] Because inspiration left intact the limitations and cultural perspectives of the sacred writers, they often portrayed God in ways that did not exactly match the actual God whom we and they worshiped. And so, Fretheim and Froelich wrote,

> The God portrayed in the text does not fully correspond to the God who transcends the text, who is a living, dynamic reality that cannot be captured in words on a page.[22]

The reader should check what was said in chapter 6 about the importance of the principle of *the unity of all of Scripture*—how tradition through the whole of Scripture must be brought to bear on its particular segments. The fact is, the text of Deuteronomy 7:1-6 portrayed the anguish of a mi-

---

[21] Terence E. Fretheim and Karlfried Froelich, *The Bible as Word of God: In a Postmodern Age* (Minneapolis: Fortress Press, 1998) 116–17. See also Eric A. Seibert, *Disturbing Divine Behavior: Troubling Old Testament Images of God* (Minneapolis: Fortress Press, 2009), 170.

[22] Fretheim and Froelich, *The Bible as Word of God*, 116.

nority group that feared disappearance and/or loss of religious identity through assimilation into a wider and more powerful group. When Deuteronomy was published (sixth/fifth centuries BCE), the seven nations no longer existed as such. For the Israel of Deuteronomy, Deuteronomy 7:1-6 did not command or authorize military conquest and extermination of the residents of the land (Israel returned home by the favor of the Persian Empire) but religious identity and distinctiveness. The focus had shifted from the *national* to the *religious*. The seven nations now stood for alienating culture and religion. Believers must mercilessly uproot whatever stood between them and their God. So much was this true that Deuteronomy 13:13-19 prescribed a similar ban of destruction for any Israelite city that turned from Yahweh to idolatry. In due course, Israel discovered a mission toward the nations (the Servant of Isaiah 49:6-7).

Verbum Domini

It is worth repeating the excerpt from *Verbum Domini* that heads this chapter. "It must be remembered," says the pope, that "*biblical revelation is deeply rooted in history*. God's plan is manifested *progressively* and it is accomplished slowly, *in successive stages* and despite human resistance. God chose a people and patiently worked to guide and educate them. Revelation is suited to the cultural and moral level of distant times and thus describes acts and customs, such as cheating and trickery, and acts of violence and massacre, without explicitly denouncing the immorality of such things" (no. 42, italics mine). The pope reminds the reader to take account also of the many "dark" deeds carried out through the centuries, even in our own day, and the fact that "in the Old Testament, the preaching of the prophets vigorously challenged every kind of injustice and violence, whether collective or individual, and thus became God's way of training his people in preparation for the Gospel" (ibid.).

Appendix: History, Archaeology, and the Bible

The appendixes, as explained in the introduction, have especially students and advanced inquirers in mind. Modern historians seek to present events "as they happened" as closely as possible, even though a historian always has a point of view. Ancient writers "used the past creatively to make a point in the present."[23] If a modern historian finds new material or has cause to alter

---

[23] Seibert, *Disturbing Divine Behavior*, 106.

or qualify earlier opinions or assertions, he/she brings out a new edition that incorporates the new perspectives or writes an article to that effect; the former work remains untouched. In ancient writings one adapted or quali-fied material by juxtaposing a second (sometimes a third) account to the original. That is how we have two accounts of the creation (Gen 1 and Gen 2–3), two accounts of the origin of kingship in Israel,[24] and three differing accounts of the rise of Saul,[25] for instance. Stories may be reused and given different functions over centuries. One may make "selective omissions"[26] or add evaluations that run against the grain of parts of the narrative itself. Ancient "history-like"[27] accounts in Scripture accept divine causality as part of history, while history as we moderns craft it does not reckon with divine causality but rather traces the network of economic, political, diplomatic, and military causes. Factual mistakes of history may, and actually do, occur in the biblical text, but these in no way take away from the truth or author-ity of Scripture (see chapter 5 on the inspiration and truth of Scripture). Scripture is as *fully* human word as it is *fully* divine word.[28] Ancient peoples believed that the earth was flat; the Bible does so too. That was the scientific understanding then, the cultural map. Cultural maps within which God's message must be understood need to be distinguished from the message itself, hence the necessity of biblical historical and cultural study.

Archaeology is one of the historical sciences that reconstruct history from the material remains of civilizations. The central claim of the Bible is that God has worked in history. Archaeology and other human disciplines may throw light on the historical context of such divine intervention. W. Waite Willis[29] traces two wrong approaches to the question. Jerry Falwell[30]

[24] An antimonarchist version (1 Sam 8; 10:17-24; 12) and a monarchist version (1 Sam 9:1–10:16). In one, the people forced the issue; in the other it was God's ordinance.

[25] Saul, king by lot and proclamation (1 Sam 10:24); Saul proclaimed king as result of victory over the Ammonites (1 Sam 11:11, 15); Saul finally crowned king after rejection by some whom the people wanted to kill but who were spared by Saul's intervention (1 Sam 11:12-14).

[26] Seibert, *Disturbing Divine Behavior*, 109. An example: Chronicles says nothing about David's adultery with Bathsheba or the subsequent murder of Uriah.

[27] The term is from James Barr, "Story and History," *Journal of Religion* 56 (April 1975) 1–17.

[28] Mowinckel, *The Old Testament as Word of God*, 79.

[29] W. Waite Willis Jr., "The Archaeology of Palestine and the Archaeology of Faith: Be-tween a Rock and a Hard Place," *What Has Archaeology to Do with Faith?*, eds. James Charles-worth and Walter Beaver (Philadelphia: Trinity Press International, 1992) 75–111, here 98.

[30] *Listen America* (New York: Doubleday, 1980) 63: "The Bible is absolutely infallible, without error in all matters pertaining to faith and practice, as well as in areas such as geog-raphy, science, history . . ."

and people of his persuasion reject the results of archaeology whenever they seem to contradict the historical accuracy of the Bible. Carl Sagan[31] and his group accept archaeological results and reject the Bible. Willis finds that both groups equate truth with factuality, and that this turns faith into assent to facts and reduces Scripture to a repository of information.[32] But God's word is *formation* to God's will, not information. God's action in history follows the pattern of the incarnation, and is subject to the ambiguities, accidents, limitations, and developments that mark history.[33] On the cross God acted by identifying with human history completely; this divine intervention can be perceived only in the response of faith. The crucifixion of Jesus was a historical fact, in a certain place and time. Archaeology may bring us to near certainty that the place called Golgotha is within the present Church of the Holy Sepulcher in Jerusalem, but it can in no way dig up the evidence that God was active on the cross of Jesus. The fact of the crucifixion there of a man called Jesus can be ascertained by history and archaeology; that this event is God's act of redemption and self-disclosure is completely beyond the ken of archaeology or history but belongs to the area of faith. Archaeology can prevent us from emphasizing as factual biblical accounts that may, at best, be improbable or may not even have been intended to be factual. In such cases, archaeology causes us to look again at the genre of the story. However, lack of archaeological evidence would not be sufficient in itself to cast doubt on the affirmations of the written witnesses.[34]

How would the story of the walls of Jericho in Joshua 6 look taking the above principles into account? When Joshua gave the order, the entire people raised a shout, the city walls collapsed, and "the people charged straight ahead into the city and captured it" (Josh 6:20). John Garstang excavated in Jericho in 1930–36. He found part of a city fortified by double walls that had been destroyed by fire around 1440 BCE and concluded that these were the walls of Joshua 6. The British archaeologist Kathleen Kenyon excavated there in 1952–58. She believed that the double city wall dated about a thousand years earlier than Garstang allotted it. Jericho had been destroyed about 1550 by the Hyksos who were chased out of Egypt

---

[31] *Cosmos* (New York: Random House, 1980).

[32] Seifert (*Disturbing Divine Behavior*, 120–24) also insists on this distinction between "truth" and "historical." A story (even fiction, like the book of Job) may convey truth as "vehicle of profound insights into our relationship with the world, each other and God" (124).

[33] Cf. Willis, "The Archaeology of Palestine," 101.

[34] Thomas W. Davis, "Faith and Archaeology—A Brief History to the Present," *BAR* 19/2 (March/April 1993) 54–59, here 57.

and was not rebuilt. During the traditional date of the entry of Israel into the Promised Land (mid-thirteenth century BCE), Jericho was a small village with no protecting walls at all! Unfortunately, Kenyon died in 1982 before publishing the full report. In 1990, Bryant Wood[35] undertook to review Kenyon's evidence. He concluded that Garstang was right after all: the city was destroyed in 1440 and the entry of Israel into Canaan should be moved to that date. Stephen Langfur[36] reviewed Wood, confirming Kenyon's findings.

A wall may collapse at the shout of the people, if God wills it. The possibility of miracles is not the issue here. Some interpreters even think of a providential earthquake.[37] J. Alberto Soggin with some scholars believe that the earliest narrative was of an armed attack that succeeded with the aid of a ruse, perhaps from within by the Rahab people.[38] The important question, though, is that of the genre and function of the narrative, what the story set out to achieve. Though composite,[39] the story as a whole attributes to God a mighty victory for Israel against a very superior power. Jericho could have proven to be Israel's Waterloo. Richard Nelson correctly sees that "Jericho's wall serves as a conceptual parallel to the Jordan, as a barrier that must be breached in order for Israel to move forward in acquiring the land."[40] The collapse of a city wall was equivalent to the defeat of that city.[41] The narrative is a typical "holy war" account. In such accounts, "Yahweh's role is stressed and Israel's is downplayed."[42] The discerning reader notices a variant account of the same episode in Joshua 24:11-12. In this account God "sent the hornet ahead of you, which drove out before you the two kings of the Amorites; it was not by your sword or by your

[35] Bryant G. Wood, "Did the Israelites Conquer Jericho? A New Look at the Archaeological Evidence," *BAR* 16/2 (March/April 1990) 44–58.

[36] Stephen Langfur, "Jericho: When Did What Walls Fall?," Near East Tourist Agency, accessed September 21, 2009, http://new.netours.com/index.php?option=com_content&task=view&id=119&Itemid=26&limit=1&limitstart=3.

[37] Garstang posited so; so did Robert G. Boling and G. Ernest Wright, *Joshua*, The Anchor Bible (New York and London: Doubleday, 1982) 215: "the tradition may perhaps more plausibly have originated in a series of protective ritual exercises which were accompanied or soon followed by an unexpected seismic event."

[38] J. Alberto Soggin, *Joshua* (Philadelphia: Westminster Press, 1972) 84.

[39] There is confusion and contradiction: who is to sound the trumpets (priests or the rearguard); when are the people to shout (after a long blast or not till Joshua gives the order). See Soggin, *Joshua*, 82.

[40] Richard D. Nelson, *Joshua: A Commentary* (Louisville: John Knox Press, 1997) 92.

[41] Ibid., 93.

[42] Ibid., 92.

bow." In this variant, the walls did not collapse at the shout of the people, yet the victory is all God's! The account also contains elements of liturgical performance. The entire people (including women and children) did the circuits and engaged in the final storming of the city. Ram's horn was used in the liturgy. On the seventh day, they processed around the city seven times before the order to shout. At least one scholar, Soggin, believes that the liturgical celebration of the event has now been superimposed upon the original military account.[43] My purpose here has not been to conclude one way or the other but to illustrate from the case of Jericho in Joshua 6 the various issues that an attentive reader should examine.

Questions for Discussion

1. Evolution versus "intelligent design." Discuss.

2. Discuss the development of faith in the resurrection of the body.

3. Discuss the morality of the storming of Shechem, Genesis 34.

4. Discuss Yahweh's anger against Uzzah, 2 Samuel 6:1-8.

5. Read Exodus 4:24-26. Does distinguishing the "textual god" from the "actual god" help?

6. The walls of Jericho. What must the believer hold, and why?

7. Outline some issues in history, archaeology, and the Bible.

8. Outline and discuss some criteria given in this chapter for dealing with the "dark" passages of the Bible.

---

[43] Soggin, *Joshua*, 86.

Fundamentalism

The *Lineamenta* mentioned fundamentalism almost in passing. *Lineamenta*, 15, noted the danger of the Scriptures being interpreted arbitrarily or literalistically as obtains in *fundamentalism*. Fundamentalism, though it desires to remain faithful to the text, is said in reality to display a lack of knowledge of the texts themselves, thus falling into serious errors.

The responses from the particular churches more insistently decried the inroads of fundamentalism everywhere, even within the Catholic Church itself. The *Instrumentum Laboris* returned to the issue of fundamentalism at least three times.[44] *Instrumentum Laboris*, 29, gave a more extended characterization and evaluation of the phenomenon of fundamentalism:

> In Bible reading, fundamentalism takes refuge in literalism and refuses to take into consideration the historical dimension of biblical revelation. It is thus unable to fully accept the incarnation itself. This kind of interpretation is winning more and more adherents . . . even among Catholics. It demands an unshakable adherence to rigid doctrinal points of view and imposes, as the only source of teaching for Christian life and salvation, a reading of the Bible which rejects all questioning and any kind of critical research.

Concern about fundamentalism was echoed frequently in the aula of the synod itself. It was said that in Latin America this tendency leads to readings of Scripture that encourage passivity[45] and discourage the social and political involvement of Christians. During the last forty years, the church in Latin America is said to have lost about 15 percent of its faithful to non-Catholic movements, based on the biblical strategies of these movements, a huge loss considering that Latin America makes up 43 percent of world Catholicism today.[46] Speaking for Oceania, Bishop Putney of Townsville (Australia) noted how Catholic evangelization was sometimes rejected because it was not distinguished from the approach of some groups who ignored the cultural context and relied on fundamentalist understandings of the word of God.[47] A synod father,[48] noting that fundamentalism was a

[44] *Instrumentum Laboris*, 20 (which takes up *Lineamenta*, 15), 29, and 43.

[45] Cardinal Maradiaga, archbishop of Tegucigalpa (Honduras), Report on the Word of God in the Americas, October 6, 2008. See further chapter 3 above.

[46] Bishop Strotmann Hoppe, bishop of Chosica (Peru), October 7, 2008.

[47] Synod assembly, October 6, 2008.

[48] Archbishop Tottunkal, archbishop major of Trivandrum of Syro-Malankar Church, president of the synod of the Syro-Malankarensi Church (India), October 6, 2008.

current within all the world religions, placed it among the new challenges that the church's mission faced in the religiously and culturally pluralistic context of Asia, especially India. Recent attacks on Christians there have been engineered by fundamentalist groups, thus manifesting intolerance of differences even unto violence. In Africa, fundamentalist and anti-Catholic groups attack the church and seek to make converts from Catholicism. A synod father noted, however, that Catholics were becoming more familiar with Scripture and this was enabling them to stand their ground when others attacked their beliefs or the Catholic Church.[49]

Biblical Fundamentalism

As used today, the term fundamentalism refers to a phenomenon among reactionary groups within the world religions that seek to restore the pristine purity of particular faiths or belief systems by demarcating "fundamentals" of that faith as a kind of litmus test between orthodoxy and heresy. Total reliance is placed on sacred texts that are considered as having divine authority.[50] Mark LeVine calls such groups "resistance identities,"[51] and they usually consist of people who feel excluded or marginalized by the dominant system and who take up arms against it, literally or metaphorically.

The term fundamentalism, however, had Christian origins. Toward the end of the nineteenth century, evangelical Christians took up arms against what they considered an erosion of faith and piety by the onset of rationalism and secularism through the historical-critical interpretation of Scripture. Between 1910 and 1925, in meetings in New York, Niagara, and Chicago, they hatched out twelve tracts titled *The Fundamentals: A Testimony to the Truth.*[52] The actual term fundamentalist was said to have been coined by Curtis Lee Laws in the July 1, 1920, edition of the *Watchman-Examiner*, a Baptist paper in New York.[53] The five "fundamentals" that they saw under attack were

---

[49] Archbishop Onayekan, archbishop of Abuja, Nigeria, October 6, 2008.

[50] Cf. Ronald D. Witherup, *Biblical Fundamentalism: What Every Catholic Should Know* (Collegeville, MN: Liturgical Press, 2001) 14.

[51] Mark LeVine, "What Is Fundamentalism, and How Do We Get Rid of It?," *Journal of Ecumenical Studies* 42/1 (Winter 2007) 21.

[52] Eugene LaVerdiere, *Fundamentalism: A Pastoral Concern* (Collegeville, MN: Liturgical Press, 2000) 5.

[53] ". . . we suggest that those who still cling to the fundamentals and who mean to do battle royal for the fundamentals shall be called 'Fundamentalists.' This name as compliment, not as disparagement" (cf. LaVerdiere, *Fundamentalism*, 7).

1) the inspiration and inerrancy of the Bible,

2) the divinity and virgin birth of Christ,

3) the substitutionary atonement of Christ's death,

4) the literal bodily resurrection of Christ from the dead, and

5) the literal return of Christ in the Second Coming.[54]

The gospel of this movement in the United States has come to be *The Scofield Reference Bible*[55] by Cyrus I. Scofield, 1909, which has undergone several revisions.[56] Scofield's interpretation is dispensationalist, that is, prophecies are seen as predictive of the far future (our times), and the history of the universe is divided into seven eras or dispensations.[57] In America today, the fundamentalist movement really tries to live a spirituality based on the Bible, in which all life, private and public, is subject to the word of God. Most televangelists and "The Bible Says" groups are fundamentalist. The movement is also associated with *Rapture* (referring to 1 Thess 4:16-17) and the Left Behind series,[58] and finds social and political expression through multiple "crusades," for example, the crusade of Scripture as the absolutely inerrant word of God (acting as bulwark against methods of interpretation of the Bible that would factor in questions of culture and history), the crusade of "family values" (hence crusade against abortion and same-sex unions), and, above all, the struggle to include "intelligent design" in school curricula as an equally "scientific" account of creation as evolution and, in some cases, the banning of the teaching of evolution altogether.

A taste of the biblical perspectives of fundamentalism can be seen in the 1978 Chicago Statement on Biblical Inerrancy.[59] This document was signed by nearly three hundred evangelical scholars who met at the Hyatt Regency O'Hare in Chicago. I give a summary of the salient points of this document:

---

[54] Cf. LaVerdiere, *Fundamentalism*, 17.

[55] New York: Oxford University Press, 1909.

[56] Cf. Witherup, *Biblical Fundamentalism*, 8.

[57] Cf. Witherup, *Biblical Fundamentalism*, 59. The dispensations are (1) innocence (Gen 1:28; the Garden of Eden); (2) conscience or moral responsibility (Gen 3:7; from Fall to Noah); (3) human government (Gen 8:15; from Noah to covenant with Abraham); (4) promise (Gen 12:1; from Abraham to Moses); (5) law (Exod 19:1; from Moses to Jesus Christ); (6) church (Acts 2:1; from death and resurrection of Jesus to the present); and (7) kingdom (Rev 20:4; begins when Christ returns to earth in victory).

[58] A series of sixteen novels by Tim LaHaye and Jerry Jenkins on the Rapture that have sold over fifty million copies.

[59] "Chicago Statement on Biblical Inerrancy with Exposition," Bible Research, accessed January 21, 2010, http://www.bible-researcher.com/chicago1.html.

Scripture is without error or fault in all its teaching, no less in what it states about God's acts in creation, about the events of world history, and about its own literary origins under God, than in its witness to God's saving grace in individual lives. . . .

The whole of Scripture and all its parts, down to the very words of the original, were given by divine inspiration. . . .

Inspiration, strictly speaking, applies only to the autographic text of Scripture. . . .

We deny that Biblical infallibility and inerrancy are limited to spiritual, religious, or redemptive themes, exclusive of assertions in the fields of history and science. We further deny that scientific hypotheses about earth history may properly be used to overturn the teaching of Scripture on creation and the flood. . . .

What Scripture says, God says . . . what Scripture says, Christ says. . . .

Canonical Scripture is the divinely inspired and therefore normative witness to Christ. No hermeneutic, therefore, of which the historical Christ is not the focal point is acceptable. . . .

Inasmuch as all Scripture is the product of a single divine mind, interpretation must stay within the bounds of the analogy of Scripture and eschew hypotheses that would correct one Biblical passage by another, whether in the name of progressive revelation or of the imperfect enlightenment of the inspired writer's mind.

I now give a brief evaluation. One can see that overemphasis on the divine element of inspiration seems to smother the human element. The view that the very words (of the original autograph), not the sentences and units in context, are inspired is called *plenary verbal inspiration* (see chapter 5 of this book). Such a view sometimes leads to conflict between reason and faith, for example, in the case of inconsistencies. On inconsistencies the Statement has this to say:

Solution of them, where this can be convincingly achieved, will encourage our faith, and where for the present no convincing solution is at hand we shall significantly honor God by trusting His assurance that His Word is true, despite these appearances, and by maintaining our confidence that one day they will be seen to have been illusions.

It should also be noted that the fundamentalist christological orientation tends to deny the Old Testament any independent valence in interpretation.

The Catholic point of view on the Old Testament is more nuanced (see chapters 2 and 4 of this book). In an insightful table,[60] Ronald D. Witherup compares the fundamentalist perspectives on the Bible with the Catholic ones as follows:

Fundamentalist Perspective on the Bible	Catholic Perspective on the Bible
The Bible *is* the word of God	The Bible is God's word in human words
Scripture *alone*	Scripture *and* Tradition
Emphasis on literalist reading of Bible	Emphasis on literal (not literalist) reading as well as deeper (and spiritual) meanings
Tendency to view inspiration narrowly	Tendency to take a broad view of inspiration
Inerrancy of the Bible in all matters	No errors in the Bible only on matters of faith and morals
Lack of historical perspective in interpretation	Historical perspective is essential for interpretation
Frequent interpretations out of context	Necessity of interpretations in context, especially the context of the sacred canon
Direct and immediate applicability of most biblical passages	Mostly indirect applicability of biblical passages
Denial of role of church in canonization of Scripture	Recognition of role of church in canonization process
Tendency to ignore history of interpretation	History of interpretation essential
Narrow and precise prophetic eschatology often linked to a time line	Broad and imprecise eschatology not linked to any specific time line
Rejection of scientific historical-critical methods of interpretation	Acceptance of scientific historical-critical methods of interpretation (among others)

However, for Catholics the Bible is error-less not "only on matters of faith and morals" (as above), which would be limited inerrancy. Chapter 5 ("The Inspiration and Truth of Scripture") saw DV 11's "for the sake of our salvation" as a formal, not material, gratification of the truth of Scripture.

[60] *Biblical Fundamentalism*, 47, used with permission.

The Church's Response to Fundamentalism

The United States Catholic Conference of Bishops addressed fundamentalism in a timely document in 1987, A Pastoral Statement for Catholics on Biblical Fundamentalism. Noting that excellent resources exist, thanks to Vatican II, the bishops wrote that

> our challenge now is to get this knowledge into the minds, hearts and lives of all our Catholic people. We need a Pastoral Plan for the Word of God that will place the Sacred Scriptures at the heart of the parish and individual life. (p. 7)

They went on to propose familiar quoting of the Bible by every catechist, lector, and minister. They acknowledged that we have not done enough in this area.

The danger of biblical fundamentalism was clearly articulated by The Interpretation of the Bible in the Church, 1, F:

> The fundamentalist approach is dangerous, for it is attractive to people who look to the Bible for ready answers to the problems of life. It can deceive these people, offering them interpretations that are pious but illusory, instead of telling them that the Bible does not necessarily contain an immediate answer to each and every problem. Without saying as much in so many words, fundamentalism actually invites people to a kind of intellectual suicide. It injects into life a false certitude, for it unwittingly confuses the divine substance of the biblical message with what are in fact its human limitations.

The language of "intellectual suicide" is perhaps slightly over-the-board, seeing that fundamentalists count many and stellar intellectual giants among them. As Eugene LaVerdiere said, they have a point, for some things are so basic that if we deny them, we are not Christians anymore (for example, the Creeds).[61] The comment of the Commission, however, illustrates an important difference in the Catholic approach to revelation: the use of the God-given light of reason (the reader should remember how in chapter 4 the natural law was seen as an element of revelation). In an apparent conflict between reason and what is considered word of God, fundamentalists hold on to what they consider the word of God, even against reason. Fundamentalists are to be praised for this courage of faith; however, the Catholic approach is to reject any dichotomy between

---

[61] Cf. LaVerdiere, *Fundamentalism*, 17.

"right reason" (*recta ratio*) and word of God, and in apparent conflicts to reexamine the foundations of both for their mutual dialogue.

Proposition 47 of the Synod on the Word of God calls for intensification of the biblical apostolate so as to provide the food of the Word to the faithful who seek it. The church should also encourage groups of sharing and meditation in order to counteract the attraction of the sects and of fundamentalism. Finally, it is necessary that priests be adequately prepared to confront these new situations, rendering them capable of proposing a biblically grounded pastoral strategy, adapted to the problems experienced by people today.

The synod's Message to the People of God, 5, broadened the canvas and called for the biblical literacy of every believer: "Every reader of sacred Scripture, even the most simple, must have a proportionate knowledge of the sacred text, recalling that the word is enveloped in concrete words, which is shaped and adapted to make it heard and understood by all of humanity. This is a necessary commitment. If it is excluded, one could fall into fundamentalism which in practice denies the Incarnation of the divine Word in history."

Verbum Domini, 44, treats the fundamentalist interpretation of Sacred Scripture. The pope says that the literalism championed by the fundamentalist approach actually represents a betrayal of both the literal and the spiritual sense. It actually opens the way for various forms of manipulation. Christianity, says the pope, "perceives in the words the Word himself, the Logos who displays his mystery through this complexity and the reality of human history."[62] The human mediation of the inspired text and its literary genres must not be neglected.

[62] Citing his Address to Representatives of the World of Culture at the Collège des Bernardins in Paris, September 12, 2008.

Questions for Discussion

1. Outline and discuss the various types of fundamentalism.
2. How is the church experiencing the phenomenon of fundamentalism?
3. Compare the fundamentalist and Catholic perspectives on the Bible.
4. Outline some of the synod's responses to biblical fundamentalism.
5. Have you read any books of the Left Behind series? Discuss its assumptions and biblical foundations.
6. Fifteen percent of Catholics in Latin America have been lost to fundamentalist Bible groups in the last forty years. As a minister or missionary there, detail your plan of response.

Chapter 10

Verbum Domini,
Part I: The Word of God

With this Apostolic Exhortation I would like the work of the Synod to have a real effect on the life of the Church: on our personal relationship with the sacred Scriptures, on their interpretation in the liturgy and in catechesis, and in scientific research, so that the Bible may not be simply a word from the past, but a living and timely word.

Verbum Domini, **5**

Chapter 1 of this book outlined the synod process and mentioned the fact that since the 1974 Fourth Ordinary General Assembly of the Synod of Bishops (On Evangelization) it has been the practice for the Holy Father, and not the synod itself, to issue a post-synodal apostolic exhortation. Benedict XVI signed the post-synodal apostolic exhortation *Verbum Domini*, On the Word of God in the Life and Mission of the Church, on September 30, 2010 (feast of St. Jerome), but released it for the public only on November 11, 2010. The association with St. Jerome may not be fortuitous; he is the father of the church most often cited (see later). It is possible that after the Blessed Virgin's response to the Word, His Holiness may be holding up to the church St. Jerome's utter insertion into the word of God in prayer and study, particularly his method of interpreting the text.

The Apostolic Exhortation

In alignment with the goals of the Synod on the Word of God (see chapter 1), His Holiness presents his aim in the apostolic exhortation to "revisit the work of the Synod in the light of its documents . . . [and] to point out certain fundamental approaches to a rediscovery of God's word in the life of the Church as a wellspring of constant renewal" (no. 1). The exhortation contains "reflections with which I have sought to gather up and examine more fully the rich fruits" of the synod (no. 121). His Holiness uses the prologue of John (John 1:1-18) as the caption for his reflection on these fruits. This use of the prologue underlines what he calls "the Christology of the word" (no. 11). Language of the word "set[s us] before the very person of Jesus. His unique and singular history is the definitive word which God speaks to humanity" (ibid.). In this couple of sentences, the pope has given a kind of summary of both this exhortation and the work of the synod itself.

The exhortation comprises three parts:

Verbum Dei (the Word of God), centered on John 1:1, 14;

Verbum in Ecclesia (the Word in the Church), centered on John 1:12

Verbum Mundo (the Word to the World), centered on John 1:18.

Part I, the topic of this chapter, unfolds in three sections: The God Who Speaks, Our Response to the God Who Speaks, and The Interpretation of Sacred Scripture in the Church.

In the following commentary, I take for granted all the discussions of the synod till now and focus on new insights, qualifications, or perspectives. A document of the magisterium treats the topic in relation to the trajectory of magisterial teaching, especially of the current pontiff; this exhortation is no exception. What is striking, though, is the constant reference to the teaching of the fathers and the medieval doctors of the church, far beyond the smattering of such references in the documents of the synod. There are sixty-one such references,[1] forty of which occur in this part I! His Holiness shows himself as one steeped in the wells of tradition, one with a sharp ecclesial sense of the church of all times and places. Incidentally he puts on display the theological richness of the patristic tradition that he would like all believers to emulate.

The tone of the exhortation is very collegial: the pope often speaks as a member of the synod, sometimes using the pronouns "we" and "us," and referring to "the recommendations which resulted from our common endeavor" (no. 1). All the fifty-five propositions of the synod are either referred to or cited in part, with a few being mentioned twice or more[2] for an additional forty-three citations, making ninety-eight references in

---

[1] Most often cited are St. Jerome (hardly surprising since the document was signed on his feast day), St. Augustine, Gregory the Great, and St. Ambrose in descending order.

[2] Besides, the *Lineamenta* is cited once, the *Instrumentum Laboris* three times, the Report before the Discussion once, the Report after the Discussion five times, the Message to the

all! The results of the voting on the propositions of the synod are not usually divulged. The fact that His Holiness referred to all of them makes one surmise that they were all approved, though the pope is always free to take account of whichever propositions he considers most apt for the animation of the entire church. Leading the list were propositions 14 and 38 (each cited five times) and propositions 4 and 55 (each cited four times)—none in full, of course, only excerpts. Proposition 14 is titled "The Word of God and Liturgy," proposition 38 "The Missionary Duty of all the Baptized," proposition 4 "The Dialogic Dimension of Revelation," and proposition 55 "Mary, *Mater Dei* and *Mater Fidei*" (Mother of God and Mother of the Faith). These four, in a sense, give the reader a bird's-eye view of the apostolic exhortation, which can be summarized as follows: through the power of the Holy Spirit,

> "The Word of God IS the mission of the Church."

the word of God, especially in the liturgy, encounters and transforms all hearers of the Word into heralds of the Word, Jesus Christ, as happened in Mary. "Heralding" the Word happens in the personal and ecclesial life of Christians and through their transforming presence to the world. The exhortation repeats in many ways Benedict XVI's appeal at the beginning of his pontificate to "open wide the doors to Christ" (no. 104), for "only in this friendship are the doors of life opened wide. Only in this friendship is the great potential of human existence truly revealed."[3]

The pope did not always merge his voice with that of the synod. The recommendations of the synod are clearly handed on as such, sometimes with subtle adaptations. Where the pope speaks in the person of his office as head, he uses the first person singular, saying, "I urge," "I encourage," or "I recommend." For example, "I recommend that competent authorities prepare ritual directories [for celebration of the Word on Sundays without a priest], drawing on the experience of the particular churches" (no. 65). Or, on the danger of a dualistic approach to Sacred Scripture, he writes, "here I would mention the most troubling consequences which are to be avoided" (no. 35). Paying close attention to the nuanced language of the exhortation helps the reader to better grasp the direction in which His Holiness wishes to take the church.

People of God five times. It is clear that besides the propositions, the pope drew material especially from the Report after the Discussion and the Message.

[3] Homily at the Mass of Inauguration, April 24, 2005.

The God Who Speaks

The Analogy of the Word

The word of God constitutes the church's inner mystery: "the Church is built upon the word of God; she is born from and lives from that word" (no. 3). Besides, as a synod father expressed it,[4] "the Word of God IS the mission of the Church." The church lives from and for the word of God!

The expression "word of God" refers to various ways in which God manifests God's self and executes God's plan "at whose center is the invitation to partake, in Christ, in the divine life" (no. 8). The different meanings of word of God are categorized in number 7:

> The Logos, the eternal Word, only Son of the Father
>
> The Incarnate Word, Jesus Christ, born of the Virgin Mary
>
> The Book of Nature: "every creature is a word of God, since it proclaims God" (no. 8)[5]
>
> Salvation history—God's deeds and words in the history of God's people handed on in tradition
>
> Sacred Scripture—the Old and New Testaments, word of God, attested and divinely inspired

The pope acknowledged the "need for further study of how the different meanings of this expression are interrelated, so that the unity of God's plan and, within it, the centrality of the person of Christ, may shine forth more clearly" (no. 7).[6]

God's plan of salvation is the unity that links all these expressions of the word of God, and within this plan the person of Jesus Christ is central. Jesus Christ is God's *Verbum abbreviatum* ("the abbreviated Word," no. 12). God, in giving us God's only Word, the Son "spoke everything at once in this sole word—and he has no more to say . . . because what he spoke before to the prophets in parts, he has spoken all at once by giving us this All who is his Son" (no. 14).[7]

Lineamenta, 9, had included, as part of the symphony of the word of God, "spirited preaching and many other forms in service to the gospel,"

---

[4] Very Rev. Fr. Antonio Pernia, SVD, superior general of the Society of the Divine Word, October 10, 2008.

[5] Citing St. Bonaventure, *Itinerarium mentis in Deum* (The Soul's Path to God), II, 12.

[6] Citing Proposition 3.

[7] Citing St. John of the Cross, *Ascent of Mount Carmel*, II.

describing preaching as "the word of God communicated by a living God to living persons in Jesus Christ by means of the Church." That "spirited preaching" referred to the Holy Spirit was made clear by *Instrumentum Laboris*, 9, which spoke of "preaching . . . under the power of the Holy Spirit." *Instrumentum Laboris* (preface) noted the christological concentration of the word of God, nevertheless affirmed that "this christological approach, linked by necessity to the pneumatological one, leads to the discovery of the Trinitarian dimension of revelation." Benedict XVI thought it better not to place the activity of the Holy Spirit as just one variant of the word of God but as part of every configuration of the word from the very beginning. The word always has a "pneumatological horizon." God's self-communication always involves the relationship of the Son and the Holy Spirit, the "two hands of the Father" as Irenaeus[8] put it (no. 15). It is worth citing part of this number 15:

> The word of God is thus expressed in human words thanks to the working of the Holy Spirit. The missions of the Son and the Holy Spirit are inseparable and constitute a single economy of salvation. The same Spirit who acts in the incarnation of the Word in the womb of the Virgin Mary is the Spirit who guides Jesus throughout his mission and is promised to the disciples. The same Spirit who spoke through the prophets sustains and inspires the Church in her task of proclaiming the word of God and in the preaching of the Apostles; finally, it is this Spirit who inspires the authors of sacred Scripture.

And so, "we cannot come to an understanding of Scripture without the assistance of the Holy Spirit who inspired it"[9] (no. 16). Hence, it is necessary to remain open to the working of the Paraclete in the church and in the hearts of believers (ibid.).

Three implications of the doctrine on the word of God are inspiration and truth of Scripture, tradition and Scripture, and private revelations.

Inspiration and Truth of Scripture

Chapter 5 of this book discussed the synod's view on the inspiration and truth of Scripture. In the documents of the synod this topic was treated in relation to the interpretation of Scripture; Benedict XVI considers this topic under the heading of "God Who Speaks," hence as an outflow of the

---

[8] *Adversus Haereses*, IV, 7, 4.
[9] St. Jerome, *Epistula*, 120, 10.

doctrine of the word of God, the divine self-disclosure. The inspiration of the Holy Spirit is what makes the text of the Bible "sacred Scripture," that is, the locus where "we can hear the Lord himself speak and recognize his presence in history" (no. 19). The inspiration of the Holy Spirit lets the human author act fully as such, while making God himself the true author. Scripture thus participates somewhat in the analogy of the incarnation: "the body of the Son is the Scripture which we have received"[10] (no. 18). The truth of Scripture is a consequence of its inspiration:

> [S]ince, therefore, all that the inspired authors, or sacred writers, affirm should be regarded as affirmed by the Holy Spirit, we must acknowledge that the books of Scripture firmly, faithfully and without error, teach that truth which God, for the sake of our salvation, wished to see confided to the sacred Scriptures.[11]

The pope went no further in explaining the doctrine of inspiration and truth of Scripture but rather acknowledged the need for a fuller and more adequate study of these realities.[12] It was noted in chapter 5 that the Pontifical Biblical Commission began studying the inspiration and truth of Scripture during its plenary session of 2009.

Tradition and Scripture

Through the prompting of the Holy Spirit, the word of truth handed on through the apostolic succession gave birth to the canon of Sacred Scripture; the Scriptures themselves are more thoroughly understood in relation to the living tradition of the church (no. 17). Apostolic tradition grows in the church in the sense that "there is a growth in insight into the realities and the words that are being passed on" (no. 18).[13] The relation between Scripture and the word of God had exercised the minds of the synod fathers who asked whether Scripture was word of God or contained the word of God. Benedict XVI describes it as follows:[14]

---

[10] St. Ambrose, *Exposition of the Gospel according to Luke*, 6, 33.

[11] Citing *Dei Verbum*, 11. See chapter 5 for the questions this number raises.

[12] Proposition 12 had asked that the Congregation for the Doctrine of the Faith clarify the concepts of inspiration and truth in the Bible, along with their reciprocal relationship.

[13] *Dei Verbum*, 8.

[14] This adapts proposition 3 slightly, for it read: "The word of God transcends the sacred Scriptures, even if Scripture contains the word of God in an entirely unique way." The Message to the People of God, 3, reads: "Therefore the word of God precedes and goes beyond the Bible which itself is 'inspired by God' and contains the efficacious divine word (cf. 2 Tim 3:16)."

Although the word of God precedes and exceeds sacred Scripture, nonetheless, Scripture, as inspired by God, contains the divine word (cf. 2 Tim 3:16) "in an altogether singular way."

It will be the task of theologians to clarify what containing the divine word "in an altogether singular way" means. The pope led the way by affirming that "the word of God is given to us in sacred Scripture as an inspired testimony to revelation" (no 18). He cites *Dei Verbum*, 21, to the effect that "together with the Church's living tradition, it constitutes the supreme rule of faith."[15] The reader may want to glance back at chapter 2 for some suggestions of theologians. A particular opinion there was that of Sandra Schneiders. She holds "word of God" to be a "root metaphor" (one that generates and holds together multiple meanings) that integrates all manners of divine self-giving and self-disclosure,[16] that is, revelation. For her, "we cannot say that the Bible is, purely and simply, revelation" (word of God) but rather "it is more correct to say that the Bible is (*potentially*) revelatory":[17]

> Sacred scripture is the sacrament of the word of God . . . the entire mystery of divine revelation . . . this mystery here comes to articulation with a clarity and transparency that focuses our attention on the mystery of divine revelation and thus fosters our attentiveness to the word of God wherever we encounter it.

Concerning tradition, the then Joseph Ratzinger had written:

> It is important to note that only Scripture is defined in terms of what it *is*: it is stated that Scripture *is* the word of God consigned to writing. Tradition, however, is described only functionally, in terms of what it *does*: it hands on the word of God, but *is* not the word of God.[18]

In a speech during Vatican II, on September 30, 1964, Cardinal Meyer sought to clarify the notion of tradition. True tradition concerns *quae substantialia sunt ecclesiae* (what belongs to the essence of the church) that proceed from the apostolic tradition. Scripture is a criterion for distinguishing what is authentic and true in tradition.[19]

---

[15] *Dei Verbum*, 21.

[16] *The Revelatory Text: Interpreting the New Testament as Sacred Scripture*, 2nd ed. (Collegeville, MN: Liturgical Press, 1999) 39.

[17] Ibid., 39, 41–42 (italics mine).

[18] Joseph Ratzinger, "The Transmission of Divine Revelation," *Commentary on the Documents of Vatican II*, vol. 3, ed. Herbert Vorgrimler (Freiburg: Herder, 1968) 181–92, here 194.

[19] Ibid., 185.

Scripture, Tradition, and the Magisterium are intimately bound together. The living magisterium is charged with "giving an authentic interpretation of the word of God, whether in its written form or in the form of tradition" (no. 33).[20]

Private Revelations

Proposition 47 indicated "the need to help the faithful distinguish well the word of God from private revelations." The pope developed a very integrative theology of private revelations, which nevertheless assigns them their place in the hierarchy of truths. "It is not their role to improve or complete Christ's definitive revelation but to help live it more fully in a certain period of history."[21] Hence their use is obligatory on no one. This is important in light of a recent tendency to universalize certain devotions based on private revelation, even to regard them, in some quarters, as tests of orthodoxy. Private revelations are judged solely in their orientation to Christ. They may nourish faith, hope, and love by introducing new emphases, giving rise to new forms of piety, and deepening older ones (no. 14). Church approval only assures that the private revelation in question contains nothing contrary to faith and morals.

Our Response to the God Who Speaks

Chapter 2 of part I is titled Our Response to the God Who Speaks. The main sections are Called to the Covenant with God; The Word of God and Faith; Sin as a Refusal to Hear the Word of God; and Mary, "Mother of God's Word" and "Mother of Faith." I comment on Sin as a Refusal to Hear the Word of God; and Mary, "Mother of God's Word" and "Mother of Faith."

Sin as a Refusal to Hear the Word of God

This emphasis is relatively new in the synod's proceedings. The divine Word discloses the sin that lurks in the human heart, thus disclosing sin as a refusal to hear the word of God (no. 26). The reader will recall the words of the Report after the Discussion cited in chapter 4:

[20] Citing *Dei Verbum*, 10.
[21] Citing the Catechism of the Catholic Church, 67.

In speaking God created humans for encounter with God. To encounter the word of God is to really understand creation and oneself. The human being is *un être appelé à l'écoute de la parole* (a being called to listen to the word). For humans this hearing is not facultative, but constitutive.[22] The word of God has an eminently vocational character: the vocation of humankind is to realize self by going out of self to embrace God's project for humans.

In other words, not to hear the word of God is not only sin but also to compromise the very integrity of one's being.

Mary, "Mother of God's Word" and "Mother of Faith"

Here His Holiness beautifully develops ideas contained in all the synod documents. The Virgin Mary, "by her 'yes' to the word of the covenant and her mission, perfectly fulfills the divine vocation of humanity" (no. 27).[23] She was so attuned to the word of God that she spoke and thought with the Word. "Mary is the image of the Church in attentive hearing of the word of God, which took flesh in her" (ibid.). What took place in Mary should daily take place in each Christian. As St. Ambrose reminds us, every Christian believer like Mary in some way interiorly conceives and gives birth to the word of God. The pope then encouraged scholars to study the relationship between Mariology and the theology of the Word, thereby opening up a fresh area of research and reflection.

The Interpretation of Sacred Scripture in the Church

Chapter 3 of part I deals with the interpretation of Sacred Scripture in the church, one of the major goals of the exhortation (see the citation at the head of this chapter). A useful background for this section is the account of recent tensions in Catholic exegesis (outlined in chapter 7). Briefly, there has been an attack on the historical-critical method as moored in the past, stuck to history, lacking theology, and alienating people from the faith. People who raised the question, what is Catholic in Catholic exegesis? tended to see the conditions of exegesis in the academe as crowding out

---

[22] One may see this in the submission of Bishop José Rodríguez, bishop of Líbano-Honda, Columbia, on October 7, 2008: "the ontological structure of human beings, of each human being, . . . is essentially dialogue . . . In the depth of our being we discover a dialogical dynamism that makes us different from other beings of our experience. And so our personal existence is, above all, as listeners. The human being is made such by his ability to listen to God."

[23] Citing proposition 55.

that ecclesial sense by which the interpretation of Scripture should be a work of building up the church. In his *Jesus of Nazareth*, xvi–xvii,[24] Benedict XVI had at least four things to say about the historical-critical method. The historical-critical method is an indispensable tool, given the historical structure of the Christian faith, but it does not exhaust the interpretive task for someone who sees the biblical writings as a single corpus of Holy Scripture inspired by God. Second, as a *historical* method, it is limited to the past and considers moving to today's present as overstepping its bounds. Third, it is bound to treat as human words the biblical words it investigates; it may sense a higher dimension than the human word but considers that beyond its specific object. Finally, it considers the individual books in the context of their historical periods but pays little attention to the unity of all these writings as one "Bible."

This section of the exhortation runs for almost forty pages, from numbers 29 to 49. Parts of the text show signs of having been worked over several times. There seem to be differing emphases in different parts—the effort to be integrative of the whole tradition in the matter has not always smoothed out the rough edges.[25] Nonetheless, seven major statements stand out clearly: interpretation as an ecclesial task, the word of God as address to believers in the present, the hermeneutic of faith, the unity of the literal sense and the spiritual sense, Scripture as the soul of theology, the saints as living interpretation of Scripture, and Bible and ecumenism.

Interpretation, an Ecclesial Task

The primary setting for scriptural interpretation is the life of the church; the ecclesial context is intrinsic to interpretation (no. 29). The intrinsic link between the Word and faith means that authentic interpretation must be situated within the faith of the church and build up that faith. The Bible was written by the people of God for the people of God, under the inspiration of the Holy Spirit (no. 30). Saint Thomas Aquinas insisted that "the letter even that of the Gospel, would kill, were there not the inward grace of healing faith."[26] Saint Bonaventure stated that without faith there is

[24] *Jesus of Nazareth: From the Baptism in the Jordan to the Transfiguration* (New York and London: Doubleday, 2007).

[25] It should be remembered that, though the responsibility is the pope's, the synod had voted a committee of twelve bishops/cardinals (to which the pope appointed three members) to help with editing the exhortation. Besides, the striking collegiality of the pope in this exhortation has been noted.

[26] *Summa Theologiae*, Ia–IIae, q. 106, art. 2.

no key to throw open the sacred text. This means that "access to a proper understanding of biblical texts is only granted to the person who has an affinity with what the text is saying on the basis of life experience."[27]

A Living and Timely Word, Not a Word from the Past

Already in the introduction to this apostolic exhortation, the pope stated that one of his concerns in writing this exhortation was that "the Bible may not be simply a word from the past, but a living and timely word" (see citation at the head of this chapter). Because God speaks and acts in history for our good and for our integral salvation, it is decisive to present the word of God in its capacity to enter into dialogue with the everyday problems that people face. In that way, the word of God becomes "a response to our questions, a broadening of our values and the fulfillment of our aspirations" (no. 23). True exegesis thus "finds the reality of faith expressed [in the text] but also seeks to link this reality to the experience of faith in our present world" (no. 37).[28] In the language of hermeneutics, one can say that the interpretive task involves a "listening" dimension that is not just *explanation* (cognitive, information) but a process of *understanding*,[29] whereby one comes to awareness and integrates a new experience into one's psyche. To cite from the exposition in chapter 7 of this book, there is no adequate interpretation of the biblical text without attending to its truth claims. Meaning ultimately involves appropriation (Ricoeur) or "transformative understanding" (Schneiders). Understanding expands the existential reality of the knower. The ultimate goal of interpretation, the existential augmentation of the reader, takes place in her or his participation, through the text, in the world before the text.[30]

The pope warns that a certain reductive approach leaves the biblical text in the past. There is even a secularized hermeneutic that is convinced that God does not intervene in human history, and so whatever appears as a divine element must be reduced to the human (no. 35). Such hermeneutic denies, for example, the institution of the Eucharist and the resurrection of Christ. It holds to a purely rationalistic exegesis in which reason is not harmonized with faith, or which sticks to one method, ignoring the

---

[27] Citing the Pontifical Biblical Commission, The Interpretation of the Bible in the Church, II, A, 2.

[28] Ibid.

[29] Cf. Anthony C. Thiselton, *Hermeneutics: An Introduction* (Grand Rapids: Wm. Eerdmans, 2009) 8.

[30] Schneiders, *Revelatory Text*, 167.

need for a comprehensive exegesis (no. 36). It needs to be remembered that the various hermeneutical approaches have their own philosophical underpinnings, and not all these presuppositions are in conformity with the faith of the church. Catholics need to examine the presuppositions of the various methods to make sure they are in conformity with the faith.

A Hermeneutic of Faith

The pope called exegetes back to Vatican Council II's biblical hermeneutic, which he referred to several times as a "hermeneutic of faith." It is contained in *Dei Verbum*, 12, which he cites over five times in this section. *Dei Verbum*, 12, ruled that the interpreter of Sacred Scripture "should carefully search out the meaning which the sacred writers really had in mind, that meaning which God had thought well to manifest through the medium of their words" (no. 34). To elucidate this, the interpreter is asked to interpret the Bible according to the same Spirit by which it was written.[31] Three fundamental criteria for interpreting the Bible according the same Spirit by which it was written are the following:

> *The content and unity of the whole of Scripture.* The whole of Scripture being one, the parts mutually explain and complement one another; later texts take up and update earlier ones.

> *The living tradition of the whole church.* Here regard is had to how the church, head and members, have interpreted Scripture across time and space and interpret it today. The *living* aspect of tradition, as we saw in chapter 7, may introduce new awareness or modify past tradition. Here belongs also the authority of the magisterium to authentically interpret the word of God, although "this teaching office is not above the word of God but serves it" (*DV*, 10).

> *The analogy of faith* or the harmony that exists between elements of the faith.

These three criteria are the roots of theological exegesis and must go hand in hand with and complete historical exegesis.

Here and there a second line of reflection is adumbrated of what interpreting the Bible according to the same Spirit by which it was written

---

[31] *Lineamenta*, 19, already stated as follows: "but the Spirit also brings home (cf. John 14:15-17, 25, 26; 15:26–16:15) to each person individually everything that is spoken in the proclamation of the word of God for the good of the whole gathering of the faithful."

involved. This is the case, for example, when Benedict XVI writes that students in formation "need to have a deep spiritual life in order to appreciate that the Scripture can only be understood if it is lived" (no. 47). Or, when he cites Origen to the effect that "the best way to know God is through love, and that there can be no authentic *scientia Christi* [knowledge of Christ] apart from growth in his love" (no. 86). Or, as said above (see "Interpretation, an Ecclesial Task"), "access to a proper understanding of biblical texts is only granted to the person who has an affinity with what the text is saying on the basis of life experience."[32] The pope adds a comment from The Interpretation of the Bible in the Church to the effect that "as the reader matures in the life of the Spirit, so there grows also his or her capacity to understand the realities of which the Bible speaks."[33] A scholar who considered this aspect in a very balanced manner was de la Potterie.[34]

The Unity of the Literal Sense and the Spiritual Sense

Language of the *literal sense* and the *spiritual sense* originated from 1 Corinthians 3:6, where Paul opposed "letter" and "spirit": the letter kills, the spirit gives life. He seemed to suggest that the Jews of his time did not accept Christ because they held on to the letter of their Scriptures, ignoring their inner religious meaning (the spirit). Hence arose, already with Origen (185–254), the distinction between the literal and spiritual senses of Scripture, and this later developed into the patristic and medieval four senses of Scripture. The reader should consult the definition and qualifications of the literal sense and the spiritual given in chapter 6 and the section on Luke Timothy Johnson in chapter 7. In chapter 6, the literal sense was described as "the meaning conveyed by the words of Scripture and discovered by exegesis, following the rules of sound interpretation" (*Catechism of the Catholic Church*, 116), while the spiritual sense was defined as "the meaning expressed by the biblical texts when read, under the influence of the Holy Spirit, in the context of the paschal mystery of Christ and of the new life which flows from it."[35]

[32] Citing the Pontifical Biblical Commission, Interpretation of the Bible in the Church, II, A, 2.

[33] Ibid.

[34] Ignace de la Potterie, "Interpretation of Holy Scripture in the Spirit in Which It Was Written (*Dei Verbum* 12c)," *Vatican II: Assessment and Perspectives*, vol. 1, ed. René Latourelle (New York: Paulist Press, 1988) 220–66.

[35] Interpretation of the Bible in the Church, II, B, 2.

His Holiness insists that to distinguish two *levels* of approach to the Bible in no way means to separate or oppose them, nor simply to juxtapose them. They exist in reciprocity (no. 35). The historical-critical and the theological aspects are merely two *dimensions,* two methodological *levels* of the one hermeneutic of faith. The pope carefully details the history of magisterial intervention in the matter of the harmony of historical and theological exegesis (no. 33) through recourse to the important address of John Paul II in presenting The Interpretation of the Bible in the Church. John Paul II outlined how Pope Leo XIII in *Providentissimus Deus* (1893) protected Catholic exegesis from the inroads of rationalism "without, however, seeking refuge in a spiritual meaning, detached from history" (no. 35). When Pius XII was faced with attacks on the part of those who proposed a so-called mystical exegesis that rejected any form of scientific approach, his *Divino Afflante Spiritu* (1943)

> was careful to avoid any hint of a dichotomy between "scientific ex-
> egesis" for use in apologetics and "spiritual interpretation meant for
> internal use"; rather it affirmed both the "theological significance of
> the literal sense, methodically defined" and the fact that "determin-
> ing the spiritual sense . . . belongs itself to the realm of exegetical
> science." (ibid.)

In this way, these popes affirmed the "incarnational principle" enunci-
ated by John Paul II, rejecting "a split between the human and the divine, between scientific research and respect for the faith, between the literal sense and the spiritual sense."[36]

This incarnational principle had been carefully maintained by the Pon-
tifical Biblical Commission in its 1993 document, The Interpretation of the Bible in the Church, when it said that, "contrary to a current view, there is not necessarily a distinction between the literal sense and the spiritual sense," at least for the New Testament and many texts of the Old Testament.[37] However, the type of literalism championed by the *fundamentalist approach* to Scripture seeks precisely to escape the closeness of the divine and the human, refusing to "[perceive] *in* the words *the* Word himself" (no. 44).

---

[36] John Paul II, Address on the Interpretation of the Bible in the Church (April 23, 1993), 5, on the occasion of the presentation of the document of the Pontifical Biblical Commission, The Interpretation of the Bible in the Church. This important address is printed at the head of The Interpretation of the Bible in the Church.
[37] II, B, 2.

The true response is the faith-filled interpretation of Sacred Scripture. For further information on fundamentalism, see chapter 9 of this book.

Scripture as the "Soul of Theology"

Dei Verbum, 24, said that "the study of the sacred page should be the very soul of sacred theology." The pope conveyed the heartfelt thanks of the synod fathers to the Pontifical Biblical Commission, past and present, and to the many exegetes and theologians who through their dedication and competence have made an essential contribution to the deeper understanding of the meaning of the Scriptures (no. 31). He noted, nevertheless, that the synod felt a need to look into the present state of biblical studies and their standing within the field of theology (ibid.). He insisted that the one flows into the other when both theology and Bible studies are done right:

> Where exegesis is not theology, Scripture cannot be the soul of theology, and conversely, where theology is not essentially the interpretation of the Church's Scripture, such a theology no longer has a foundation. (no. 35; citing Benedict XVI, Intervention at the Fourteenth General Congregation of the Synod, October 14, 2008)

So, the study of Scripture must present the word of God as addressed to today's world, to the church, and to each of us personally (no. 47). If exegesis would "perceive the divine word in the text,"[38] doctrine would have the function of arranging this divine Word in some systematic and unfolding order in intimate relation to tradition. Students need a deep spiritual life to appreciate that Scripture can only be understood if it is lived. "Emphasis must be placed on the indispensable interplay of exegesis, theology, spirituality, and mission" (no. 82).[39] Academic formation must induce a "profoundly ecclesial spirit," taking due account of the interventions of the magisterium and imparting instruction based on the conviction that "sacred Tradition, sacred Scripture and the magisterium of the Church are so connected and associated that one of them cannot stand without the others" (no. 47).[40] In the mind of the pope, the organic link between Scripture, tradition, and magisterial teaching should be the model for organizing theology. The pope recalled the synod recommendation that

[38] John Paul II, *Allocutio* of April 23, 1993, on the occasion of the release of The Interpretation of the Bible in the Church (now in The Interpretation of the Bible in the Church, 1993, page 15, no. 9).

[39] Citing proposition 32.

[40] Citing *DV*, 10.

episcopal conferences promote a closer working relationship between pastors, exegetes, and theologians (proposition 28), and grounded this in a similar proposal of *Dei Verbum*, 23, that called for Catholic exegetes and other workers in the field of sacred theology to work diligently with one another and under the watchful eye of the magisterium.

Among other things, proposition 32 had hoped for "a renewal of academic programs . . . so that the systematic study of theology is better seen in the light of sacred Scripture." His Holiness preferred tactical changes to structural ones. The problem, as he saw it, was one of the relationship between biblical studies and scriptural prayer, the reciprocity of scientific exegesis and the personal relationship with God's word induced by *lectio divina* (no. 82).

The Saints and the Interpretation of Scripture

Number 48 on the saints and the interpretation of Scripture is a beautifully written text, advancing thoughts contained in all the synod documents. The principle is *viva lectio est vita bonorum* (the life of saints is a living interpretation of Scripture).[41] The saints are the most profound and living exegesis of the Word. "Every saint is like a ray of light streaming forth from the word of God" (no. 48). The Holy Spirit who inspired the sacred authors is the same Spirit who impels the saints to offer their lives for the gospel. Great currents of spirituality in the church's history originated with an explicit reference to Scripture. For example, St. Anthony the Abbot's life was changed by simply hearing Matthew 19:21: "If you wish to be perfect, go, sell your possessions, and give the money to the poor, and you will have treasure in heaven; then come, follow me." Saint Thérèse of the Child Jesus discovered her vocation as love at the heart of the church by reading 1 Corinthians 13. Of course, as said earlier, the Blessed Virgin Mary remains the "Mother of Faith" who "by her 'yes' to the word of the covenant and her mission, perfectly fulfills the divine vocation of humanity" (no. 27).[42] Later, in number 83, His Holiness called the consecrated life "a living 'exegesis' of God's word,"[43] in that "every charism and every rule springs from it and seeks to be an expression of it."[44]

[41] St. Gregory the Great, *Moralia in Job*, XXIV, VIII, 16.

[42] Citing proposition 55.

[43] Citing his Homily for the World Day of Consecrated Life (February 2, 2008) and John Paul II, post-synodal apostolic exhortation *Vita Consecrata* (1996) 82.

[44] Citing Congregation for Institutes of Consecrated Life and for Societies of Apostolic Life, Starting Afresh from Christ: A Renewed Commitment to Consecrated Life in the Third Millennium (2002) 24.

Some Questions That Arise

Reviewing the material on the interpretation of the Bible, it appears that the citation of the view of *Divino Afflante Spiritu* concerning the "theological significance of the literal sense, methodically defined . . . [and that] determining the spiritual sense . . . belongs itself to the realm of exegetical science" indicates a point of tension in recent exegesis. One issue among scholars had been the question whether the literal sense was also carrier of religious meaning and to what extent exegetical method was able to access the divine meaning of Scripture.[45] Some tended to distinguish the historical sense (meaning linked with the author in the past) from the literal sense (see Luke Timothy Johnson in chapter 7); others opined that the literal sense concerned merely questions of grammar and semantics. The strong affirmation about "the theological significance of the literal sense, methodologically defined," looks like a conscious rebuttal of certain views in the field.

The patristic four senses of Scripture are treated in number 37. They have not been structurally integrated into the criteria of theological exegesis in *Dei Verbum*, 12 (see "A Hermeneutic of Faith" above), but have been given beside these, appearing almost as a parallel scheme for theological exegesis or as, perhaps, another way of studying Sacred Scripture as a whole and in the light of faith. Further, the dictum of St. Thomas Aquinas that "all the senses of sacred Scripture are based on the literal sense"[46] is mentioned, but it is not clear to what extent this was meant to be a touchstone for discerning the valid use of these four senses. The four senses are described as the literal, allegorical, moral, and anagogical (*anagogē* means "leading," that is, to our final end) senses. The literal sense is described as "the meaning conveyed by the words of Scripture and discovered by exegesis, following the rules of sound interpretation" (no. 37; *Catechism*, 116). It is the foundation for all the other senses of Scripture. The allegorical sense gives "a more profound understanding of events by recognizing their significance in Christ"—for example, the Red Sea as a type of Christ's victory or sign of Christian baptism. In hermeneutics, such is called typology.[47] The moral

---

[45] The saying in *Verbum Domini*, 38, "there is need to transcend the letter for the word of God can never simply be equated with the letter of the text," unless understood within the context, would seem to cohere with some difficulty with all the assertions concerning the unity of literal and spiritual sense and that the literal sense itself has theological significance.

[46] *Summa Theologiae*, I, q. 1, a. 10, ad. 1.

[47] In chapter 4, we distinguished typology from allegory—one is rooted in correspondences seen in events, institutions, and person; the other merely discovers literary correspondences.

sense instructs us how to act justly. The anagogical sense views realities
and events in the light of their eternal significance, leading us toward our
true homeland, for example, the church on earth as sign of the heavenly
Jerusalem (*Catechism*, 117). The last three make up the spiritual sense, thus
leaving mainly two senses, the *literal sense* and the *spiritual sense*. The pope
cites the medieval couplet in which this teaching is enshrined (no. 37):

> The letter speaks of deeds; allegory about the faith; the moral about
> our actions; anagogy about our destiny.[48]

The Pontifical Biblical document The Jewish People and Their Sacred
Scriptures in the Christian Bible, 20, singled out an element of the patristic
use of typology/allegory for comment, namely, the issue of "detaching
each detail from its context and severing the relationship between the
biblical text and the concrete reality of salvation history. Interpretation
then became arbitrary." The teaching may have been animated by faith,
"but such teaching was not based on the commented text. It was superimposed on it" (ibid.).

Types are "persons, institutions, and events of the Old Testament which
are regarded as divinely established models or pre-representations of corresponding realities in New Testament salvation history."[49] Not all scholars
are agreed that typology is a valid hermeneutical move. For example, R. T.
France has this to say on the matter:

> If every type were originally intended explicitly to point forward to an
> antitype, it might be correct to classify typology as a style of exegesis.
> But this is not the case. There is no indication in a type, as such, of
> any forward reference; it is complete and intelligible in itself.[50]

On the contrary, there is no doubt that following the lead of the Scriptures themselves we may discover typological meanings retrospectively.
Sidney Greidanus[51] insists, correctly, that a type must first have symbolic
meaning in Old Testament times, that is, it must first be a symbol before

[48] *Littera gesta docet, quid credas allegoria, moralis quid agas, quo tendas anagogia.*

[49] Walter Eichrodt, "Is Typological Exegesis an Appropriate Method?" in *Essays in Old Testament Hermeneutics*, ed. Claus Westermann, 224–45, here 225 (Richmond: John Knox, 1963).

[50] *Jesus and the Old Testament: His Application of the Old Testament Passages to Himself and His Mission* (London: Tyndale, 1971) 41.

[51] *Preaching Christ from the Old Testament: A Contemporary Hermeneutical Method* (Grand Rapids: Wm. Eerdmans, 1999) 250–60.

one may posit an antitype in the New. The Pontifical Biblical Commission put it this way:

> The Old Testament itself progressively opens up a perspective of fulfillment that is final and definitive. The Exodus . . . becomes the symbol of final salvation. Liberation from the Babylonian Exile and the prospect of an eschatological salvation are described as a new Exodus. Christian interpretation is situated along these lines.[52]

For the comments of His Holiness on Christians, Jews, and the Sacred Scriptures (no. 43), the reader should see chapter 4 of this book.

The Bible and Ecumenism

On the Bible and ecumenism (no. 46), the pope endorsed the proposal of the synod fathers that "shared listening to the Scriptures . . . spurs us on towards the dialogue of charity and enables growth in the dialogue of truth" (proposition 36). He agreed with the synod fathers that there should be an increase in ecumenical study, discussions, and celebrations of the word of God, though adding "with due respect for existing norms and the variety of traditions." Celebrations of the word of God should be moments of intense prayer and hope for a future in God's time when we can all share the one table and one cup. Common translations of the Bible into the vernacular have ecumenical importance; however, there

> *"Desire is not enough"*
>
> *Readiness for "sacrifice [of] laws and structures"*
>
> *"Fusion of two pieces of gold to achieve a new entity in unity"*

should be no dissimulation of differences, for example, in the understanding of the decisive role of the magisterium in the authoritative interpretation of the Bible.

Among proposals from the floor of the synod, a synod father[53] urged that the churches of East and West agree upon a common day for the celebration of Easter. Another[54] relayed the question of his Orthodox neighbors as to what extent the church's diplomatic apparatus conformed to the word of God and urged, "desire is not enough. We have to be willing

---

[52] The Jewish People and Their Sacred Scriptures in the Christian Bible, no. 21.
[53] Bishop Felix Toppo, SJ, bishop of Jamshedpur, India.
[54] Bishop Fragkiskos Papamanólis, OFM, bishop of Syros, Greece, October 15, 2008.

to sacrifice laws and structures to prepare for the blessed day we Christians will be united . . . [as] a fusion of two pieces of gold to achieve a new entity in unity."

Questions for Discussion

1. What are the pope's goals in this exhortation? How does he place himself in relation to the synod?

2. Discuss the analogy of the word. What questions does it seek to answer?

3. Outline the role of the Holy Spirit in relation to the word of God.

4. What is tradition? Discuss its relation to Scripture.

5. Discuss the seven aspects of the interpretation of Scripture in the church.

6. How, in your opinion, can Scripture become the "soul of theology"?

7. "Determining the spiritual sense belongs to the realm of exegetical science." Discuss.

8. What steps could the church take toward ecumenism? What should be avoided?

Chapter 11

Verbum Domini,
Part II: The Word in the Church

The Church . . . is a community that hears and proclaims the word of God . . . from the Gospel she discovers ever anew the direction for her journey . . . only those who first place themselves in an attitude of listening to the word can go on to become its heralds.

Verbum Domini, 51

This chapter comments on part II of the apostolic exhortation *Verbum Domini,* titled *Verbum in Ecclesia* (The Word in the Church). The caption for this second part is John 1:12: "But to all who received him he gave power to become children of God." It comprises three chapters: The Word of God and the Church; The Liturgy, Privileged Setting for the Word of God; and The Word of God in the Life of the Church.

The Word of God and the Church

The ear is the organ that defines the church: she is the community of those who hear and proclaim the word of God. In a profound sense, the church is "the home of the Word."[1] The goal of the Word is a new creation: "to all who received him he gave power to become children of God" (John 1:12). To receive him is to undergo radical transformation, to be conformed to him (no. 50). Saint Augustine put it succinctly, as always: "you were created through the word, but now through the word you must be recreated" (ibid.).[2] The Holy Spirit induces in each member of the faithful

[1] Message to the People of God, III, 6.
[2] *Tractate on John's Gospel,* I, 12.

147

a deep and living friendship with Christ, the Word, who is always present in the life of the church. Hearers of the Word become heralds of the Word.

The Liturgy, Privileged Setting for the Word of God

This second chapter of part II compares in length with the chapter on the interpretation of Scripture in the church in part I. I comment on the following seven salient features: the Holy Spirit, the sacramentality of the Word, the word of God and the Eucharist, the word of God and silence, the word of God and the other sacraments, the word of God and the Liturgy of the Hours, and celebrations of the word of God.

The Holy Spirit Makes the Word Effective

Christ himself "is present in his word, since it is he who speaks when Scripture is read in Church" (no. 52),[3] but it is the Holy Spirit, who by interiorly working on the soul of the believer makes the Word "effective in the hearts of the faithful," bringing home to each person what has been proclaimed "for the good of the whole gathering" (ibid.). In so doing, the Spirit makes the Word a *living* word that promotes the encounter of the believer with his or her Lord. We saw in chapter 10 that the same Holy Spirit enlightens the heart of the believer to understand the Scriptures and to respond to the God who calls through the words of Scripture.

The Sacramentality of the Word

The synod fathers expressed the hope that the sacramentality of the Word could be promoted (proposition 7). Benedict XVI obliged with an outline of such a theology of the Word. The starting point is the concept of the Hebrew *dabar*, which means both word and event: what God *says*, God *does*—God's word in history has a performative character (nos. 53, 56). In the mystery of revelation, God discloses God's self through "deeds and words having an inner unity" (*DV*, 2). In the church's sacramental life there is, through the action of the Holy Spirit, the unity of gesture and word (no. 53). "The Word of God can be perceived by faith through the 'sign' of human words and actions" (no. 56). The sacramentality of the Word bears analogy with the real presence of Christ under the appearances of bread and wine (ibid.). In the church's great tradition it is said that "God's Scripture is also understood as the Body of Christ" (*corpus Christi intel-*

---

[3] Citing Vatican II, Constitution on the Sacred Liturgy, *Sacrosanctum Concilium*, 7.

ligitur etiam . . . Scriptura Dei).[4] In John 6, Jesus proclaimed himself "the Bread of Life." The discourse that follows presents Jesus as nourishment for pilgrims on the heavenly journey, "not only in the Eucharist but also in reading sacred Scripture."[5]

The Word of God and the Eucharist

"Word and Eucharist are thus so deeply bound together that we cannot understand one without the other" (no. 55). We see this already in the two disciples on the road to Emmaus in Luke 24. The stranger first set the hearts of the disciples on fire with the Word as he "interpreted to them the things about himself in all the scriptures" (Luke 24:27). Then at the breaking of bread "their eyes were opened, and they recognized him" (Luke 24:31). Under these guiding principles, the pope made determinations on some practical matters of the eucharistic liturgy.

In the construction of churches, bishops are to take care that the sacred space eloquently "present[s] the Christian mystery in relation to the word of God." The acoustics are to promote the proclamation of the Word (no. 68, citing proposition 40). The *ambo*, "from which the word of God is proclaimed, . . . should be fixed, and decorated in aesthetic harmony with the *altar*," thus displaying the twofold table of the Word and of the Eucharist. "The readings, the responsorial psalm and the *Exsultet* are to be proclaimed from the ambo," which "can also be used for the homily and the prayers of the faithful" (ibid.).[6]

The proposal of the synod to give a place of honor to the Sacred Scriptures, even outside of liturgical celebrations,[7] is good, provided that such place of honor in no way obstructs the "central place proper to the *tabernacle* containing the Blessed Sacrament."[8]

The current *Lectionary* puts on display the interplay of the Old and New Testaments "in which Christ is the central figure, commemorated in his paschal mystery" (no. 57).[9] The synod reaffirmed the practice never to replace readings drawn from Scripture with other texts, no matter how

---

[4] No. 54, note 191.

[5] St. Jerome, *Commentary on Ecclesiastes*, III. PL 23, 1092A.

[6] Cf. *General Instruction of the Roman Missal*, 309.

[7] Proposition 14.

[8] Here Benedict XVI refers to his post-synodal apostolic exhortation *Sacramentum Caritatis* (February 22, 2007) 69.

[9] *Order of Readings of the Mass*, 66.

significant.[10] "This is an ancient rule of the Church which is to be main-tained" (no. 69).

"The *Responsorial Psalm* is also word of God, and hence should not be replaced by other texts; indeed it is most appropriate that it be sung" (ibid.). Preference in liturgical celebrations is to be given to songs of clear biblical inspiration, which through music reinforce the message of the word of God (no. 70). In this connection, the pope mentioned the Gregorian chant as an example of "those songs handed down by the church's tradition which respect this criterion" (ibid.).

The *gospel* is proclaimed by a priest or deacon; in the Latin rite, the first and second readings are proclaimed by an appointed reader, man or woman. The synod "stressed the need for the adequate training of those who exercise the *munus* [office] of reader in liturgical celebrations" (no. 58). In fact, the *Order of the Readings of Mass*, 55, specified that "this training should be biblical and liturgical, as well as technical" (art of public reading).

The *homily* helps the faithful realize that God's word is present and at work in their everyday lives. The preacher must feel "a compelling desire to present Christ, who must stand at the center of every homily" (no. 59). The quality of homilies needs to be improved. The preacher is to prepare for the homily by meditation and prayer, so as to "be the first to hear the word of God which he proclaims."[11] Whenever possible,[12] a brief homily is to be given at weekday masses with the people. The synod hoped that a Directory on the Homily could be elaborated (proposition 15). His Holiness asked the competent dicasteries to prepare one along the lines of the Eucharistic Compendium.

The Word of God and Silence

Proposition 14 drew attention to the *General Instruction on the Roman Missal*, 56, which called for silence after the first and second readings, and also after the homily. The pope commented that the word of God could only be spoken and heard in silence, outward and inward (no. 66). Silence, when called for, should be considered "a part of the celebration."[13]

---

[10] Proposition 14: no text of spirituality or literature can equal the value and riches contained in Sacred Scripture, which is the word of God.

[11] Citing proposition 15.

[12] Proposition 15 said categorically, "there should be a homily at every mass *cum populo*, even during the week."

[13] Cf. *General Instruction of the Roman Missal*, 45.

In fact, the Liturgy of the word should be celebrated in a way that favors meditation.[14]

The Word of God and the Other Sacraments

The individual penitent is encouraged to prepare for the sacrament of reconciliation by meditating on a suitable text of Sacred Scripture and to use a prayer based on the words of Scripture for expressing contrition (no. 61). The rite already provides for Scripture texts that may be read or listened to at the beginning of confession. Whenever possible or opportune, individual confessions could take place within penitential celebrations of the word of God. Similarly, when circumstances permit, community celebrations of the anointing of the sick can be done within a celebration of the Word.

The word of God is at the very origin of *marriage* (cf. Gen 2:24). In fact, the union of the Christian couple is sign of the mystery of the union of Christ with the church (no. 85; cf. Eph 5:31-32). In the face of attacks on the family, it is the word of God that anchors in Christ "the faithful, reciprocal and fruitful" love of the Christian couple (ibid.).

The Word of God and the Liturgy of the Hours

As the public prayer of the church, the *Liturgy of the Hours* sanctifies the entire day through a rhythm of hearing the word of God and praying the Psalms. Participation by the faithful in this celebration can only lead to greater familiarity with the word of God. His Holiness recommends that, wherever possible, parishes and religious communities promote this prayer with the participation of the faithful, especially on the First Vespers of Sundays and Solemnities (no. 62).

Celebrations of the Word of God

The synod had recommended "celebrations of the word of God on pilgrimages, special feasts, popular missions, spiritual retreats and special days of penance, reparation or pardon" (proposition 18). His Holiness endorsed all this (no. 65). Popular piety, "not to be confused with liturgical celebrations," may also profit from the proclamation of the word of God (ibid.). Celebrations of the Word are a fitting way to prepare for the Sunday Eucharist. They are also a very good way to meditate on and pray the Lectionary, especially during the great liturgical seasons of Advent,

---

[14] Ibid., 56.

Christmas, Lent, and Easter. They are to be highly recommended where there is no priest on Sundays and holy days of obligation, keeping in mind indications already set forth in the apostolic exhortation *Sacramentum Caritatis* with regard to Sunday celebrations in the absence of a priest. The synod had recommended that ritual directories be formulated, based on the experience of the churches in which well-formed catechists regularly conduct Sunday assemblies around the word of God (proposition 18). His Holiness gave determination to this by recommending "that the competent authorities prepare ritual directories, drawing on the experience of the particular churches," while avoiding the danger of the confusion of such celebrations of the Word with the celebration of the Eucharist (no. 65). On the contrary, the celebrations should be privileged moments of prayer for God to send holy priests after God's own heart (ibid.). An experience from Honduras mentioned during the synod showed that vocations to the priesthood actually grew from the institution since 1966 of "Delegates of the Word." These Delegates were laypeople who have been given a special biblical formation and authorized by the bishop to animate various ecclesial communities.[15] The program became a source of priestly vocations, such that Bishop Plante said that "in my diocese of Choluteca, for example, all young priests were Delegates of the Word."

The Word of God in the Life of the Church

In section 3 of part II, I highlight six specifications of His Holiness, namely, frequent reading of Scripture and the biblical formation of Christians, the Bible as soul of pastoral activity, the word of God and charisms in the church, the prayerful reading of Sacred Scripture and *lectio divina*, the word of God and Marian prayer, and the word of God and the Holy Land.

Biblical Formation of Christians: Biblical Spirituality

The Bible is the means "by which God speaks daily to believers."[16] It is "the first source of all Christian spirituality. It gives rise to a personal relationship

---

[15] Bishop Guido Plante of Choluteca, Honduras, October 11, 2008, gave their origin as follows: In March 1966 in the wake of Vatican II's Constitution on the Sacred Liturgy, Bishop Marcelo Gérin of Choluteca trained seventeen peasants and sent them to celebrate Holy Week in isolated communities without a priest. The enthusiasm was so great that the communities requested celebrations each Sunday. Thus arose the Delegates of the Word of God, now over ten thousand in Honduras and neighboring countries.

[16] St. Jerome, *Epistula*, 133, 13.

with the living God and with his saving and sanctifying will."[17] Benedict XVI echoed the synod fathers in their hope for the flowering of "a new season of greater love for sacred Scripture on the part of every member of the People of God so that their prayerful and faith-filled reading of the Bible will, with time, deepen their personal relationship with Jesus" (no. 72).[18] When one makes frequent encounter with Christ in his word the center of one's spiritual life, one is impelled toward the highest ideals of Christian living (ibid.).

What has been said will require the biblical formation of Christians. The pope echoed the recommendation of the synod fathers that "centers of formation should be established where laity and missionaries could be trained to understand, live and proclaim the word of God," this possibly through use of existing academic structures (no. 75). Also, "where needed, specialized institutes for biblical studies should be established to ensure that exegetes possess a solid understanding of theology and an appropriate appreciation for the contexts in which they carry out their mission."[19] The reading of the Bible has improved greatly among Catholics since Vatican II, though for many spirituality is still nurtured by private devotions and hagiography. The pope's determination here, if followed, will change the face of Catholic spirituality.

The Bible as Soul of Pastoral Activity

The synod fathers called for the Bible to inspire all pastoral activity (proposition 30). Rather than new programs or meetings, the pope saw this as really calling for "examining the ordinary activities of Christian communities . . . to see if they are truly concerned with fostering a personal encounter with Christ, who gives himself to us in his word" (no. 73). Fostering such encounters with Christ through pastoral activity will be the best way to deal with the proliferation of *sects*.

Luke's description of Christ's meeting with the two disciples on the way to Emmaus (Luke 24:13-35) gives us the model of a *catechesis* centered on the explanation of the Scriptures (no. 74).[20] The *General Directory for Catechesis* contains valuable guidelines for a biblically inspired catechesis and is to be consulted for this.[21] It also shows the relationship in catechesis between Sacred Scripture and the *Catechism of the Catholic Church*:

[17] John Paul II, *Vita Consecrata*, 94, cited in *Instrumentum Laboris*, 52.

[18] Proposition 9.

[19] Proposition 31.

[20] Cf. proposition 23.

[21] In fact, the document of the Pontifical Biblical Commission, The Interpretation of the Bible in the Church, 123, affirmed that "Scripture provides the starting-point, foundation

Sacred Scripture as, "the word of God written under the inspiration of the Holy Spirit," . . . and the *Catechism of the Catholic Church,* as a significant contemporary expression of the living Tradition of the Church and a sure norm for teaching the faith, are called, each in its own way and according to its specific authority, to nourish catechesis in the Church of today.[22]

His Holiness did not pick up the part of proposition 23 that called for a formal postbaptismal mystagogy, perhaps because this was overtaken by the many opportunities being created for Christians to be formed by the word of God through the Bible and in relation to the *Catechism of the Catholic Church.*

The Word of God and Charisms in the Church

The word of God "calls each one of us personally, revealing that life itself is a vocation from God" (no. 77). It impels each one to holiness "in and through the definitive choices by which we respond to his love in our lives," and the tasks and ministries we undertake to build up the church and our world (ibid.). In other words, in every vocation in the church, the Word calls us to be saints (cf. Rom 1:7).

Ordained ministers must remember that "the word of God is indispensable in forming the heart of a good shepherd and minister of the word" (no. 78).[23] To *bishops,* the pope recommended frequent personal reading and study of Sacred Scripture in imitation of Mary, "*Virgo Audiens* [Listening Virgin] and Queen of the Apostles" (ibid.). *Priests,* who are first of all ministers of the Word, consecrated and sent to announce the Good News of the kingdom, must approach the Word with docile and prayerful hearts so that it may deeply penetrate their thoughts and feelings and bring about a new outlook in them—the mind of Christ.[24] The *Directory for the Permanent Diaconate,* 74, notes that "a characteristic element of diaconal spirituality is the word of God, of which the *deacon* is called to be an authoritative preacher." It rules that deacons are to be introduced to "sacred Scripture and its correct interpretation; to the relationship between Scripture and Tradition, in particular to the use of Scripture in preaching, in catechesis

---

and norm of catechetical teaching. One of the goals of catechesis should be to initiate a person in a correct understanding and fruitful reading of the Bible."

[22] *General Directory for Catechesis,* 128.

[23] Proposition 31.

[24] Cf. John Paul II, post-synodal apostolic exhortation *Pastores Dabo Vobis,* 26.

and in pastoral activity in general."[25] The synod fathers proposed that *candidates for Holy Orders* "must learn to love the word of God. Scripture should thus be the soul of their theological formation, and emphasis must be given to the indispensable interplay of exegesis, theology, spirituality and mission" (no. 82).[26] The pope concurs. They are to be trained in *lectio divina*; however, "such attention to prayerful reading of Scripture must not in any way lead to a dichotomy with regard to the exegetical studies which are a part of formation" (ibid.). Rather, they are to be "helped to see *the relationship between biblical studies and scriptural prayer.*" To this end, the study of Scripture is to be through methods that foster such an integral approach. As pointed out in chapter 10 of this book, His Holiness quietly bypassed calls for structural changes of curricula.[27]

The *consecrated life* presents "a living 'exegesis' of God's word" (no. 83).[28] "Every charism and every rule springs from it and seeks to be an expression of it"[29]; each opens up a new pathway of Christian living marked by the radicalism of the gospel. The pope echoed the synod when he recommended that "communities of consecrated life always make provision for solid instruction in the faith-filled reading of the Bible" (ibid.; proposition 24).The *lay faithful* do their part in the building up of the kingdom by engaging in temporal matters and participating in earthly activities. They "need to be trained to discern God's will through a familiarity with the word of God, read and studied in the church under the guidance of her legitimate pastors" (no. 84). The pope echoed the synod recommendation that, "wherever possible, dioceses themselves should provide an opportunity for continued formation to lay persons charged with particular ecclesial responsibilities" (ibid.). The synod also urged that every household own a Bible to be kept in a worthy place and used for reading and prayer. Small communities of families may also be formed through common prayer and meditation on passages of Scripture.

---

[25] *Directory for the Permanent Diaconate*, 81.

[26] Proposition 32.

[27] Proposition 32 apparently included a call for such, when it said, "a renewal of academic programs is also hoped for . . . so that the systematic study of theology is better seen in the light of Sacred Scripture. Moreover, a revision of courses in seminaries and houses of formation must be attentive that the word of God have its deserved place in the various dimensions of formation."

[28] Benedict XVI, Homily for the World Day of Consecrated Life (February 22, 2008).

[29] Congregation for Institutes of Consecrated Life and for Societies of Apostolic Life, *Starting Afresh from Christ: A Renewed Commitment to Consecrated Life in the Third Millennium* (May 19, 2002) 24.

The Prayerful Reading of Sacred Scripture and Lectio Divina

By comparison with the *Instrumentum Laboris* and the interventions in the assembly of the synod, this apostolic exhortation seems to have fewer references to *lectio divina*[30]; besides, it always distinguishes it as just one form of the prayerful reading of Scripture. The apparent paucity of references is deceptive, for in the pope's mind every engagement with Scripture involves a *lectio divina* process, and biblical exegesis itself should already be a form of prayerful attentiveness to the word of God. Faith-filled study of Scripture begins from prayerful listening to God's word and leads naturally to the response of prayer. There is thus a close relationship between *lectio divina* and a true hermeneutic of faith (see no. 82).

The pope warned against an individualistic approach to *lectio divina* that would forget that "God's word is given to us precisely to build communion" (no. 86). He detailed and explained the basic steps of *lectio divina*—reading, meditation, prayer, contemplation, ending in action. Chapter 8 of this book deals extensively with the synod and *lectio divina*.

The Word of God and Marian Prayer

Marian prayer is to be encouraged among the faithful, above all in the life of families. It is an aid to meditating on the holy mysteries found in the Scriptures. In praying the Rosary, "it is fitting that the announcement of each mystery be accompanied by a brief biblical text pertinent to that mystery." This encourages "the memorization of brief biblical passages relevant to the mysteries of our Lord's life" (no. 88). Marian prayers of the Eastern tradition that contemplate the entire history of salvation in the light of the *Theotokos* (Bearer of God, Mother of God) are likewise worthy of being appreciated and widely used, for example, the *Akathist* Hymn to the Mother of God and the *Paraklesis* prayers.

The Word of God and the Holy Land

The synod fathers spoke of the Holy Land as "the Fifth Gospel" (proposition 51). It was the land where the mystery of salvation was accomplished, and from which the word of God spread to the ends of the earth (no. 89). It participates somewhat in the "incarnational principle" enunciated by John Paul II, for its very contours and culture became part of the Word made

---

[30] Outside numbers 86–87, which treats *lectio divina* expressly; *Verbum Domini* mentions it only four times (nos. 35, 46, 82, and 83).

flesh. "The Holy Land today remains a goal of pilgrimage for the Christian people, [and] a place of prayer and penance." The whole church expresses its solidarity with Christian communities in the Holy Land and encourages them to be "a beacon of faith for the universal Church."[31]

Lectio, reading

Then meditatio

Oratio, prayer

Contemplation

Fruit expressed in actio

[31] Benedict XVI, Homily at Mass in the Valley of Josaphat, Jerusalem (May 12, 2009).

Questions for Discussion

1. The Holy Spirit and the word of God. Discuss.

2. Outline what the pope expects of formation to biblical exegesis in the future.

3. Explain the sacramentality of the word. Any implications?

4. No literature, sacred or secular, compares with Sacred Scripture. Discuss.

5. The shortage of priests in places has led to Sunday celebrations of the Word without a priest. Discuss other possible responses to this fact.

6. What is biblical spirituality? How may the enactments of the pope promote biblical spirituality among Catholics?

7. Discuss Bible and catechesis. Illustrate with the example of some texts how you would do biblical catechesis.

Chapter 12

Verbum Domini,
Part III: The Word to the World

His word engages us not only as *hearers* of divine revelation, but also as its *heralds*.

Verbum Domini, 91

The caption for this third and last part of the exhortation is John 1:18: "No one has ever seen God. It is God the only Son, who is close to the Father's heart, who has made him known." It has four chapters: The Church's Mission: To Proclaim the Word of God to the World; The Word of God and Commitment in the World; The Word of God and Culture; and The Word of God and Interreligious Dialogue.

One thing stands out through the pope's entire treatment of the church's mission: its *christological* density. The person of Christ is at the center of mission as he is at the center of the word of God. The kingdom of God is *autobasileia*, the very person of Jesus. Mission is the proclamation of Christ. Proclamation is not just by word but even more by lives and structures transformed by Christ. All the tasks of mission boil down to one: friendship with Christ and transformation, through his Spirit, of the entire lives of individuals and communities, their cultures and structures.

The Church's Mission:
To Proclaim the Word of God to the World

"No one has ever seen God. It is God the only Son, who is close to the Father's heart, who has made him known" (John 1:18). Jesus of Nazareth, as St. Irenaeus tells us,[1] is, so to speak, the "exegete" of the God whom "no one has ever seen" (no. 90). Christ exegetes the Father by becoming

---

[1] *Adversus Haereses*, IV, 20, 7.

158

"the image of the invisible God" (Col 1:15): "God has shown himself in person. And now the way to him is open. The novelty of the Christian message does not consist in an idea but in a fact: God who has revealed himself" (no. 92).[2] As such, Christ becomes for humankind "the *Logos* of Hope" (no. 91). "*Logos* of Hope" (reason for hope) comes from 1 Peter 3:15: "Always be ready to make your defense to anyone who demands from you an accounting for the hope that is in you." But *Logos* capitalized is the Johannine reference to the eternal Word become flesh! The pope, reading 1 Peter 3:15 in light of John 1:1, 14, means by *Logos* of Hope the Word made flesh as the hope and destiny of humankind. The reason for hope concerns the kingdom of God (Mark 1:14-15), which, in the words of Origen,[3] is *autobasileia*, the very person of Jesus. The hope for humankind is that the light of Christ illumines every area of human life: the family, schools, culture, work, leisure, and the other aspects of social life (no. 93).[4] Everyone on earth, know it or not, needs this *Logos* of Hope who is nothing short of humankind's ultimate destiny and joy. Hearers of this Word, all believers necessarily become his heralds (no. 91), for we cannot but share what, by God's grace, we ourselves have received. The church is thus missionary by her very nature, not as "an optional or supplemental element in her life" but by the very logic of the life that she has received and by which she lives (no. 93). Being missionary "entails letting the Holy Spirit assimilate us to Christ himself, and thus to share in his own mission" (ibid.). It is with our entire life that we share the Word (the pope emphasizes this entire transforma-

> *"Christian witness communicates the word attested in the Scriptures. For their part, the Scriptures explain the witness which Christians are called to give by their lives."*

tion of the lives of individuals and groups). And since the very nature of the church is mission, "the entire People of God is a people which has been 'sent'" (no. 94). Every baptized person, according to his or her proper state in life, "is called to give an incisive contribution to the proclamation of Christ" (ibid.). The synod wishes to promote the consciousness that every

---

[2] Benedict XVI, Address to Representatives of the World of Culture at the Collège des Bernardins in Paris (September 12, 2008).

[3] *On the Gospel according to Matthew*, 17:7. PG, 13, 1197B.

[4] Benedict XVI, Homily for the Opening of the Twelfth Ordinary General Assembly of the Synod of Bishops (October 5, 2008).

family, parish, community, association, and ecclesial movement is called to proclaim Christ (ibid.).

An urgent task of mission today is missionary outreach to peoples and cultures that do not yet "know" Christ, the *missio ad gentes* (no. 95). Throughout history, the consecrated life, among others, has been outstanding for taking up the *missio ad gentes* in the most difficult situations (no. 94). The church is duty bound, even at the risk of persecution, to continue "her prophetic defense of people's right and freedom to hear the word of God" that saves (no. 95). Then there is the *new evangelization* among the "baptized but insufficiently evangelized" and among nations now losing their Christian identity under the influence of a secularized world (no. 96). *Witness* is crucial in today's world, "for the word of God reaches men and women through an encounter with witnesses who make it present and alive."[5] Witness is to Jesus of Nazareth, his life and teaching, kingdom and promises (no. 98). There is a reciprocity between word and witness: "Christian witness communicates the word attested in the Scriptures. For their part, the Scriptures explain the witness which Christians are called to give by their lives" (no. 97). The whole church is grateful to Christians who "lived their faith and bore outstanding witness to the Gospel even under regimes hostile to Christianity or in situations of persecution," especially in Asia and Africa (no. 98). The reader may be interested in one such story recounted by a synod father:[6]

> The Soviets allowed no religious books, no Holy Scriptures, no catechisms, hoping that without the printed word the faith would die. A Latvian priest, Viktors, was arrested for possessing the Holy Bible. The agents threw the Holy Scriptures on the floor and ordered the priest to step on it. The priest refused and instead knelt down and kissed the book. For this gesture the priest was condemned to ten years hard labor in Siberia. Ten years later he returned to his parish and celebrated the Holy Mass. Having read the Gospel, he lifted up the Lectionary and said, "The word of God!" The people cried and thanked God. They did not dare applaud, because that would be seen as another provocation. The word of God lives!

The Word of God and Commitment to the World

As Christians, we have responsibility before Christ who is the Lord of history. His word commits us to the world, to serving him in "the least

[5] Citing proposition 38.
[6] Bishop Antons Justs, bishop of Jelgava, Lettonia, October 10, 2008.

of his brethren" (Matt 25:40) and committing ourselves to justice, reconciliation, and peace. We must spare no effort in creating a more just and more liveable world (no. 99). This work of creating a more just society, though, "is not the direct task of the church" but rather primarily that of the lay faithful who engage in social and political life (no. 100). As the synod recommended,[7] these lay faithful need to be trained in the school of the Gospel and to "receive a suitable formation in the principles of the church's social teaching" (ibid.). Christians must defend and promote *"the human rights of every person*, based on the natural law written on the human heart" (no. 101). "Catholics and men and women of goodwill must commit themselves to being an example of reconciliation for the building of a just and peaceful society," especially where there are wars and conflicts (no. 102). Above all is love of neighbor, especially the poor, taking to heart the saying of St. Augustine that "whoever claims to have understood the Scriptures, or any part of them, without striving as a result to grow in this twofold love of God and neighbor, makes it clear that he or she has not yet understood them" (no. 103).[8]

The synod was particularly attentive to young people who are the future of the church and the world. "Youth is a time when genuine and irrepressible *questions* arise about the meaning of life and the direction our own lives should take" (no. 104). For youth, the word of God can become a compass pointing out the path to follow (ibid.). There is need to promote Christ's friendship with the young by presenting God's word to them in a way that enlightens each one's particular call from God and choice of the direction of life, including that of total consecration to God.

Today's world is marked by movements of migration. The synod fathers stated that migrants are entitled to hear the proclamation of Christ, "proposed, not imposed" (no. 105). The Christians among them need "forms of pastoral care which can enable them to grow in faith and to become in turn messengers of the Gospel" (ibid.). His Holiness suggests that a mobilization of all dioceses involved is essential, so movements of migration may become an opportunity to discover new forms of presence and proclamation. This might initially call for structural contacts between the home churches and the receiving churches.

The Father of life is humankind's physician par excellence. In times of pain and suffering, ultimate questions about the meaning of one's life make themselves acutely felt. Human words sometimes fail, but the

---

[7] Proposition 39.
[8] *On Christian Doctrine*, I, 35, 39.

word of God allows those in suffering "to share in a special way in Christ's redemptive suffering for the salvation of the world (cf. 2 Cor 4:8–11:14)" (no. 106).

The word of God makes us look with new eyes at the entire created cosmos, which contains traces of that Word through whom all things were made (cf. John 1:2; no. 108). As the synod fathers reminded us, "accepting the word of God . . . gives rise to a new way of seeing things, promotes an authentic ecology which has its deepest roots in the obedience of faith . . . [and] develops a renewed theological sensitivity to the goodness of all things, which are created in Christ."[9]

The Word of God and Culture

"Every authentic culture, if it is truly to be at the service of humanity, has to be open to transcendence and, in the end, to God" (no. 109). God's word, far from destroying culture, pushes it to seek ever more appropriate, meaningful, and humane forms of expression. "Down the centuries the word of God has inspired different cultures, giving rise to fundamental moral values, outstanding expressions of art and exemplary life-styles" (ibid.).

Schools and universities are a particular setting for the encounter between the word of God and culture (no. 111). "Pastors should be especially attentive to this milieu, promoting a deeper knowledge of the Bible and a grasp of its fruitful cultural implications for the present day" (ibid.). Religious education is not to be neglected; it is often the sole opportunity for students to encounter the message of faith. In it, "emphasis should be laid on knowledge of sacred Scripture, as a means of overcoming prejudices, old and new" (ibid.). "Religion teachers should be given careful training" (ibid.). Because in many countries the training of teachers is an affair of the state, this determination may call for structures and networks in order to provide for the religious and theological training of teachers.

Sacred art in the West and icons in the East have been ways of presenting the word of God. The pope encourages "the competent offices and groups to promote in the Church a solid formation of artists with regard to sacred Scripture" (no. 112). The synod fathers called for a proper knowledge of the communications media and asked for greater efforts to be made in gaining expertise in the various sectors involved, particularly in the new media, such as the internet. "Discovering new methods of transmitting the Gospel message is part of the continuing evangelizing outreach of those who believe"

[9] Proposition 54.

(no. 113). The pope cautions, however, that "the virtual world will never be able to replace the real world" (ibid.); evangelization should use the new media to create "personal contact which remains indispensable." In the world of the internet, the face of Christ needs to be seen and his voice heard, for "if there is no room for Christ, there is no room for man" (ibid.).[10]

The word of God has a profoundly intercultural character. "It is capable of encountering different cultures and in turn enabling them to encounter one another" (no. 114).[11] It transforms cultures from within. Inculturation is thus no superficial adaptation or a confused syncretism. True inculturation follows the model of the incarnation: culture transformed and regenerated by the gospel brings forth from its own living tradition original expressions of Christian life, celebration, and thought.[12]

God's word also transcends cultural limits (no. 116). It makes us enter the communion of the church, "which means going beyond the limits of individual cultures into the universality that connects all, unites all, makes us all brothers and sisters" (ibid.). A new exodus is demanded: "we leave behind our own limited standards and imaginations in order to make room for the presence of Christ" (ibid.). What His Holiness says here needs to be understood in a manner that does not make it look as if Christ achieves universality by erasing particularities, instead of achieving unity in robust diversity, which was the very promise of Pentecost.

"Over the past 40 years since Dei verbum *the United Bible Societies have completed 134 translations in collaboration with the Catholic Church. In only 438 of the world's 7,000 languages is there a translation of the complete Bible. Currently the United Bible Societies is involved in 646 translation projects worldwide."*

Translations of the Bible into the vernacular are a distinct work of the church's mission. During the synod, it was clear that many local churches still lacked a complete translation of the Bible in the vernacular. A synod father[13] reported on the situation: "Over the past 40 years since *Dei verbum*

[10] John Paul II, Message for the XXXVI World Communications Day (January 24, 2002).

[11] Citing Benedict XVI, post-synodal apostolic exhortation *Sacramentum Caritatis*, 78.

[12] The text unfortunately reads "'acculturation' or 'inculturation' will truly be a reflection of the incarnation of the Word . . ." In the English language, acculturation is not inculturation but rather a process of socialization into a culture.

[13] Rev. Archibald Miller Milloy, secretary general of the United Bible Societies, Great Britain, October 14, 2008.

the United Bible Societies have completed 134 translations in collaboration with the Catholic Church. In only 438 of the world's 7,000 languages is there a translation of the complete Bible. Currently the United Bible Societies is involved in 646 translation projects worldwide." The synod considered it important that specialists be trained who are committed to translating the Bible into the various languages. His Holiness added his own voice, encouraging the investment of resources in this area, in particular recommending support for the work of the Catholic Biblical Federation with the aim of further increasing the number of translations of Sacred Scripture and their wide diffusion (no. 115), as much as possible in cooperation with the different Bible Societies.

The Word of God and Interreligious Dialogue

An essential part of the proclamation of the Word consists in "dialogue and cooperation with all people of good will, particularly with the followers of the different religious traditions of humanity" (no. 117). A synod father[14] gave a powerful theological foundation for such dialogue. He said that the inner communion or dialogue within the Trinity embraces creation and history, such that mission "is the Triune God's ongoing dialogue with the world and with humanity." Thus, "the Church exists in order to collaborate with God's ongoing dialogue with the world . . . for the Gospel we proclaim is God's invitation to dialogue." In other words, the mission of the church must be understood in terms of following God's continuing dialogue with the world and humanity.

> *"The Bible gives us a basic 'language course' for discovering the 'sparks of the Word' in human culture, in interreligious dialogue, and in our own life history" (Very Rev. Heinz Steckling, OMI, superior general of the Oblate Missionaries, October 8, 2008).*

In this vein, *Lineamenta*, 30, had called for an effort to know non-Christian religions and their respective cultures so as to discern the seeds of the Word present in them. *Lineamenta*, 32, relied on *Gaudium et Spes* (Vatican II's Pastoral Constitution on the Church in the Modern World), 4, 11, in saying that "the word of God can be read in the events and signs

---

[14] Very Rev. Fr. Antonio Pernia, SVD, superior general of the Society of the Divine Word, October 10, 2008.

of the times with which God manifests himself in history."[15] His Holiness, however, echoed propositions 50 and 53 in treating interreligious dialogue from the point of view of what the religions can contribute to human peace and welfare. They should foster "a mentality that sees Almighty God as the foundation of all good, the inexhaustible source of the moral life, and the bulwark of a profound sense of universal brotherhood" (no. 117). The pope also echoed the synod fathers when he insisted on the need to acknowledge the freedom to profess one's religion, privately and publicly, and to guarantee effective freedom of conscience to all believers (proposition 50; *Verbum Domini*, no. 120). Besides, respect and dialogue require reciprocity in all spheres, "especially in that which concerns basic freedoms, more particularly religious freedom" (ibid.). Reciprocity means that each religious group is willing to grant the others basic rights of worship it claims for itself.

His Holiness echoed the synod fathers' proposal that conferences of bishops (wherever "appropriate and helpful") "encourage meetings aimed at helping Christians and Muslims to come to better knowledge of one another, in order to promote values which society needs for a peaceful and positive coexistence" (no. 118). A synod father[16] recounted some positive signs in Catholic-Muslim dialogue: growing self-criticism within the Muslim world, the "Common Word" letter of over 140 Muslim leaders to the Christian leaders, the visit of the king of Saudi Arabia to the pope, and the conscious call and initiative from Muslim circles for dialogue with Christians at various levels. He called for intensifying theological reflection on Islam as a religion, particularly reflection on what *Nostra Aetate* (Vatican II's Declaration on the Relationship of the Church to Non-Christian Religions) meant by God speaking to Muslims. Pursuing this would, of course, explore how God might be self-revealing in the religions of humankind, not just in and through the church. Cardinal Bozanic's Report on the Word of God in Europe (see chapter 3) spoke of how the word of God is received, interpreted, and celebrated in *lectio divina*, meaning by this not only the reading of the sacred text (though this is always essential for ecclesial discernment) but also listening to the God who continuously acts upon history and who unveils the divine presence in every event. By such *lectio divina* we allow "God to read us," said he. The synod did not ignore such continuing dialogue of God with humanity and history in the Holy Spirit, though it appeared to tend to concentrate on God's word in

---

[15] See also *Instrumentum Laboris*, 58.

[16] Archbishop John Onaiyekan, archbishop of Abuja, Nigeria, October 15, 2008.

the church and *through the church* to the world. An integrative theology of interreligious dialogue still needs to be developed, for example, along the lines of the references to the ongoing presence and activity of the Holy Spirit that affect "not only individuals but also society and history, peoples, cultures and religions," as enunciated by John Paul II.[17] As the Report after the Discussion affirms (see chapter 2), "the very fullness of revelation [in Christ] carries with it the deepest demand for dialogue with all reality in authentic search for saving truth."[18]

[17] John Paul II, *Redemptoris Missio*, On the Permanent Validity of the Church's Missionary Mandate, 28.

[18] "*Justement, la plenitude de la revelation porte elle-même l'exigence la plus profonde d'un dialogue avec toute réalité en quête authentique de la vérité salvique*," 7.

Questions for Discussion

1. What, according to this exhortation, are the grounds of the church's mission?

2. What are the tasks of mission today according to this exhortation? Can you discern any hierarchy in these tasks as described in this exhortation?

3. How does the word of God call Christians to commitment to the world?

4. Discuss the exhortation's doctrine of inculturation.

5. Discuss the exhortation's doctrine of interreligious dialogue.

6. Single out and discuss one aspect that struck you in this chapter.

Chapter 13

Conclusion

May every day of our lives thus be shaped by a renewed encounter with Christ, the Word of the Father made flesh: he stands at the beginning and the end, and "in him all things hold together" (Col 1:17). Let us be silent in order to hear the Lord's word and to meditate upon it, so that by the working of the Holy Spirit it may remain in our hearts and speak to us all the days of our lives. In this way the church will always be renewed and rejuvenated, thanks to the word of the Lord which remains for ever (cf. 1 Pet 1:25; Is 40:8).

Verbum Domini, 124

By way of conclusion, it seems fitting to list the determinations through which His Holiness has seen fit to promote "an ever greater love of the word of God" (*Verbum Domini*, 5), "as a wellspring of constant renewal" (*Verbum Domini*, 1) in the church. I call them determinations, not enactments, for the making of law does not pertain to the genre of apostolic exhortation, even though here and there His Holiness clearly indicates the road to be followed and paths to be avoided. Only the "to-do" list where new emphases or new structures and strategies are indicated will be given here, not just where the determinations of His Holiness or the synod propositions reiterated or clarified a point of doctrine or affirmed what was already on the books. That is not to ignore how much the doctrinal perspectives of the synod are part of the hoped-for renewal, but hopefully the chapters of this book have shown what an influence on practice the rich practical theology of the synod was and will be.

The determinations will be divided into two. First come determinations by the initiative and authority of the Supreme Pontiff, then those where the pope expressly "echoes" the synod fathers or hands on their recommendations as such. It should be noted that synod proposals become effective in the church only if assumed by the pope and in the manner in which he does so. In chapter 10, it was remarked how His Holiness used terms like "I urge," "I recommend," "I encourage," and very rarely resorted to prescriptive language. The determinations will be given as the text of the apostolic exhortation gives them, and this sometimes varies subtly from the language of the synod propositions or other documents of the synod.[1] The scope and reach of the Synod on the Word of God in the Life and Mission of the Church is breathtaking, as one can see from the list below. Many of the recommendations the synod fathers can carry out themselves, individually or in their episcopal conferences, without further let from above. A few of these recommendations require coordination of efforts and the further teasing out of strategies.

In a sense, it is regrettable that synods follow one another in rapid succession every three years (not to talk of special synods in between), for this leaves little room for a sustained attention to the results of each synod. It seems to take almost a decade before one can begin to gauge the resonance of some general synods in the entire church. It is the hope of the present writer that the impact of the synod of bishops on the life and mission of the church will be swift and sure. The entire church joins His Holiness and the synod fathers in praying that the labors of the synod will make the church "always be renewed and rejuvenated, thanks to the word of the Lord which remains for ever." There follow the two groups of determinations.

His Holiness

Determination	Number of *Verbum Domini*
The synod has been convoked for further reflection on the theme of God's word, in order to review the implementation of the directives of *Dei Verbum* and to confront new challenges of the present time	3
Further study needed, from the theological standpoint, on how the different meanings of "word of God" are interrelated, with the person of Christ as center	7

---

[1] An unofficial text of the Propositions appeared in Italian marked as "provisional and unofficial." The English text given in this chapter is that of the English translation of the pope's exhortation.

Fervent hope for fruitful research on inspiration and truth of Scripture	19
"I would encourage scholars as well to study the relationship between *Mariology and the theology of the word*"	27
Avoid a reductive approach to hermeneutic that leaves the text in the past	35
Avoid "a positivistic and *secularized hermeneutic*" that a priori excludes miracles and/or divine intervention in human history	35; 36
Avoid danger of seeking to derive the truth of Sacred Scripture from use of one method alone, ignoring the need of a more comprehensive exegesis Remember that "hermeneutical approaches have their own philosophical underpinnings, which need to be carefully evaluated"	36
Typological interpretation relates the Old Testament to the New, though the Old Testament must retain "its own inherent value as revelation, as our Lord himself reaffirmed (cf. *Mk* 12:29-31). Consequently, the New Testament has to be read in the light of the Old"	41
"Dark" passages of the Bible: "I encourage scholars and pastors to help all the faithful to approach [them] through an interpretation which enables their meaning to emerge in the light of the mystery of Christ"	42
Dialogue with the Jews: it would be good, wherever appropriate, "to create opportunities for encounter and exchange in public as well as in private," thus promoting "growth in reciprocal knowledge, mutual esteem and cooperation, also in the study of the sacred Scriptures"	43
"Promoting common translations of the Bible is part of the ecumenical enterprise"	46
"It is important that the criteria [for theological exegesis] indicated in Number 12 of the Dogmatic Constitution *Dei Verbum* receive real attention and become the object of deeper study"	47
"As well as learning the original languages in which the Bible was written and suitable methods of interpretation, students need to have a deep spiritual life, in order to appreciate that the Scripture can only be understood if it is lived"	47

continued from page 169

Determination	Number of *Verbum Domini*
"I urge that the study of the word of God, both handed down and written, be constantly carried out in a profoundly ecclesial spirit, and that academic formation take due account of the pertinent interventions of the magisterium"	47
I encourage pastors "and all engaged in pastoral work to see that all the faithful learn to savour the deep meaning of the word of God which unfolds each year in the liturgy"	52
"Need for a deeper investigation of the relationship between word and sacrament in the Church's pastoral activity and in theological reflection"	53
"Wherever necessary, the competent offices and groups can make provision for publications aimed at bringing out the interconnection of the Lectionary readings, all of which are to be proclaimed to the liturgical assembly as called for by the liturgy of the day. Other problems or difficulties should be brought to the attention of the Congregation for Divine Worship and the Discipline of the Sacraments" Proposition 16: it is recommended that an examination be made "of the Roman Lectionary to see if the current selection and ordering of the readings is truly adequate to the mission of the church in this historical moment. In particular, the bond between the Old Testament and the pericopes of the gospels should be reconsidered, so that they do not imply an overly restrictive reading of the Old Testament or an exclusion of certain important passages"	57
The training of readers in liturgical celebrations should be biblical, liturgical, and technical (cf. *Ordo Lectionum Missae*, 55)	58
Whenever possible, a brief homily at weekday masses *cum populo* Proposition 15: "There should be a homily at every mass *cum populo*, even during the week"	

"In continuity with the desire expressed by the previous Synod, I ask the competent authorities, along the lines of the Eucharistic Compendium, also to prepare practical publications to assist ministers in carrying out their task . . . for example a Directory on the homily" Proposition 15: "in continuity with the teaching of the Post-synodal Apostolic Exhortation *Sacramentum Caritatis*, the synod fathers hope that a 'Directory on the Homily' can be elaborated"	60
To express contrition it would be good for a penitent to use "a prayer based on the words of Scripture" (cf. *The Rite of Penance*, 19) When possible, it would be good to have individual confessions "within penitential celebrations as provided for by the ritual, with due respect for the different liturgical traditions"	61
It is good that in hospitals and parishes, according to circumstances, community celebrations of Anointing of the Sick be held, in which greater space is given to the celebration of the Word	61
I "encourage communities of consecrated life to be exemplary in the celebration of the Liturgy of the Hours," thus becoming "a point of reference and an inspiration for the spiritual and pastoral life" of the church	62
I recommend that, wherever possible, parishes and religious communities promote the First Vespers of Sundays and Solemnities with participation of the faithful	62
Sunday celebrations of the Word in the absence of a priest. "I recommend that competent authorities prepare ritual directories, drawing on the experience" of particular churches, *while avoiding the danger of these being confused with celebrations of the Eucharist* Proposition 18: "The synod fathers recommend that ritual directories be formulated, based on the experience of the churches in which well-formed catechists regularly conduct Sunday assemblies around the Word of God"	65

continued from page 171

Determination	Number of *Verbum Domini*
"Silence, when called for, should be considered 'a part of the celebration'" (*General Instruction of the Roman Missal*, 45). "Hence I encourage Pastors to foster moments of recollection whereby, with the assistance of the Holy Spirit, the word of God can find a welcome in our hearts" Proposition 14: "The use of silence after the first and second reading, and also at the close of the homily, should be encouraged, as is suggested by the *General Instruction of the Roman Missal*"	66
The ambo "should be fixed, and decorated in aesthetic harmony with the altar. . . . The readings, the responsorial psalm and the Exsultet are to be proclaimed from the ambo; it can also be used for the homily and the prayers of the faithful"	68
"To all my brother Bishops I recommend frequent personal reading and study of sacred Scripture, in imitation of Mary, *Virgo Audiens* and Queen of the Apostles"	79
"Permanent deacons are to be introduced to Scripture and its correct interpretation, the relationship between Scripture and Tradition, the use of Scripture in preaching, catechetics and pastoral activity" (cf. Congregation for Catholic Education, *Fundamental Norms for the Formation of Permanent Deacons*, 11)	81
"I urge that Marian prayer be encouraged among the faithful, above all in the life of families." It is fitting that a brief biblical text pertinent to the mystery accompany the announcement of each mystery	88
I call everyone's attention "to the importance of defending and promoting the *human rights of every person*, based on the natural law written on the human heart"	101
The word of God and migrants. "A mobilization of all dioceses involved is essential, so that movements of migration [become] an opportunity to discover new forms of presence and proclamation"	105

The word of God and culture meet in schools and universities. Pastors are to be "attentive to this milieu, promoting a deeper knowledge of the Bible and a grasp of its fruitful cultural implications also for the present day" Religious education must not be neglected and "religion teachers should be given careful training"	111
"I encourage the competent offices and groups to promote in the Church a solid formation of artists with regard to sacred Scripture" Proposition 40: Profound gratitude to liturgical artists. "It's necessary to arouse in every cultural area a new season in which art can rediscover biblical inspiration and be an instrument able to proclaim, sing, and promote contemplation of the manifestation of the Word of God"	112
The face of Christ needs to be seen and heard on the internet	113

The Synod Fathers as "Echoed" by His Holiness

Proposition	Synod Proposition	Verbum Domini
The synod acknowledges "with gratitude the great benefits which [*Dei Verbum*] has brought to the life of the Church, on the exegetical, theological, spiritual, pastoral and ecumenical plane"	2	3
Need to help the faithful better "grasp the different meanings of the expression ['word of God'], but also to understand its unitary sense"	3	7
"Need to help the faithful distinguish the word of God from private revelations"	47	14
Deeper study needed of inspiration in connection with the truth of Scripture Synod Proposition 12: "the Synod proposes that the Congregation for the Doctrine of the Faith clarify the concepts of 'inspiration' and 'truth' in the Bible, along with their reciprocal relationships"	12	19

continued from page 173

Proposition	Synod Propo- sition	*Verbum Domini*
To attain the synod's aim, which is "to renew the Church's faith in the word of God," we need to look to Mary, Mother of God's Word and Mother of Faith, "in whom the interplay between the word of God and faith was brought to perfection"	55	27
"Need to look into the present state of biblical studies and their standing within the field of theology"	cf. 26	31
"Comparable attention needs to be paid to the theological dimension of the biblical texts"	26	34
"Renewed attention to the Fathers of the Church and their exegetical approach" may help recover "an adequate scriptural hermeneutic"	6	37
"The Jewish understanding of the Bible can prove helpful to Christians for their own understanding and study of the Scriptures"	52	41
"Dark" passages of the Bible: "hermeneutical key [is] the Gospel and the new commandment of Jesus Christ brought about in the paschal mystery"	29	42
Episcopal conferences to foster "closer working relationship between pastors, exegetes and theologians" in order to promote greater communion in service to the Word	28	45
"There should be an increase in ecumenical study, discussion and celebrations of the word of God, *with due respect for existing norms and the variety of traditions . . . care must be taken that they are not proposed to the faithful as alternatives to the celebration of Holy Mass on Sundays or holydays of obligation"* The phrases in italics have been added by His Holiness	36	46

"The ecumenical importance of *translations of the Bible in the various languages*" Proposition 36: the common commitment to translation and distribution of the Bible should be intensified	36	46
The synod fathers hope that a theological reflection on the sacramentality of the Word can be promoted	7	56
The synod requested that the issue of the Lectionary in the liturgies of the Eastern Catholic churches "be 'examined authoritatively,' *in accordance with the proper tradition and competences of the* sui iuris *churches, likewise taking into account the ecumenical context*" The phrase in italics has been added by the pope	16	57
The synod "stressed the need for the adequate training of those who exercise the *munus* of reader in liturgical celebrations"	14	58
The synod asks that the Liturgy of the Hours "become more widespread among the People of God," particularly Morning Prayer and Evening Prayer	19	62
All pastors are encouraged to promote times devoted to the celebration of the Word	18	65
"Celebrations of the word of God on pilgrimages, special feasts, popular missions, spiritual retreats and special days of penance, reparation or pardon"	18	65
Bishops to take care of acoustics and that church space be adapted to proclamation of Word, meditation, and celebration of the Eucharist	40	68
"Place of honor [to be given] to the sacred Scriptures, even *outside of liturgical celebrations*" Pope adds: "without prejudice to the central place proper to the tabernacle containing the Blessed Sacrament"	14	68

continued from page 175

Proposition	Synod Proposition	Verbum Domini
"The readings drawn from sacred Scripture may never be replaced by other texts" Pope adds: "This is an ancient rule of the Church which is to be maintained. The *Responsorial Psalm* is also the word of God, and hence should not be replaced by other texts; indeed it is most appropriate that it be sung"	14	69
"Special attention [to] be given to those who encounter problems in participating actively in the liturgy" Pope adds: "I encourage our Christian communities to offer every possible practical assistance to our brothers and sisters suffering from such impairments, so that they too can be able to experience a living contact with the word of the Lord"	14	71
The synod fathers "recommended a greater 'biblical apostolate,' not alongside other forms of pastoral work, but as *a means of letting the Bible inspire all pastoral work*"	30	73
"Possibly through the use of existing academic structures, centres of formation should be established where laity and missionaries can be trained to understand, live and proclaim the word of God" "Where needed, specialized institutes for biblical studies should be established to ensure that exegetes possess a solid understanding of theology and appropriate appreciation for the contexts in which they carry out their mission"	33	75
"In Eucharistic Congresses, whether national or international, at World Youth Days and other gatherings, it would be praiseworthy to make greater room for the celebration of the word and for biblically-inspired moments of formation"	45	76

"Scripture should . . . be the soul of . . . theological formation, and emphasis must be given to the indispensable interplay of exegesis, theology, spirituality and mission" "Seminarians [to be] helped to see *the relationship between biblical studies and scriptural prayer*"	32	82
"Communities of consecrated life [to] always make provision for solid instruction in the faith-filled reading of the Bible"	24	83
"Wherever possible, dioceses themselves should provide an opportunity for continued formation to lay persons charged with particular ecclesial responsibilities"	33	84
"The Synod urged that *every household have its Bible*, to be kept in a worthy place and used for reading and prayer"	21	85
"Formation of small communities of families, where common prayer and meditation on passages of Scripture can be cultivated"	21	85
Documents of the synod mention a number of methods of *lectio divina*		87
"The Synod reaffirmed that 'the mission of proclaiming the word of God is the task of all of the disciples of Jesus Christ based on their Baptism'" Pope adds: "A consciousness of this must be revived in every family, parish, community, association and ecclesial movement"	38	94
"The Synod Fathers restated the need in our day too for a decisive commitment to the *missio ad gentes*"	49	95
"Many Christians . . . need to have the word of God once more persuasively proclaimed to them," because they are "baptized, but insufficiently evangelized." Hence the need of a new evangelization	38	96

Scripture in the Church

continued from page 177

Proposition	Synod Proposition	Verbum Domini
The lay faithful have the task of changing society and politics according to the gospel. They are to be given "a suitable formation in the principles of the Church's social teaching"	39	100
"Catholics and men and women of goodwill must commit themselves to being an example of reconciliation for the building of a just and peaceful society"	8	102
"Young people need witnesses and teachers who can walk with them, teaching them to love the Gospel and to share it, especially with their peers, and thus to become authentic and credible messengers"	34	104
"Accepting the word of God . . . gives rise to a new way of seeing things, promotes an authentic ecology which has its deepest roots in the obedience of faith . . . develops a renewed theological sensitivity to the goodness of all things, which are created in Christ"	54	108
The synod called for a proper knowledge of the media of social communications, particularly the internet Pope adds: awareness that "the virtual world will never be able to replace the real world, and that evangelization will be able to make use of the *virtual world* . . . to create meaningful relationships only if it is able to offer the *personal contact* which remains indispensable"	44	113
It is important "to train specialists committed to translating the Bible into the various languages" Pope adds: "I would encourage the investment of resources in this area. In particular I wish to recommend supporting the work of the Catholic Biblical Federation, with the aim of further increasing the number of translations of sacred Scripture and their wide diffusion"	42	115

"Conferences of Bishops, wherever it is appropriate and helpful, to encourage" Christian-Muslim meetings, to know each other better and "to promote the values which society needs for a peaceful and positive coexistence"	53	118

I end with the prayer in 2 Thessalonians 3:1 that "the word of the Lord may spread rapidly and be glorified." Amen.

Bibliography

Abbott, Walter M., ed. *The Documents of Vatican II*. London and Dublin: Geoffrey Chapman, 1966.

Achtemeier, Paul J. *Inspiration and Authority: The` Nature and Function of Christian Scripture*. Peabody: Hendrickson, 1999.

Alter, Robert. *The Art of Biblical Narrative*. New York: Basic Books, 1981.

Anderson, Bernhard W., ed. *The Old Testament and Christian Faith: A Theological Discussion*. New York: Harper & Row, 1963.

Ausloos, Hans, and Bénédicte Lemmelijn. *The Book of Life: Biblical Answers to Existential Questions*. Grand Rapids: Wm. Eerdmans, 2010.

Barr, James. *Beyond Fundamentalism*. Philadelphia: Westminster Press, 1984.

———. *Fundamentalism*. Philadelphia: Westminster Press, 1978.

———. *Holy Scripture: Canon, Authority, Criticism*. Oxford: Clarendon Press, 1983.

———. "Story and History." *Journal of Religion* 56 (April 1975) 1–17.

Benedict XVI. Address to Representatives of the World of Culture at the Collège des Bernardins in Paris, September 12, 2008. AAS 100 (2008).

———. *Jesus of Nazareth: From the Baptism in the Jordan to the Transfiguration*. New York and London: Doubleday, 2007.

———. *Sacramentum Caritatis* (On the Eucharist as the Source and Summit of the Church's Life and Mission). Vatican City: Libreria Editrice Vaticana, 2007.

———. The Word of God in the Life and Mission of the Church: *Verbum Domini*. Frederick, MD: The Word Among Us, 2010.

Billings, J. Todd. *The Word of God for the People of God: An Entryway to the Theological Interpretation of Scripture*. Grand Rapids: Wm. Eerdmans, 2010.

Binz, Stephen J. *Conversing with God in Scripture: A Contemporary Approach to Lectio Divina*. Ijamsville, MD: The Word Among Us Press, 2008.

Boland, André, Jacques Rousse, and Hermann Josef Sieben. "Lectio Divina." In *Dictionnaire de Spiritualité Ascétique et Mystique, Doctrine et Histoire*, 470–510. Tome 9. Paris: Edition Beauchesne, 1975.

Boling, Robert G., and G. Ernest Wright. *Joshua*. The Anchor Bible. New York and London: Doubleday, 1982.

Borg, Marcus J. *Reading the Bible Again for the First Time: Taking the Bible Seriously but Not Literally*. San Francisco: HarperSanFrancisco, 2001.

Bradley, L. Richard. "The Curse of Canaan and the American Negro." *Concordia Theological Monthly* 42 (1971) 100–110.

Brown, Raymond. "'And the Lord Said'? Biblical Reflections on Scripture as the Word of God." *TS* 42 (1981) 3–19.

Caba, José. "Historicity of the Gospels (*Dei Verbum* 19): Genesis and Fruits of the Conciliar Text." In *Vatican II: Assessment and Perspectives: Twenty-five Years After (1962–87)*, edited by René Latourelle, 299–320. New York: Paulist Press, 1988.

Catechism of the Catholic Church. New York, London, and Sydney: Doubleday, 1994.

Collins, Raymond F. "Inspiration." In *The New Jerome Biblical Commentary*, 2nd ed., edited by Raymond Brown, Joseph Fitzmyer, and Roland Murphy, 1023–33. Englewood Cliffs: Prentice Hall, 1990.

Congregation for Catholic Education and Congregation for Clergy. *Basic Norms for the Formation of Permanent Deacons: Directory for the Ministry and Life of Permanent Deacons.* Vatican City: Libreria Editrice Vaticana, 1998.

Congregation for Institutes of Consecrated Life and for Societies of Apostolic Life. *Starting Afresh from Christ: A Renewed Commitment to Consecrated Life in the Third Millennium.* Vatican City: Libreria Editrice Vaticana, 2002.

Congregation for the Clergy. *General Directory for Catechesis.* Vatican City: Libreria Editrice Vaticana, 1997.

Davis, Thomas W. "Faith and Archaeology—A Brief History to the Present." *BAR* 19/2 (March/April 1993) 54–59.

De Lubac, Henri. *Medieval Exegesis: The Four Senses of Scripture.* 3 vols. Grand Rapids: Wm. Eerdmans, 1998.

Dulles, Avery. *Models of Revelation.* New York: Doubleday, 1983.

Falwell, Jerry. *Listen America.* New York: Doubleday, 1980.

Fitzmyer, Joseph A. "Historical Criticism: Its Role in Biblical Interpretation and Church Life." *Theological Studies* 50 (1989) 246–59. Also in Fitzmyer, *The Interpretation of Scripture: In Defense of the Historical-Critical Method*, 59–73. New York: Paulist Press, 2008.

———. *The Interpretation of Scripture: In Defense of the Historical-Critical Method.* New York: Paulist Press, 2008.

Flannery, Austin, OP, ed. *Vatican Council II: The Basic Sixteen Documents.* New York: Costello, 1996.

Fretheim, Terence E., and Karlfried Froelich. *The Bible as Word of God: In a Postmodern Age.* Minneapolis: Fortress Press, 1998.

Goldingay, John. *Key Questions about Christian Faith: Old Testament Answers.* Grand Rapids: Baker Academic, 2010.

Hanson, A. T., and R. P. C. Hanson. *Reasonable Belief: A Summary of the Christian Faith.* Oxford: Oxford University Press, 1980.

John Paul II. *Ecclesia in Oceania.* Vatican City: Libreria Editrice Vaticana, 2001.

———. *Pastores Dabo Vobis* (On the Formation of Priests in the Circumstances of the Present Day). Vatican City: Libreria Editrice Vaticana, 1992.

———. *Redemptoris Missio* (On the Permanent Validity of the Church's Missionary Mandate). Vatican City: Libreria Editrice Vaticana, 1990.

————. *Vita Consecrata* (On the Consecrated Life and its Mission in the Church and the World). Vatican City: Libreria Editrice Vaticana, 1996.

Johnson, Luke Timothy, and William S. Kurz. *The Future of Catholic Biblical Scholarship: A Constructive Conversation*. Grand Rapids: Wm. Eerdmans, 2002.

Knight, George A. F. *A Christian Theology of the Old Testament*. 2nd rev. ed. London: SCM, 1964, 1959.

Langfur, Stephen. "Jericho: When Did What Walls Fall?" Near East Tourist Agency. Accessed September 21, 2009. http://new.netours.com/index.php?option=com _content&task=view&id=119&Itemid=26&limit=1&limitstart=3.

Latourelle, René. "Le Christ signe de la revelation selon la constitution *Dei Verbum*," *Gregorianum* 47/4 (1966) 685–709.

————. *Theology of Revelation*. New York: Alba House, 1966.

LaVerdiere, Eugene. *Fundamentalism: A Pastoral Concern*. Collegeville, MN: Liturgical Press, 2000.

Leithart, Peter J. *Deep Exegesis: The Mystery of Reading Scripture*. Waco, TX: Baylor University Press, 2009.

Letter & Spirit: For the Sake of Our Salvation; The Truth and Humility of God's Word 6 (2010).

LeVine, Mark. "What Is Fundamentalism, and How Do We Get Rid of It?" *Journal of Ecumenical Studies* 42/1 (Winter 2007) 15–28.

Levison, John R. "Spirit and Inspired Knowledge." In *Filled with the Spirit*, 178–201. Grand Rapids: Wm. Eerdmans, 2009.

Lumko Institute. "The Lumko 'Seven Step' Method." Catholic Biblica Federation. Accessed January 6, 2010. http://www.c-b-f.org/start.php? CONTID=11_01_02_00 &LANG=en.

Marsden, George M. *Fundamentalism and American Culture: The Shaping of Twentieth Century Evangelicalism, 1870–1925*. New York: Oxford University Press, 1980.

————. *Understanding Fundamentalism and Evangelicalism*. Grand Rapids: Wm. Eerdmans, 1991.

Martin-Achard, Robert. *From Death to Life: A Study of the Development of the Doctrine of the Resurrection in the Old Testament*. London and Edinburgh: Oliver and Boyd, 1960.

Martini, Cardinal Carlo M. "The Central Role of the Word of God in the Life of the Church: Biblical Animation of the Entire Pastoral Ministry." *Bulletin Dei Verbum* 76/77, nos. 3–4 (2005) 33–38.

————. *La Parola di Dio alle Origini della Chiesa*. Rome, 1980.

————. "*Lectio divina*." *Bulletin Dei Verbum* 10 (1989) 16–18.

Marty, Martin E., and R. Scott Appleby. *The Fundamentalisms Project*. Chicago: University of Chicago Press. 5 vols. Vol. 1, *Fundamentalisms Observed*, 1991. Vol. 2, *Fundamentalisms and Society: Reclaiming the Sciences, the Family, and Education*, 1993. Vol. 3, *Fundamentalisms and the State: Remaking Politics, Economics, and Militance*, 1993. Vol. 4, *Accounting for Fundamentalisms: The Dynamic Character of Movements*, 1994. Vol. 5, *Fundamentalisms Comprehended*, 1995.

McKenzie, John L. "The Social Character of Inspiration." In *Myths and Realities: Studies in Biblical Theology*, 59–69. Milwaukee: Bruce, 1963.

———. "The Word of God in the Old Testament." In *Myths and Realities: Studies in Biblical Theology*, 37–58. Milwaukee: Bruce, 1963.

Megivern, James J., ed. *Official Catholic Teachings: Bible Interpretation*. Wilmington: McGrath, 1978.

Meier, John P. *A Marginal Jew: Rethinking the Historical Jesus: The Roots of the Problem and the Person*. Vol. 1. New York: Doubleday, 1991.

Morrison, John D. "The Nature of Holy Scripture in Roman Catholic Discussion from Vatican II to the New Catechism." *Trinity Journal* 24/NS (2003) 259–82.

Mowinckel, Sigmund. *The Old Testament as Word of God*. New York and Nashville: Abingdon Press, 1959. Swedish original: Oslo, 1938.

Murphy, Roland E. "What Is Catholic about Catholic Biblical Scholarship—Revisited," *BTB* 28 (1998) 112–19.

Nelson, Richard D. *Joshua: A Commentary*. Louisville: John Knox Press, 1997.

Neuner, J., and Jaques Dupuis, eds. *The Christian Faith: Doctrinal Documents of the Catholic Church*. 5th revised and enlarged ed. London: HarperCollinsReligious, 1990.

Nickelsburg, George W. E. *Resurrection, Immortality, and Eternal Life in Intertestamental Judaism and Early Christianity*. Expanded ed. Harvard: Harvard University Press, 2006.

O'Collins, Gerald. "Revelation Past and Present." In *Vatican II: Assessment and Perspectives: Twenty-five Years After (1962–87)*, edited by René Latourelle, 125–37. New York: Paulist Press, 1988.

O'Meara, Thomas F. *Fundamentalism: A Catholic Perspective*. New York: Paulist Press, 1990.

Osiek, Carolyn. "Catholic or catholic? Biblical Scholarship at the Center." *JBL* 125/1 (2006) 5–22.

Paintner, Christine Valters, and Lucy Wynkoop. Lectio Divina: *Contemplative Awakening and Awareness*. New York: Paulist Press, 2008.

Pannenberg, Wolfhart. *Revelation as History: Basic Questions in Theology*. Vol. 1. Philadelphia: Fortress Press, 1970.

Pius XII. *Divino Afflante Spiritu* (On the Most Opportune Way to Promote Biblical Studies). Vatican City: Libreria Editrice Vaticana, 1943.

Pixley, George V. *On Exodus: A Liberation Perspective*. Maryknoll: Orbis, 1983.

Pontifical Biblical Commission. Instruction Concerning the Historical Truth of the Gospels. Vatican City: Libreria Editrice Vaticana, 1964.

———. The Interpretation of the Bible in the Church. Vatican City: Libreria Editrice Vaticana, 1993.

———. The Jewish People and Their Sacred Scriptures in the Christian Bible. Vatican City: Libreria Editrice Vaticana, 2002.

Potterie, Ignace de la. "Interpretation of Holy Scripture in the Spirit in Which It Was Written (*Dei Verbum* 12c)." In *Vatican II: Assessment and Perspectives: Twenty-five*

Years After (1962–87), vol. 1, edited by René Latourelle, 220–66. New York: Paulist Press, 1988.

Priest, Josiah. *Bible Defense of Slavery.* Glasgow, KY: W. S. Brown, 1853. Reprint, Detroit: Negro History Press, 1969, 33. Cited from L. Richard Bradley, "The Curse of Canaan and the American Negro," *Concordia Theological Monthly* 42 (1971) 100–110, here 393.

Rahner, Karl. *Foundations of the Christian Faith.* New York: Seabury Press, 1978.

———. *Inspiration in the Bible (Questiones Disputatae,* 1). 2nd ed. New York: Herder and Herder, 1966.

———. "Revelation." In *Encyclopedia of Theology: The Concise Sacramentum Mundi,* edited by Karl Rahner, 1453–73. New York: Seabury Press, 1975.

Ratzinger, Joseph Cardinal. "Biblical Interpretation in Crisis: On the Question of the Foundations and Approaches of Exegesis Today." In *Biblical Interpretation in Crisis: The Ratzinger Conference on Bible and Church,* edited by Richard John Neuhaus, 1–23. Grand Rapids: Wm. Eerdmans, 1989.

———. "The Transmission of Divine Revelation." In *Commentary on the Documents of Vatican II,* vol. 3, edited by Herbert Vorgrimler, 181–92. New York: Herder and Herder, 1969.

Rigaux, Béda. "*Dei Verbum,* Chapter IV." In *Commentary on the Documents of Vatican II,* vol. 3, edited by Herbert Vorgrimler. New York: Herder and Herder, 1969.

Robinson, H. Wheeler. *Inspiration and Revelation in the Old Testament.* Oxford: Clarendon Press, 1946. Reprint, 1960.

Sagan, Carl. *Cosmos.* New York: Random House, 1980.

Sanders, James A. "Hermeneutics." In *Interpreters' Dictionary of the Bible,* supplementary vol., edited by George A. Buttrick and Keith Crim, 402–7. Nashville: Abingdon Press, 1976.

———. "Torah and Christ." *Int* 29/4 (1975) 372–90.

Schneiders, Sandra M. *The Revelatory Text: Interpreting the New Testament as Sacred Scripture.* 2nd ed. Collegeville, MN: Liturgical Press, 1999.

Schökel, Luis Alonso. *The Inspired Word: Scripture in the Light of Language and Literature.* New York: Herder and Herder, 1965.

Schüssler Fiorenza, Elisabeth. *In Memory of Her: A Feminist Theological Reconstruction of Christian Origins.* New York: Crossroad, 1983.

Scullion, John. *The Theology of Inspiration.* Notre Dame: Fides Publishers, 1970.

Seibert, Eric A. *Disturbing Divine Behavior: Troubling Old Testament Images of God.* Minneapolis: Fortress Press, 2009.

Shanks, Hershel et al. *The Rise of Ancient Israel.* Washington, DC: Biblical Archaeology Society, 1992.

Sheppard, Gerald T. "Canonization: Hearing the Voice of the Same God through Historically Dissimilar Traditions." *Int* 36 (1982) 21–33.

Soggin, J. Alberto. *Joshua.* Philadelphia: Westminster Press, 1972.

Thiselton, Anthony C. *Hermeneutics: An Introduction.* Grand Rapids: Wm. Eerdmans, 2009.

USCCB. A Pastoral Statement for Catholics on Biblical Fundamentalism. Washington, DC: USCCB 1987.

Vorgrimler, Herbert, ed. *Commentary on the Documents of Vatican II*. Vol. 3. New York: Herder and Herder, 1969.

Waltke, Bruce K., and James M. Houston. *The Psalms as Christian Worship: A Historical Commentary*. Grand Rapids: Wm. Eerdmans, 2010.

Williamson, Peter S. "Catholic Principles for Interpreting Scripture." *CBQ* 65 (2003) 327–49.

―――. *Catholic Principles for Interpreting Scripture: A Study of the Pontifical Biblical Commission's "The Interpretation of the Bible in the Church."* Subsidia Biblica 22. Rome: Pontifical Biblical Institute, 2001.

Willis, W. Waite Jr. "The Archaeology of Palestine and the Archaeology of Faith: Between a Rock and a Hard Place." In *What Has Archaeology to Do with Faith?*, edited by James Charlesworth and Walter Beaver, 75–111. Philadelphia: Trinity Press International, 1992.

Wimsatt, William K., and Monroe C. Beardsley. "The Intentional Fallacy." Sewanee Review 54 (1946) 468–88. Revised and republished in *The Verbal Icon: Studies in the Meaning of Poetry*, 3–18. Lexington, KY: University of Kentucky Press, 1954.

Witherup, Ronald D. *Biblical Fundamentalism: What Every Catholic Should Know*. Collegeville, MN: Liturgical Press, 2001.

Wittenberg, Gunther. "'. . . Let Canaan be his slave' (Gen 9:26). Is Ham also Cursed?" *Journal of Theology for Southern Africa* 74 (1991) 46–56.

Wood, Bryant G. "Did the Israelites Conquer Jericho? A New Look at the Archaeological Evidence." *BAR* 16/2 (March/April 1990) 44–58.

Wright, G. Ernest. *The God Who Acts: Biblical Theology as Recital*. London: SCM, 1952.

The Fathers and Medieval Doctors of the Church

St. Ambrose. *Exposition of the Holy Gospel according to Saint Luke*. Translated by Theodosia Tomkinson. Etna, CA: Center for Traditionalist Orthodox Studies, 1998.

St. Augustine. *Quaestiones in Heptateucum*. Patrologia Latina, 34.

St. Augustine. *Teaching Christianity: De Doctrina Christiana*. Translated by Edmund Hill, OP. New York: New City Press, 1996.

St. Bonaventure. *Itinerarium mentis in Deum* (The Soul's Journey to God). Introduction and commentary by Philotheus Boehner, OFM. New York: St. Bonaventure University, 1956.

St. Cyprian. *To Donatus*. In *Ante-Nicene Fathers: Fathers of the Third Century*, vol. 5, edited by Alexander Roberts and James Donaldson. New York: Charles Scribner's Sons, 1919.

Irenaeus. *Against Heresies*. In *The Ante-Nicene Fathers: The Apostolic Fathers with Justin Martyr and Irenaeus*, vol. 1, edited by Alexander Roberts and James Donaldson. New York: Charles Scribner's Sons, 1908.

St. John of the Cross. *Ascent of Mount Carmel*. Translated by Allison Peers. New York: Image Books, 1958.

Index